Human Development
and Capabilities

Globally, universities are the subject of public debate and disagreement about their private benefits or public good, and the key policy vehicle for driving human capital development for competitive knowledge economies. Yet what is increasingly lost in the disagreements about who should pay for university education is a more expansive imaginary which risks being lost in reductionist contemporary education policy. This is compounded by the influences on practices of students as consumers, of a university education as a private benefit and not a public good, of human capital outcomes over other graduate qualities and of unfettered markets in education. Policy reductionism comes from a narrow vision of the activities, products and objectives of the university and a blinkered vision of what is a knowledge society.

Human Development and Capabilities, therefore, imaginatively applies a theoretical framework to universities as institutions and social practices from human development and the capability approach, attempting to show how universities might advance equalities rather than necessarily widen them, and how they can contribute to a sustainable and democratic society. Picking through the capability approach for human development, in relation to universities, this book highlights and explores three main ideas:

- Theoretical insights to advance thinking about human development and higher education
- Policy implications for the responsibilities and potential contributions of universities in a period of significant global change
- Operationalizing a new imaginary

This fresh take on the work and purpose of the university is essential reading for anyone interested in university education, the capability approach and human development, particularly postgraduates, university policy makers, and researchers and academics in the field of higher education.

Alejandra Boni is an Associate Professor at the Universidad Politécnica de Valencia, Spain, and member of the Development, Cooperation and Ethics Study Group.

Melanie Walker is Senior Research Professor at the University of the Free State, South Africa, and South African Research Chair in human development and higher education.

Human Development and Capabilities

Re-imagining the university of the twenty-first century

Edited by Alejandra Boni
and Melanie Walker

Routledge
Taylor & Francis Group

LONDON AND NEW YORK

First published 2013
by Routledge
2 Park Square, Milton Park, Abingdon, Oxon OX14 4RN

Simultaneously published in the USA and Canada
by Routledge
711 Third Avenue, New York, NY 10017

Routledge is an imprint of the Taylor & Francis Group, an informa business

© 2013 Alejandra Boni and Melanie Walker

British Library Cataloguing in Publication Data
A catalogue record for this book is available from the British Library

Library of Congress Cataloging in Publication Data
Human development and capabilities : re-imagining the university of the
twenty-first century / edited by Alejandra Boni and Melanie Walker.
p. cm.
1. Education, Higher--Aims and objectives. 2. Education and globalization. I.
Boni, Alejandra. II. Walker, Melanie.
LB2322.2.H86 2013
378--dc23
2012025705

ISBN: 978-0-415-53632-5 (hbk)
ISBN: 978-0-415-53633-2 (pbk)
ISBN: 978-0-203-07508-1 (ebk)

Typeset in Galliard
by Swales & Willis Ltd, Exeter, Devon

Printed and bound in Great Britain by MPG Printgroup

To our lovely and enlarged families

Contents

Illustrations

Tables

Figures

Contributors

Andrea Abbas is Reader in Education in the Centre for Educational Research and Development at the University of Lincoln, UK. She is a sociologist of higher education whose empirical research uses sociological theory and innovative research methods to explore how higher education might effectively promote social justice.

Paul Ashwin is Senior Lecturer in Higher Education in the Department of Educational Research, Lancaster University, UK. His research includes: *Analysing Teaching – Learning Interactions in Higher Education: Accounting for Structure and Agency* (Continuum 2009) and the 'Pedagogic quality and inequality in university first degrees' project (http://www.pedagogice quality.ac.uk).

Sergio Belda is an architect with an MS in Development Policies and Processes from the Universidad Politécnica de Valencia, Spain. He is an assistant researcher within the Development, Cooperation and Ethics Study Group at the same university. His area of research is the human rights-based approach, social mobilization, critical development practice and urban planning.

Alejandra Boni is an Associate Professor at the Universidad Politécnica de Valencia, Spain, and member of the Development, Cooperation and Ethics Study Group. She is conducting research on development education, capabilities and universities and has published several articles on the topic. She is also Associate Editor of the *Journal of Human Development and Capabilities*.

Vivienne Bozalek holds a PhD from Utrecht University, the Netherlands and is currently Professor and Director of Teaching and Learning at the University of the Western Cape, South Africa. Her areas of research include social justice, political ethics of care perspectives, critical family studies, innovative pedagogical approaches, and feminist and participatory research methodologies.

Veronica Crosbie is a lecturer in English for Speakers of Other Languages and Intercultural Studies at Dublin City University, Ireland. She recently completed an EdD with the University of Sheffield, UK on capabilities in higher education.

Her research interests include capabilities in education, identity development, intercultural communication, cultural adaptation, drama in education and online portfolios for language learners.

Iván Cuesta holds an MS in Renewable Energy, Development Studies and Political Science. He lectures in non-governmental organizations and organizational change for a Masters degree in International Cooperation at the Universidad Politécnica de Valencia, Spain. His research interest is in critical development management and infrastructures in Africa.

Luisa S. Deprez is Professor of Sociology, Women and Gender Studies, and Faculty Associate, Muskie School of Public Service, at the University of Southern Maine, USA. Her research interests include scholarship and teaching focusing on US welfare policy and poverty, and the application of the capability approach to enrich knowledge and practice in higher education.

Stephanie Paul Doscher is Associate Director of Global Learning Initiatives at Florida International University, USA. She holds an EdD in Education Administration and Supervision from the same university. Ms Doscher's research interests include education for human capability development, educational ethics, and assessment strategies for global education.

Des Gasper is Professor at the International Institute of Social Studies (The Hague) of Erasmus University, Rotterdam, the Netherlands. His research focuses on development ethics, with special reference currently to migration and climate change. Recent publications include *Transnational Migration and Human Security* (co-editor T-D. Truong; Springer 2011) and *Development Ethics* (co-editor A. L. St. Clair; Ashgate 2010).

Shanti George, an independent researcher based in The Hague, has taught at universities in India, the Netherlands and Zimbabwe, and has conducted field research in all these settings, in addition to research with a global purview. Her books have been published by Oxford University Press, Sage and the International Foster Care Organization.

Geoffrey Hinchliffe is an Honorary Lecturer at the University of East Anglia, UK. He has worked in higher education for 15 years in outreach, student employability and academic practice. He also teaches undergraduates in the School of Education at the same University. His research background is in the philosophy of education and he has published a number of articles in this area, several of which draw on the capability approach.

Hilary Landorf is an Associate Professor of Global Education and Director of Global Learning Initiatives at Florida International University, USA. She holds a PhD in International Education from New York University, USA and degrees from the University of Virginia, USA and Stanford University, USA. Her research interests include integrative global learning and human capability development.

José-Félix Lozano holds a PhD in Ethics from the University of Valencia, Spain. He is an Associate Professor in Development Ethics, Business Ethics and Social Corporate Responsibility at the Universidad Politécnica de Valencia, Spain. He has published several articles in the *Journal of Business Ethics* and *Science and Engineering Ethics*, among others.

Monica McLean is Professor of Education at the University of Nottingham, UK. Her recent projects have investigated the relevance of the capability approach to professional education in South Africa and quality and inequality in UK universities. Her approach is outlined in *Pedagogy and the University: Critical Theory and Practice* (Continuum 2008).

Jordi Peris is Associate Professor at the Universidad Politécnica de Valencia, Spain, and team leader of the Development, Cooperation and Ethics Study Group. He is also co-director of the Master's Degree in International Cooperation with specialization in Development Processes and Project Management.

Jadicha Sow Paino is an independent researcher based in Valencia, Spain. She holds an MS in Politics and Development Process and has conducted research in Mexico on the capability approach and higher education. She is currently conducting research on development education and participatory methods.

Alberta Maria Carlotta Spreafico is a researcher at the Human Development, Capability and Poverty International Research Centre and the Institute of Advanced Study, Pavia, Italy; Chair of Human Development Programs at Henry Ford Hospital, Detroit, USA and at WINFOCUS, Italy. Alberta focuses on applying the human capability development approach to education policies, socio-economic analysis and healthcare development programmes.

Elaine Unterhalter is Professor of Education and International Development in the Faculty of Policy and Society at the Institute of Education, University of London, UK. Her current research is on gender, the capability approach, human development and education in Africa, particularly South Africa. She is the author of the prize-winning book *Gender, Schooling and Global Social Justice* (Routledge 2007).

Melanie Walker is Senior Research Professor at the University of the Free State, South Africa, and South African Research Chair in Human Development and Higher Education. She is a fellow of the Human Development and Capability Association and guest editor of a 2012 special issue for the *Journal of Human Development and Capabilities* on 'Education and Capabilities'.

Li Wang is a lecturer in the Institute of Educational Leadership and Policy, Zhejiang University, China. She has published papers on education policy and inequality in China in journals such as the *International Journal of Educational Development*, *Asia Pacific Journal of Education and Globalisation*, and *Societies and Education*.

Diane R. Wood is Professor of Instructional Leadership and Professional Development at the College of Education, Towson University, MD, USA. Her scholarship focuses on the development of teachers' professional inquiry communities and on educational implications of the capability approach in early childhood through graduate school.

Acknowledgements

This book had its genesis in May 2010, when we met in one of the Italian city of Pavia's beautiful squares. We were both in Pavia for the first meeting of an EU-funded Marie Curie Actions project, EDUWEL, and took the opportunity to begin the discussion about a book on higher education and human development. This was followed by a further meeting in London in June 2011, where we firmed up the proposal for our publisher and listed potential contributors, a third meeting in The Hague in September 2011, and a final meeting in Nottingham in December 2011, by which time we had read and suggested revisions to nearly all the changes and drafted the introduction and our joint chapter. Further discussions took place via e-mail, with Sandra in Spain and Melanie, by then in South Africa. So the origins of this book and its contributors make for a truly cosmopolitan production!

As always, books are the products of many conversations, not just with contributors but with colleagues and graduate students near and far. We would therefore especially like to acknowledge firstly all the contributing authors to this book and secondly the Human Development and Capability Association community for being a continuing source of inspiration for a better higher education. We must also thank Hans-Uwe Otto of the University of Bielefeld, who has brought capability researchers together so many times for challenging seminars, for new connections, and who was instrumental in EDUWEL. Susanne Gottuck has always been a source of support and good ideas for both of us. We would also like to thank the early-stage researchers in Working Group 3 of EDUWEL for constantly surprising us in the best possible way: Aurora Fogues, Petya Ilieva, Ana Sofia Ribeiro Santos, Lukas Ertl and Krystian Szadowski.

Sandra would like to thank her colleagues and doctoral students of the Development, Cooperation and Ethics Study Group, especially Félix Lozano, Jordi Peris, Andrés Hueso and Alvaro Fernández; Des Gasper, John Cameron, Alex Frediani and Peter Taylor, all of them have contributed to enrich knowledge and expand possibilities of application of the human development and capability approach. She would also like to thank the Spanish Ministry of Education for a postdoctoral grant in 2009 at ISS in The Hague.

Melanie would like to thank Monica McLean, Elaine Unterhalter, Caroline Suransky, Merridy Wilson-Strydom, Lis Lange, Sonja Loots, Marie Brennan, Lew

Zipin, Fazal Rizvi and Linda East; also Lesley Powell, Tham Nguyen and Melis Cin for their support in various ways, and for inspiring conversations. In particular, she would like to thank the University of the Free State, especially the inspiring vice-chancellor Jonathan Jansen for 'fetching her', and Professors Frans Swanepoel, Nicky Morgan and Driekie Hay for making her feel welcome and ensuring the support to enable her to complete the book in the midst of the upheaval of relocating countries.

Elmarie Viljoen provided meticulous editorial support, while Philip Mudd from Routledge has been encouraging of the project from the outset.

Finally, both want to thank their wonderful extended families in Spain, South Africa and Australia – human and canine – for welcome distractions, love and support.

Alejandra Boni and Melanie Walker

Chapter 1

Introduction

Human development, capabilities and universities of the twenty-first century

Alejandra Boni and Melanie Walker

Various answers are offered nowadays concerning the appropriate role, goals and performance indicators for universities. We have found competing visions dominated, however, by a focus on economic competitiveness and efficiency. The Council of the European Union (2007), the OECD (2007), the World Bank (2002) are examples of this perspective, which, as Naidoo (2003: 250) suggests, is 'the perception of higher education as an industry for enhancing national competitiveness and as a lucrative service that can be sold in the global marketplace'. This vision has arguably eclipsed the social and cultural objectives of higher education captured in these overlapping ideas: a public good (benefiting the public at large; for example, by educating doctors for public service or by enhancing democratic life and human rights); a social good (making diverse contributions to others and to future persons beyond one's own interests; for example, through service learning in communities or regional development); and a commitment to the common good and associational life. Such non-market goods go beyond and subsume market benefits, but without excluding benefits such as the formation of human capital investments in one's future, economic opportunities and income (Sen 1999 and see McMahon 2009).

The view of the university that we therefore propose in this book resonates with public, social and common-good values and ideals but it is also based explicitly and distinctively on the principles of the human development approach (Haq 1999). It is different from the prevailing reductionist view of higher education as a business whose product is increased revenues and profit, but notwithstanding the challenges presented by the current conjuncture of global politics and inequalities, our perspective is neither utopian nor naive. Universities everywhere have the potential to act for reproductive or transformative ends. There are numerous official documents signed by university leaders that support the validity of such a proposal. For example, the preamble of the Magna Charta of European Universities,[1] prepared in 1988, and several other international declarations like the World Declaration on Higher Education for the Twenty-First Century: Vision and Action, signed in 1998,[2] and the Talloires Declaration of 2005.[3] Along the same lines we find interesting work carried out by several universities which, in recent years, have been promoting university social responsibility policies that involve university learning, research, social outreach and governance (i.e. AUJSAL 2009).

Besides international declarations, many academic studies of higher education have elaborated and defended this expansive perspective on what a university might and should be. Among them, we note the liberal visions of Nussbaum (1997); Kezar *et al.*'s (2005) model of a higher education institution for the public good or Brennan (2002) on the transformative university. We can add to this a small but growing literature exploring higher education from a human capabilities perspective (e.g. Walker 2006, 2009; Flores-Crespo 2007; Boni and Gasper 2012; Boni *et al.* 2012; Walker 2012a). The common point of all these authors is that the university should not be distant from the tremendous problems the world faces nowadays – environmental challenges, social injustices, armed conflicts, intolerance, abuses of and lack of respect for human rights – and that it should have an active role, engaged in local and global spaces, to foster and support a just and sustainable society.

However, we do not want to simplify the complex debate on what should be the role of a university. We acknowledge the great diversity among higher education institutions all around the world, under pressure from recent processes of massification, privatization, and public expenditure reduction. We want to stress the ethical perspective of a university both in its micro-dimension (the university seen as an organization together with all its immediate stakeholders), and in its relationship with its wider partners at the local, national and global levels. We argue in this chapter that the human development framework and, inside this, the capability approach (CA) can valuably contribute to define and characterize what a good university might be, and can stimulate new avenues to reach it.

Human development and the capability approach

The human development approach arises from a tradition in humanist social philosophy and humanist economics (e.g. Haq 1999; Nussbaum 2000; Gasper 2009). It stresses: (1) a plurality of values, not only the values of economic utility as expressed and promoted within markets; (2) a human-wide concern and solidarity, as in human rights philosophy – the field of reference is all humans, wheresoever in the world, and in particular all those affected by one's actions; and (3) it recognizes the normality and centrality of interconnections – side effects of markets mean that market calculation is insufficient even if we only use a value of economic utility. Human development thinking contains thus a concern not only for an increase in people's skills (human resource development) or the so-called 'human sectors' (e.g. nutrition, health, education). It rests on a broad and plural conception of human well-being, and sees development as the promotion and advance of well-being. The United Nations Development Programme's standard definition of the core dimensions of human development includes: *empowerment*, meaning the expansion of capabilities (ability to attain valued ends), expansion of valued functionings (attained valued ends), and participation (sharing in specifying priorities); *equity* in distribution of basic capabilities, and, *security* and *sustainability* of people's valued attainments and opportunities. Penz *et al.*'s (2011) synthesis of work on human development ethics slightly extends this list by highlighting human rights and cultural freedom. Arguably, these were already largely subsumed within the UNDP formulation within the range of valued ends to be promoted, equitably distributed, sustained and secured, but are now further highlighted (Boni and Gasper 2012).

Intertwined with the human development approach is the concept of capabilities or the real possibilities and opportunities of leading a life which a person has reason to value (Sen 1999). Human capability formation *is* human development; human development demands human capabilities. Capabilities refer to different combinations of functions which can be achieved, whereas functions are 'the different things that a person can value doing or being' (Sen 1999: 3). These beings and doings together constitute what makes a person's life valuable. The distinction between achieved functionings and capabilities is between the realized and the effectively possible; in other words, between achievements on the one hand and freedoms or valuable options from which one can choose on the other (Robeyns 2005). In other words, capabilities are the freedom to enjoy valuable functionings. Capabilities are specific positive freedoms – the freedom to do or be what one values. Freedom thus plays a substantive role in development. Freedom is an end in itself, and not only a means for another type of utility. Thus, for a society to develop, the main sources of freedom deprivations must be reduced and eliminated.

In higher education, both capability – potential and opportunity – and functioning – being able to exercise valued capabilities – may be important. For example, it would not be enough for students to value a capability for voice but be prevented from exercising their voice in learning contexts through particular educational and social arrangements which value some identities more than others. If we cannot observe the functioning of voice, we may wish to ask questions both about the underlying capability but also about teaching and learning conditions. Functioning directs our attention to individuals, and also to pedagogical relations and social arrangements which may enable or constrain learning and participation. As Sen (1999: xi–xii) emphasizes, there is 'a deep complementarity between individual agency and social arrangements . . . [and] the force of social influences on the extent and reach of individual freedom'.

One interesting aspect of the CA is that it focuses primarily on the opportunities aspect instead of stressing the results and products of the interventions (Crocker 2008). It is in that process where the CA takes into account social inequalities generated by diversity, and where equality does not mean equal income, but equal human capabilities (Sen 1999). However, Sen explains that while capability is important for evaluating the opportunity aspect of freedom, it cannot deal fully with the process aspect of freedom, since capabilities are individual advantages, which do not tell us enough about the fairness of the processes involved in capability formation. He writes as follows:

Freedom is valuable for at least two distinct reasons. First, more freedom gives us more opportunity to achieve those things that we value, and have reason to value. This aspect of freedom is concerned primarily with our ability to achieve, rather than the process through which that achievement comes about. Second, the process through which things happen may also be of importance in assessing freedom.

(Sen 1999: 336)

Thus, if we wish to develop a theory of justice in higher education we would need to pay attention to both process and opportunity aspects of freedom.

Another central concept in the CA is agency, defined as the ability to act according to what one values or – in Sen's (1985: 206) words – 'what a person is free to do and achieve in pursuit of whatever goals or values he or she regards as important'.

Consequently, 'people who enjoy high levels of agency are engaged in actions that are congruent with their values' (Alkire 2007: 3) and this becomes an essential aspect in the effective realization of human development and human capabilities. Two elements of agency are especially important to enhance capabilities and pursue human development goals: reflexivity and responsibility. On one side, critical reflexivity and Freire's conscious awareness of being an agent become relevant in the framework of collective action. In this regard, deliberation and reflective dialogue become core elements for developing agency because 'not just any behaviour that an agent "emits" is an agency achievement' (Crocker 2008: 11). There must be a certain reflection and conscious deliberation of the reasons and values upholding agency: 'what is needed is not merely freedom and power to act, but also freedom and power to question and reassess the prevailing norms and values' (Drèze and Sen 2002 cited in Crocker 2008: 11). The second element is the responsibility towards others. Ballet et al. (2007) propose to broaden Sen's concept of agency by considering responsibility as a constitutive characteristic of the person at the same level as freedom. This has important consequences as it generates a distinction between weak and strong agency. While weak agency would refer solely to developing individual goals and capabilities, strong agency would include the exercise of responsibility towards others' capabilities and society as a whole. Agency becomes strong agency when it aims to expand freedom of others within a network of social interactions where commitment and responsibility take place (Peris et al. 2012).

In this review of the main elements of the CA, we refer regularly to the contributions of Nussbaum (2000), who presents a list of 'ten central human functional capabilities' for a truly human life. These are the core requirements for a decent life and they represent a minimal agreement on social justice. Central to a CA is the conviction that a society that does not guarantee the active cultivation of these central capabilities, cannot be considered a just society, whatever its level of affluence. There is an extremely interesting debate on the appropriateness of making a list of the core capabilities. Sen has always refused to do that as he considers that dialogue and public debate are the only way to legitimate the capabilities that must be prioritized in each particular situation. Nussbaum on her side considers that there is a solid philosophical basis for elaborating a proposal of core capabilities and, moreover, she states that proposing a list entails political benefits as it provides a reference for the design and evaluation of public policies (Lozano *et al*. 2012). What we need to acknowledge is both ways of approaching capabilities theory have been extremely useful and complementary in educational fields as we can see in several chapters of this book (by Bozalek, Crosbie and Spreafico).

Higher education through the lenses of human development and capabilities

Human development values, capabilities, agency, all are key concepts to re-imagine a different vision of the university, beyond the goal to prepare people as part of a workforce. While education can enhance human capital, people benefit from education in ways that exceed its role in human capital for commodity production. If we pursue Sen's argument that ultimately what matters 'is what freedom does a person have', then a human capital model does not do well. Even acknowledging the importance of a job to social inclusion prospects – and the obverse, unemployment to social exclusion – an educational focus on employability and jobs tells us nothing about the quality of work, or whether or not people are treated fairly and with dignity at work.

Capabilities implies a larger scope of benefits from education, which include enhancing the well-being and freedom of individuals and peoples, improving economic production and influencing social change. This point has been captured by Nussbaum in her recent book *Not for Profit: Why Democracy Needs Humanities*:

> Cultivated capacities for critical thinking and reflection are crucial in keeping democracies alive and wide awake. The ability to think well about a wide range of cultures, groups and nations in the context of the global economy and of the history of many national and group interactions is crucial in order to enable democracies to deal responsibly with the problems we currently face as members of an interdependent world. And the ability to imagine the experience of another – a capacity almost all human beings possess in some form – needs to be greatly enhanced and refined if we are to have any hope of sustaining decent institutions across the many divisions that any modern society contains.
>
> (Nussbaum 2010: 10)

Using Sen's and Nussbaum's inspiration, there have been several contributions to re-imagining the spheres of university work: pedagogy and curriculum, research, social engagement, as well as internal governance and even the physical environment of the institutions. For instance, Walker (2012a) discusses what could be a professional committed to social justice, what she calls a 'public-good professional'.

On curriculum, Nussbaum's proposal of the three capabilities for democratic citizenship (2006) has inspired several contributions. For instance, Boni et al. (2012) used them to think of a cosmopolitan curriculum; Gasper and George (2010) link those three capabilities with a sustainable future, while Walker (2012b) explains dimensions for curriculum design.

The CA, complemented and made more robust by critical pedagogies, has been useful to rethink the pedagogical process. Both critical pedagogy and capabilities have concerns with the voices of those who have to struggle to be heard and included. Both have concerns with human flourishing and how equality and social arrangements have to change. Critical pedagogy is better at showing how power-in-process works pedagogically, and that education may be oppressive as well as transformative. Critical pedagogy is sharper at dealing with contextual dynamics of language, discourse and power. Critical pedagogy has a clearer conceptualization of collective as well as individual agency so that individual critical thinking is linked to increasing social criticality. (Examples of the link between critical pedagogies and the CA can be found in the chapters by Deprez and Wood and Peris et al.). However, the CA, while broadly oriented to justice through its emphasis on capability (potential to function) does not prescribe one version of the good life but allows for plurality in choosing a life we have reason to value. The importance of capability over functioning is emphasized – not a single idea of human flourishing but plural and diverse possibilities, a concern with facilitating choices, not 'dragooning people' (Nussbaum 2000: 59).

Research and knowledge generation is another area in which the CA and human development can make a valuable contribution. Whose knowledge needs to be produced and who needs to be engaged in that process? As Delanty (2001) suggests, universities can have a role as a place of interconnectivity in society, opening up sites of communication in society rather than becoming a self-referential bureaucratic organization. This means that universities may foster a democratization of knowledge, which implies the participation of more and more actors in the social construction of reality. A human development perspective, with its core values of well-being, participation, empowerment and sustainability, could be a good framework to rethink research and knowledge 'transfers', and connected to it, the social engagement of a university. Moreover, in producing rigorous knowledge, the public domain is 'one of the best sites from which to engage in certain kinds of intellectual work . . . the best or only place to alter one's thoughts' (Alcoff 2002: 530). Although arguably more wedded to a role for philosophers, Nussbaum (2000) nonetheless also proposes that because public policies (including higher education policies) are the products of intuitions and theories both examined and unexamined, it seems 'sensible', 'to deliberate about which theories we want to hold onto, which intuitions are most deeply rooted in our moral sensibility' and through public deliberation 'to choose the view that stands the test of argument' (Nussbaum 2000: 300).

Sen is a powerful ally in making the case for the crucial importance of public reasoning and rational scrutiny of research goals, values, processes and knowledge

– both theoretical and empirical – to democratic life. As he argues systematically in *The Idea of Justice* (2009: 392): 'When we try to determine how justice can be advanced, there is a basic need for public reasoning, involving arguments coming from different quarters and divergent perspectives.' Sen (2009: 401) does not argue for complete agreements on every issue, but rather 'reasoned scrutiny'. It is then up to us as a community of higher education researchers to think through how his broadly framed emphasis on public reasoning and open impartiality for evaluating and advancing our research – theoretically and practically – would work in our specific situation, our obligations to public as well as academic scholarship and education's contributions to equity, justice and democratic life. This would be in contrast to current debates, which are reductive and instrumental – focusing on unidirectional instrumental knowledge transfer for economic development and growth.

The last contribution of human development and capabilities is on university policy or governance. This affects the internal way of taking decisions, what we can call the democratic procedures, and also the kind of policies that affect internal (teachers, students, administrative staff) and external actors (private and public organizations, civil society, etc.). Sen (2009) argues that the advancement of justice depends on inclusive democracy – deepening democracy depends on discussion and collective reasoning that injects more information and knowledge, diverse perspectives and plural voices into debates. Rich dialogic and participatory processes enable the formation of a capability for all voices to be heard in decision making, thereby making possible and also valuing people's ability to express their points of view, to argue and defend these, and to do so in a 'capability-friendly' environment which fosters not only individual development, but through collaboration and group working supports a collective agenda too. Human development and CA thinking could also be very inspiring to see which values could be the goals of a university policy. Once again, equity, well-being, participation, sustainability could be key principles that inform university policies when we think of access, dealing with diversity, quality and so forth.

About the book

This book is a real and clear example of how powerful a human development and the CA perspective is and could be to inform policies and practices of higher education institutions. From its beginning the book was imagined (as the human development paradigm) with an interdisciplinary and plural perspective. Its 22 authors come from different backgrounds: education, ethics, engineering and economics, among others. Southern and Northern perspectives are included because authors and experiences are based on countries like China, South Africa, United States, Mexico, England, Spain, Ireland and the Netherlands. And, lastly, our will has always been to try to recruit distinguished scholars alongside young authors because both are important to re-imagining the twenty-first century university.

This book is structured in three sections: the first engages with theoretical debates linked with human development and the CA and other theoretical proposals; the second is centred on policy debates and practices; and the third is a selection of seven case studies where the CA has been useful to re-imagining a different pedagogy. While the case studies cannot include examples of all aspects of the university curriculum they do hopefully point in the direction of what is possible and doable.

Part I opens with Walker and Boni's proposal to situate the chapters which follow. They outline the challenges dominant policy currently offers to the notion of public good. These challenges are situated in language, human capital, status and unequal knowledge. The authors outline an alternative oriented to the public and social good. They suggest focusing on development ethics to produce a switch in the 'Polanyi pendulum' towards public good starting from university teaching. In the second chapter, McLean, Abbas and Ashwin introduce the idea of 'pedagogic rights' to evaluate the extent to which processes of teaching and learning in formal educational systems reproduce or interrupt social hierarchies. They argue that university-level knowledge acquisition is an important element of human development and capability expansion and that combining the concepts of human capabilities and access to pedagogic rights can provide an analytic framework to evaluate pedagogic efforts aimed at human development. In the third chapter, Unterhalter discuss the question of what is wrong with global inequality in higher education and she gives ethical arguments to rebut assumptions that say global inequalities are not a problem in higher education. This theoretical part ends with Gasper's contribution, which stresses the importance of value change in addressing social change. Using the work of the Great Transition project he highlights the vital role of national and global citizens' movements driven by the energies of young people, which implies potential major roles for progressive education and, conversely, a negative role for anti-progressive education.

Part II begins with two chapters focusing on how, from the CA, we can obtain a different vision of graduate attributes and graduate employability. On the one hand, Bozalek examines the similarities and differences of graduate attributes and the human CAs and contends that the human CA has the potential to offer a different and enhanced conception of higher education when considered in relation to a graduate attribute approach. On the other hand, Hinchliffe explores the possibility of developing a CA to graduate employability. Starting with a four-dimensional concept of graduate identity that comprises value, intellect, social engagement and performance, his chapter suggests that the enactment of these four strands or dimensions is best captured through the CA. Wang follows, analysing widening access to higher education through a capability perspective and social exclusion theory. She uses China as a case study to consider educational inequality in higher education admissions, but argues that the framing of the issue is more widely relevant and applicable. Finally, Lozano and Boni's chapter aims to contribute to reflections on the social responsibility of higher education institutions. Using human development and CA, they offer a definition of university social responsibility and examine some public policy implications.

Part III begins with Spreafico, who proposes a contextual methodology inspired by human development for deriving a list of capabilities. Her case study is Barnard College, a women's liberal arts college in New York, where she derived a research-based list of nine education capabilities that this institution intends to foster. Deprez and Wood then discuss how the CA invites both teachers and students to become publicly engaged 'intellectuals' concerned with contributing to the creation of a just society. In their chapter, using an heuristic approach, they reflect on what they have tried and learned in their efforts to incorporate the CA into the classrooms. In their chapter Landorf and Doscher show how they used the CA to help their university identify student learning needs and prepare itself to meet those needs. They focus on the dialogic process followed at Florida International University, inspired by participatory dialogue and democratic deliberation, and its impact not only among students but also among staff and faculty. The following contribution connects critical global citizenship to classroom practices; Crosbie investigated a higher education language classroom to see to what extent it can be viewed as a site that lends itself to capability enhancement. She sketches a story of an engagement between teacher and students about matters concerning social justice, community and diversity in the context of an English to speakers of other languages module centred on the theme of globalization.

The next two chapters use human development and the CA perspective to analyse development aid and graduate degrees. In the first case, Peris, Belda and Cuesta explore how the notion of reflexive and transformative agency could be helpful to inform a critical development practice in the field of development management. Their analysis is based on a study of a master's degree in development in a Spanish university. The second chapter is authored by George, who explores one of the older schools of development studies in Europe, the Institute of Social Studies at The Hague. The research used in-depth interviews with a wide selection of graduates of the institute to argue that relatively small-scale initiatives in non-conventional education provided at schools or centres of development studies can generate dynamics that pull against the status quo and against the relationships that sustain it. Finally, the chapter by Sow Paino uses the CA to explore how non-formal education spaces, such the Community Learning Centres sustained by a Mexican university, can expand the capabilities of a group of women.

This case and all the others presented in this book are real examples of how human development and the CA can inspire a new imaginary to contest the status quo and offer new avenues towards public good and social justice. Universities, we think, are well positioned to help face local and global challenges regarding human and social development. They ought to be oriented to human and social challenges and be spaces for critical thought, reflection, action, unravelling complexity, and robust but respectful argument. At stake here is by doing particular kinds of educational things universities educate particular kinds of graduates who are both professionals and citizens. We suggest that the 'particular kinds of things' ought to be to educate people who act responsibly towards others, who contribute in different ways to creating and securing capabilities to all in society, and who value the building of a society which works in this way, faced as we are with staggering inequalities, poverty and vulnerability. If we manage this we would go some way – even if imperfectly – to creating multidimensional capabilities for economic growth, equity and the broader democratic good. We therefore invite readers to take up the challenge to dialogue and 'public reasoning' and to add to the human development and capabilities theorizing, policy analysis and case studies presented in this book.

Notes

1   Available at http://www.aic.lv/bolona/Bologna/maindoc/magna_carta_univ_.pdf [accessed 2 May 2012].
2   Available at http://www.unesco.org/education/educprog/wche/declaration_eng.htm [accessed 2 May 2012].
3   Available at http://www.tufts.edu/talloiresnetwork/?pid=17 [accessed 2 May 2012].

References

Alcoff, L. (2002) 'Does the public intellectual have intellectual integrity', *Metaphilosophy*, 33(5): 521–32.
Alkire, S. (2007) 'Concepts and measures of agency', OPHI Working Paper Series. Available at http://www.ophi.org.uk/wp-content/uploads/OPHI-wp09.pdf [accessed 2 May 2012].
AUJSAL (2009) *Políticas y Sistema de Autoevaluación y gestión de la responsabilidad social universitaria,* Córdoba: Alejandría Editorial.
Ballet, J., Dubois, J.L. and Mahieu, F. (2007) 'Responsibility for each other's freedom: agency as the source of collective capability', *Journal of Human Development and Capabilities*, 8(2): 185–201.
Boni, A. and Gasper, D. (2012) 'Rethinking the quality of universities: how can human development thinking contribute?', *Journal of Human Development and Capabilities*, 13(3): 451–70.
Boni, A., McDonald, P. and Peris, J. (2012) 'Cultivating engineers' humanity: fostering cosmopolitanism in a technical university', *International Journal of Educational Development*, 32(1): 179–86.
Brennan, J. (2002) 'Transformation or reproduction? Contradictions in the social role of the contemporary university', in J. Enders and O. Fulton (eds) *Higher Education in a Globalizing World: International Trends and Mutual Observations*, Dordretch, Boston, London: Kluwer Academic Publishers, pp. 73–86.
Council of the European Union (2007) *Council Resolution on Modernising Universities for Europe's Competitiveness in a Global Knowledge Economy*, Brussels: Council of the European Union.
Crocker, D. (2008) 'Sen's concepts of agency', paper presented at the Human Development and Capability Association Conference, New Delhi, 10–13 September 2008.
Delanty, G. (2001) *Challenging Knowledge: The University in the Knowledge Society*, Berkshire and New York: Society for Research into Higher Education and Open University Press.

Flores-Crespo, P. (2007) 'Situating education in the human capabilities approach', in M. Walker and E. Unterhalter (eds) *Amartya Sen's Capability Approach and Social Justice in Education*, New York: Palgrave Macmillan.

Gasper, D. (2009) 'Human development', in J. Peil and I. van Staveren (eds) *Handbook of Economics and Ethics*, Cheltenham: Edward Elgar.

Gasper, D. and George, S. (2010) 'Cultivating humanity? Education and capabilities for a global "Great Transition"', Working Paper 503, The Hague: Institute of Social Studies.

Haq, Ul M. (1999) *Reflections on Human Development*, 2nd edn, Dehli: Oxford University Press.

Kezar, A., Chambers, A.C. and Burkhardt, J.C. (2005) *Higher Education for the Public Good: Emerging Voices From a National Movement*, San Francisco: Jossey Bass.

Lozano, J.F., Boni, A., Peris, J. and Hueso, A. (2012) 'Competencies in higher education: a critical analysis from the capabilities approach', *Journal of Philosophy of Education*, 46, (1):132–47.

McMahon, W. (2009) *Higher Learning, Greater Good: The Private and Social Benefits of Higher Education*, Baltimore: Johns Hopkins University Press.

Naidoo, R. (2003) 'Repositioning higher education as a global commodity: opportunities and challenges for future sociology of education work', *British Journal of Sociology of Education*, 24(2): 249–59.

Nussbaum, M. (1997) *Cultivating Humanity. A Classical Defense of Reform in Liberal Education*, Cambridge, MA: Harvard University Press.

—— (2000) *Women and Human Development*, Cambridge: Cambridge University Press.

—— (2006) 'Education and democratic citizenship: capabilities and quality education', *Journal of Human Development*, 7(3): 385–96.

—— (2010) *Not For Profit*, Princeton: Princeton University Press.

OECD (2007) *Higher Education and Regions: Globally Competitive, Locally Engaged*, Paris: Organization for Economic Co-operation and Development.

Penz, P., Drydyk, J. and Bose, P. (2011) *Displacement by Development: Ethics, Rights and Responsibilities*, Cambridge: Cambridge University Press.

Peris, J., Fariñas, S., López, E. and Boni, A. (2012) 'Expanding collective agency in rural indigenous communities in Guatemala: a case for El Almanario approach', *International Development Planning Review*, 34(1): 84–102.

Robeyns, I. (2005) 'The capability approach: a theoretical survey', *Journal of Human Development*, 6(1): 93–117.

Sen, A. (1985) *Commodities and Capabilities*, Amsterdam: North Holland.

—— (1999) *Development as Freedom*, New York: Knopf.

—— (2009) *The Idea of Justice*, London: Allen Lane Penguin Books.

Walker, M. (2006) *Higher Education Pedagogies*, Maidenhead, UK: Open University Press and The Society for Research into Higher Education.

—— (2009) 'Making a world that is worth living in: humanities teaching and the formation of practical reasoning', *Arts and Humanities in Higher Education*, 8(3): 231–46.

—— (2012a) 'Universities, professional capabilities and contributions to the public good in South Africa', *Compare*, 42(6): 819–38.

—— (2012b) 'Universities and human development ethics: a capabilities approach to curriculum', *European Journal of Education*, 47(3): 448–61.

World Bank (2002) *Constructing Knowledge Societies: New Challenges for Tertiary Education*, World Bank: Washington.

Part I

Theoretical insights

Chapter 2

Higher education and human development
Towards the public and social good

Melanie Walker and Alejandra Boni

You trivialize us and trivialize the bird that is not in our hands. Is there no context for our lives? No song, no literature, no poem full of vitamins, no history connected to experience that you can pass along to help us start strong? . . . Think of our lives and tell us your particularized world. Make up a story. Narrative is radical, creating us at the very moment it is being created. We will not blame you if your reach exceeds your grasp . . . We know you can never do it properly – once and for all. Passion is never enough; neither is skill. But try.

(Toni Morrison, Nobel Literature Prize Lecture, 1993)

A lively debate?

How did we get to this point of the more or less global capture of higher education by economic arguments and neoliberal policy? While such capture may vary in the degree of its severity it can be found almost everywhere, including lurking underneath where commitments to universities as public goods still survive.

Nonetheless the argument is by no means concluded. Recently, there has been a rush of books, articles and reviews all deeply critical of the state of higher education, especially in the USA and the UK (e.g. Collini 2010; Folbre 2010; Nussbaum 2010; Docherty 2011; Grafton 2011; Holmwood 2011). There are books and papers taking up the challenge of transforming universities (e.g. Calhoun 2006; GUNI 2008; Burawoy 2011; Saltmarsh and Hartley 2011; Boni and Gasper 2012). For earlier statements on the public value and role of universities we can turn to declarations such as the Magna Charta of European Universities (1998),[1] the international Tailloires Declaration (2005),[2] and the 1998 UNESCO declaration on higher education for the twenty-first century,[3] reconfirmed in 2003 (UNESCO, 2004). While a theoretically pluralistic literature, it has in common a concern for what it is that universities do as places both where critical knowledge is created, and where contributions to equity in society and democratic life are both possible and desirable. Thus, in arguing for transformation, GUNI (2008) proposes that critical discourses can be generated in higher education to enable societies to continually reflect on and advance towards social transformation and truly 'human development'. As Amartya Sen (1999) has pointed out, a 'good' education can make a dramatic difference to human abilities and achievements; it can transform individual lives and contribute rather crucially to social change, including in the direction of equity and social justice.

While all these books and papers capture not only the global inequalities discussed by Unterhalter in Chapter 3 – of resources, status and esteem and missing orientations to global injustices – they further point to the significant historical and contextual stratification of higher education within countries, most especially across dimensions of resources and status. It is then unsurprising that global inequalities are not high on the agenda of most universities, especially in developed countries when they tolerate considerable inequalities in their own higher education systems. Unterhalter and Carpentier (2010) characterize the issue of global inequalities in higher education not just as a dilemma (e.g. commodification versus critical knowledge, or regulation versus democratic governance) but as a 'tetralemma', which they explain as comprising: (1) economic growth; (2) equity; (3) democracy; and (4) sustainability – all pulling higher education in different directions so that resolving one dimension means compromising or abandoning at least one other. In other words, the problem is very complicated and does not admit to easy solutions.

At best, dominant policy currently offers a rather reductionist and 'thin' public good which expels the poor, poorer countries, high-quality teaching, and the ethical–global from public policy (even accepting contested views in any one country about the fate of universities). At worst, higher education promotes social inequalities (Holmwood 2011), and the 'human lifeworld' of the university (Habermas 1989) is 'colonised' by money and power so that the capacity for communicative reason and social change is compromised. Yet, to shift from an individual and competitive paradigm to one which is social and collective (Escrigas 2008) requires a public culture and graduate ethic of public service that places human dignity and the alleviation of remediable injustices at its core. It requires our engagement with capability deprivation and the moral urgencies of poverty, human security, environmental sustainability and fair access to technology.

Challenges to higher education as a social and public good

The challenges we now outline should be read as multidimensional – each influences and reinforces at least one other problem, making each more corrosive and harder to contest.

How we think and speak about higher education

The language we use to talk about higher education has changed; this of course is not surprising in that language and meaning has always shifted and changed over time and historical context. Lakoff (2011: 185) points out the more we use words defined in terms of some 'frame-circuit' (e.g. neoliberalism) the more our words strengthen the frame and 'at some point, those frames become permanent'. Framing therefore matters a great deal, 'since frames are neural structures we think with' (Lakoff 2011: 188). Frames will open out or constrain how we think about and understand the problem of universities today, including national and global inequalities.

To take just one example, that of government and university 'incentives' and 'incentivizing'. As philosopher Ruth Grant (2011) explains, incentives are designed to persuade us to behave in certain ways rather than using direct coercion. She points out that 'incentivizing' is the market's alternative to coercion and the means used by those with power (policy makers holding the purse strings and university leaders in control of university policies) to persuade so that academics end up responsible for 'choosing' to act in ways which advance the strategies decided by university leadership. In the UK, academics are incentivized to produce particular kinds of publications for the Research Excellence Framework, rather than forced to do so. Even if academics do not fully buy into incentivizing, the effects for career advancement are such that many accept and use the language anyway, even if we resist the message. There are numerous other examples which speak to the naturalization of the language we use to speak about universities and our own academic careers. Thus, recently, it has been discomforting to note how quickly in England the language of 'price' (for a university course) has superseded that of 'fees'. This arguably fundamentally changes the nature of the agreement between students and a university. Price is what one pays for a commodity. To take another example, to advance our careers, as our heads of department keep reminding us, we must be 'entrepreneurial'. Toni Morrison (1993: 1) captures this imperative compellingly, although not speaking specifically of higher education. We could borrow her words to argue that higher education 'moves relentlessly toward the bottom line and the bottomed-out mind'. And most seriously, it shapes, diminishes and reduces what higher education may be and do for future persons.

Most worryingly, those of us who work in universities end up using not Morrison's song, literature or poetry, but a pervasive, seemingly inescapable corporatized, marketized framing, which is everywhere we turn – even though Morrison reminds us that language is agency and has consequences. It becomes harder to see how we sustain public values or the good of higher education over time when we find it increasingly hard even to talk about universities in other ways. As Burawoy (2011: 40) concedes, 'the reflexive moment' is currently outweighed by the 'instrumental moment'.

Human capital

A second key challenge lies in the current dominance of a human capital framework in higher education policy and practices explained in Chapter 1. It is now widely argued by policy makers that higher education is the key arena for making countries competitive knowledge-based (and capitalist) economies, capable of combining economic growth and better jobs with greater social cohesion. Yet, economic growth and human capital on the one hand, and flourishing on the other, are arguably incommensurable goods. Transformation or 'conversion' in the direction of human capital in universities, Brown (2011: 23) argues, 'interpellates the subject only as a speck of human capital, making incoherent the idea of an engaged citizen, and educated public, or education for public life'. Yet, ironically, the logic of a strong human capital approach is to withdraw public funding from all or most education provision, which is regarded as just another marketable service which ought to be free to charge, 'whatever fees the market will bear' (Gamble 2010: 707).

However, the current higher education concern with 'employability' (see Chapter 6 – Bozalek; and Chapter 7 – Hinchliffe) and jobs tells us nothing about the quality of work, of decent work, or whether or not people are treated fairly and with dignity. While economic structures are important as an aspect of plural well-being – fair economic opportunities promote identity and belonging, and a productive business environment and reducing human insecurity are central to well-being – we need economic structures and activities that increase well-being rather than reduce it. A strong economy ought to be a means to good lives, not an end in itself. As Sen (2009) has reminded us, we cannot evaluate resources as an end; we need rich and full information about how resources are being realized in actual human lives, activities and achievements.

Status

Somewhat contrary to the claim above, Marginson (2010) suggests that the larger enemy of the public good for universities is not the economic market but the status hierarchy which plays strongly to the self-interest of universities, among universities, and among nations. He suggests that status competition has moved in everywhere. Even though the status hierarchy, in our view, is driven by the economic purposes of universities and the competition globally for resources for higher education, so that economic purposes and status seem to be inextricably interwoven, his claim about status still holds. Status might frame the problematic of funding as requiring cuts to universities which are insufficiently research productive (even though we would argue that the underlying problematic is still economic).

Of course 'world class' universities which attract resources and large numbers of international students and internationally known staff will for the foreseeable future continue to do very well, as it is precisely their graduates who will be better placed to deploy the positional good of an elite university education to economic ends. They are helped in this by the impact and effects of various world league table rankings of universities, while these same rankings will continue to marginalize those who fall outside the top 200 or even the top 500. Whatever else league tables measure, they all measure research quality and currently are all much better at measuring research quality than teaching quality, and none serve the South well or do much about equity. Adam Habib (2011: 28) explains that rankings are not truly comparative but privilege one reality of higher education and impose its indicators across multiple global systems, overlooking history and contextual specificity. In his view the most benign effect of the various rankings systems would be to promote institutional uniformity. 'The most dangerous', he writes, 'would be the derailment of the development agenda and the continued reproduction of poverty, inequality and marginalization in the developing world'.

Unequal knowledge

The fourth challenge related to how we speak about universities, and the inter-locking challenges of human capital and status drivers is that of unequal know-ledge, in terms of access, production and dissemination and use. Knowledge is the currency of the powerful; it is another tradable commodity (Vessuri 2008). Moreover, as Vessuri (2008) explains, science and technology may contribute both to improving society through addressing water and food security, for example, but also to the problems societies face today; for example, developing chemical and biological weapons. Furthermore, the flow of technology to developing countries does not seem to contribute to narrowing the knowledge divide, indeed in the longer term such flows may well constrain home-based technological learning and innovation capacity building. Yet, academic knowledge could be understood and utilized as a public good and global public good (Marginson 2010; and see Chapter 1). A global public good would fulfil three criteria: it covers more than one country; it benefits a broad spectrum of countries but also a broad spectrum of the global population; and it meets the needs of present generations without jeopardizing those of future persons (Anand 2004).

The emphasis on human capital and status further shapes and reshapes knowledge produced, in that research becomes less relevant to teaching, the public good, and making a better world, while career advancement increasingly turns on investing most of one's human capital in research activity, rather than knowledge transfers through dedicated undergraduate teaching. As Brown (2011: 33) explains, it is then accepted that not only does teaching 'steal precious time from this [research] investment but too much undergraduate teaching also stigmatizes academics as lacking "market smarts"'.

Advancing the common good: a moral and ethical turn to development ethics

Yet, those of us who value our university teaching know how transformative a university education can be; how universities may be spaces where relations of equality, respect for difference and concerns for contributing to society might be nurtured, and where original, creative and life-enhancing knowledge may be produced. How these residues of a 'subjugated' discourse (Williams 1977) about universities survive under current policy conditions is tremendously important. We therefore want to try and sketch elements of a framing of higher education for the future persons with rich, flourishing lives comprising plural goods, which include economic opportunities but are not limited to these.

Development ethics, we suggest, can work to insert the moral and ethical into our debates, requiring us to ask questions about human well-being and what is intrinsically good, and not just instrumentally valuable (Crocker 2009). Moreover, development ethics places strong emphasis on the process by which we arrive at decisions as much as on good outcomes. Crocker (2009: 51) argues that development ethics is 'centrally concerned with understanding and combating human poverty and promoting well-being throughout the world'. Decontextualized, however, this has the ring of a possible mission statement, so quite what could a development ethics do for higher education?

The common good

We want to turn to a consideration of the notion of the common good as explored by Deneulin and Townsend (2007) from the perspective of development ethics. They agree that human well-being requires global public goods – scientific knowledge as the product of collective action – secured by international cooperation, as well as national public goods. They distinguish global public goods from common goods, which, they say, 'inhere truly in action in common, rather than being its product'. When collective action to produce scientific knowledge ceases the knowledge is still available, but when the action that inheres in the common good ceases the common good does not survive because it cannot be consumed and commodified. They argue, contrary to Marginson (2010), that the concept of global public goods leaves development ethics unchanged because global public goods are still commodities. Instead, they emphasize the need for underlying conception of human well-being which is both individual and communal/social. Moreover, public goods, they argue, cannot be provided satisfactorily through market mechanisms but require a process of public action. Collective action is crucial to the common good – and for our purposes, universities contributing to a common good and forming public and collective values (and here status hierarchy and the competition stand seriously in the way).

Deneulin and Townsend (2007: 25) emphasize that what matters is not the outcome of collective action (although we would say, *not only* the outcome) but 'the good of the community which comes into being in and through that enterprise'. Not unlike Dewey's (1927) associational life: individuals form associations, but they are also formed by associations. Common goods, Deneulin and Townsend argue, exist because of shared, solidaristic and collaborative actions; this may be through a one-off but more importantly it is the common good which endures over time, and which 'inheres in the relationships themselves' rather than the outcomes. They argue that 'if the good is to exist at all, then enabling those who theoretically are members of the relevant community to participate in practice is prerequisite' (Deneulin and Townsend 2007: 30). What matters to human well-being is the good life in common. Public good emerges when people come together in deliberation and action to take care of something – higher education, environmental challenges and so on. It is the actual coming together which is the common good and essential for any public-good role for universities or their social contributions. Dewey's (1927) point was that human fulfilment required 'associated life'; it followed, he argued, that a central pedagogical task was to cultivate, through education, an 'articulate public'.

This resonates with a view of universities as intellectual communities of students and scholars who enter into processes of inquiry and intellectual engagement with each other (Calhoun 2006: 33) in ways which are not just about the outputs but the intrinsic worthwhileness of the process, and the associational life. This kind of sharing, says Calhoun (2006), 'is a distinctive part of what it means to be a university' – the process which is the common good – and 'the reason why universities are effective producers of high quality and high creativity research' – the outcome also which is knowledge goods/global public goods and Dewey's articulate public.

Unterhalter (2011) further introduces Moellendorf's (2009) principle of associational justice which, we think, strengthens Dewey's associational life and the idea of a common good. She suggests that Moellendorf's principle has – at least until recent times – been relatively uncontroversial for what it is that higher education does nationally, and might now be argued for as a principle for international higher education. Arguably, this principle still persists as a subjugated discourse (even though we are less sure that it was especially widespread in higher education in former times), which we might work to restore. For Moellendorf a common-good association would jointly produce goods and powers that are useful to all – thus higher education nationally would produce goods and powers that are useful to all, not just some members of the society, and then, by extension, do the same in an international arena. He would be critical, we think, of the obsession with status and rankings which produces exclusions and reduces associational justice, privileging the advantages conferred on some simply by virtue of the accident of citizenship. Of course, given the extent of higher education mobilities this accident of citizenship may be more complicated or nuanced, but it is still broadly true that such mobilities work to the advantage of developed countries (Unterhalter and Carpentier, 2010), and that students and academics by accident of citizenship in poorer countries find mobility quite difficult on the one hand and, on the other, in neoliberal times may struggle to raise or sustain the quality of their own higher education systems.

Moellendorf's principle complements higher education justice and equity as we conceptualize this, drawing on Sen (1999, 2009) and Nussbaum (2011). We propose that higher education ought to form people's capabilities – their freedoms to be and to do in ways they have reason to value (Sen 1999), and to achieve well-being and agency. Capabilities ask that we consider what people are actually able to be and do individually and in comparison with others, how valuable capabilities are distributed across a university and society, and what educational (curriculum, pedagogy and so forth) and social arrangements are required to support capability formation. Capabilities are intrinsically and not only instrumentally valuable in terms of us having valuable and worthwhile choices. Thus, a human development (Haq 2003) and capabilities (Nussbaum 2011; Sen 1999, 2009) perspective foregrounds *both* economy *and* society; human well-being, equality, justice (local and global) and the sustainability of democratic societies are the aims, but as importantly, is the language or 'frame'. The second feature is to understand the obligations to others conferred by the advantage of having a university education. It requires, as Nussbaum (2011) explains, that we ask how we build a society that values capabilities and functionings for all. For Sen (2009), if we have the effective power to improve lives (as graduates do, for example, as doctors, lawyers and teachers), they also have the obligation to act to do so. Graduates as 'other-regarding' agents take on obligations to develop the capabilities of all citizens to participate fully, asking what they should do to help others in defending or promoting freedoms. The good of others is not a constraint on their own good, but integral to it.

This complements Moellendorf's argument that justice requires us to make available all the goods and resources that are necessary for individual autonomy or, we might say, people's capabilities. He further upholds the recognition and respect due to each person by virtue of our inherent dignity (here he is well aligned with Nussbaum's similar concern). This raises a moral concern in evaluating actions for their impact for human dignity and respect for all persons. Moellendorf would then assign to all of us the responsibility to develop distributive measures or institutions that would work to reduce inequalities.

Thus, development ethics offers a different and richer interdisciplinary framing of higher education as a common good and contributing through associational processes and public values to global public goods which would be available to all. In this way higher education would be a public good contributing to the social good locally and globally, and to rich human development and capability formation across societies.

However, this is well and good but who will the argument convince? Is change possible in the face of neoliberalized higher education and the spread of consumer values, in most especially but not confined to developed countries? Certainly, academic colleagues in Europe are pessimistic, notwithstanding attempts to mobilize opinion and support through campaigns like that for the public university in the UK,[4] and evidence of more reflexive universities elsewhere, such as in South Africa (Burawoy 2011).

The possibility of change: Polanyi's pendulum

We find keeping in the mind the action and process elements of the common good and an associational justice principle especially encouraging and bring this further to bear on Karl Polanyi's (1944) pendulum. *The Great Transformation* is an impressive historical critique of market liberalism (such as currently drives higher education policy) through a detailed study of economic and social changes in

Europe, from the preindustrial world to the great transformation of the Industrial Revolution. Polanyi explains that there has never been a self-regulating market because of the 'double movement' as people resist the rolling back of the state; it is rather the product of a school of thought in economics. He argues empirically that there cannot be a market utopia (as David Willetts, for example, might want in 2012 for UK higher education) because of the dire consequences of untempered market capitalism on people's lives and relationships ('labour'), on the environment ('nature') and on an unregulated financial system ('money'):

> To allow the market mechanism to be the sole director of the fate of human beings and their natural environment, indeed, even of the amount and use of purchasing power, would result in the demolition of society, for the alleged commodity 'labour power' cannot be shoved about, used indiscriminately or even left unused, without affecting also the human individuals who happens to be the bearers of this peculiar commodity.
>
> (Polanyi 1944: 76)

Dire possibilities 'for the forms of life of the common people' if the pendulum swings too far in one direction have historically generated countermeasures of state intervention and democratic politics and struggles to protect people and society 'against the perils inherent in a self-regulating market system' (Polanyi 1944: 79–80). Thus, for Polanyi there is a 'pendulum effect' which ensures that societies will over the longer term swing back from a totalizing neoliberal market model when the human costs become too great for societies to sustain themselves, and political conditions reverse these policies. Frances Stewart explains:

> Polanyi's main thesis is that each system, whether dominated by the market or by the state, has consequences that provoke intellectual, political and policy reactions which, in turn, lead to a reaction against the ruling model and a return to its opposite.
>
> (Stewart 2010: 373)

Following Polanyi's analysis, in the longer term society – and we might add higher education – cannot be run as an adjunct to the market; a pure market economy would destroy society and nature. Stewart (2010) argues that Polanyi's analysis continues to apply into the twenty-first century. There is at least some contemporary evidence in the UK. Recently, Gamble (2010: 705) has noted that severe funding cuts to public services in the UK 'mobilise coalitions of special interests against them, both within and outside government'; they can end up being temporary because of the pressures to balance the competing demands of markets (cuts) and citizens (increases in public spending). But importantly, Stewart (2010) also notes Polanyi's view that policy change against market domination requires long-term political movements, political struggle and political conflict to promote human development, human security and human well-being. She suggests that human development achievements have tended to be the worst 'when the market was supreme' (Stewart 2010: 387), because state action is required to advance human development, together with public action by citizens, and this needs democratic structures. 'Democratic discussions', Stewart (2010: 392) writes, 'without underlying political organization are not likely to give the deprived sufficient space, or lead to policies in their favour' (perhaps the limits of the lively debate Burawoy notes in higher education). Political will beyond an 'aspirational consensus' is required for actual changes.

Thus, Polanyi's analysis, while offering hope to universities as places which can foster democratic discussions, also notes the limits where this does not extend to public engagement and political struggles. Universities of course are not political parties and there is a delicate balancing act required for universities to maintain and sustain their autonomous knowledge-producing role and to play a major public role without 'servitude' (Burawoy 2011: 36) or at the expense of critical and expert professional knowledge. We nonetheless have grounds for qualified hope if universities and the people who work and study in them can find ways to promote democratic and associational ways of being and doing, and values to advance our human capacity to come to reasonable agreements with others and collectively to make social change in the interests of all, advancing, in short, Sen's (2009) 'public reasoning'.

So where do we begin? Teaching and curriculum

We now situate possibility within a fight for the definition of 'university' which takes the possibility of expansive, transformative higher education (GUNI 2008) as its frame, while offering a cautionary note regarding where reductive human capital policy and thin market exchange norms might direct us. We propose specifically that a human development ethics, operationalized through the human capability approach, expands our conceptual language. It offers guidance not only for transformative educational development and the graduate achievements that ought to have priority in addressing the incommensurable goods but also the 'virtuous circle' (Ranis *et al.* 2000) of both advancing the economy *and* of creating flourishing lives. As Vessuri (2008: 127) explains: 'There is broad agreement that mankind faces three main challenges in these early years of the 21st century: freedom from want, freedom from fear and freedom of future generations to sustain their lives on this planet.' Teaching for the public good is one critical space in which universities might begin to address these urgent challenges. Through curriculum and quality teaching we also do what Alcoff (2002: 533) has described as the public obligations of scholarship and 'publicly engaged work'.

In all this it may be that university teaching is one sure way to reinstate the public good and to advance the social good – to once again understand the hugely transformative potential of good teaching on undergraduates and postgraduates alike. This is the space in which we might educate, form and shape engaged public citizens, as critical reasoners and democratic citizens who understand their obligations to others, who are equipped to ask what the public implications of their actions are, and are morally prepared to ask of their actions and those of others, is it right? McLean *et al.*'s (2011) research with sociology students at different kinds of English universities demonstrates that students do value being able to think more broadly about the world; they do value finding ways to contribute to society alongside their acquisition of disciplinary knowledge. Boni and Taylor (2011) and Boni *et al.* (2012) show how technical studies could be based on a transformative curriculum with a cosmopolitan outlook, while Walker's (2009) research on humanities teaching points to the transformative potential of university education. A number of chapters in this collection (by Landorf and Doscher, Spreafico, Deprez and Wood, Crosbie, Peris *et al.*, Sow and George) similarly show what it is possible to realize in practice. University teaching could be the one public good we could do something about. Nor should we overlook that universities educate and train professionals who will take up positions of responsibility in society. Their professional contributions to society and the decisions and actions they pursue could be oriented through their university education to the public good and advancing the common good, as Walker (2011) has argued in developing a public-good professional capabilities index. The hope is to produce professionals whose solidarity, rationality and reflection will make them more likely to act as agents for transformation in a world that faces serious political and social problems.

Moreover, academics, we think, notwithstanding the Bologna Process in Europe and other moves towards control, still retain a great deal of control over the curriculum, and this is an important site of power and control (Walker 2012). Curriculum foregrounds knowledge, how it is selected and how it is mediated pedagogically and acquired by students. Put most simply, curriculum frames what counts as valid knowledge and what is worth learning, and more expansively the range of formal learning opportunities available to students. Importantly, statements about what should be included in a curriculum exemplify what things powerful groups (e.g. academic disciplines or professional bodies) think students should learn and thereby promote particular student identities. A curriculum is thus always grounded in a moral perspective on what version of the good life is desirable. Thus, it encapsulates value judgements about what sorts of knowledge are considered important; for example, the ethical dimensions of biotechnology advances, or the equal importance of exposure to arts and science knowledge for all students, or which literatures are studied. But a curriculum further indicates with what attitudes and values students are expected to emerge in respect of the knowledge and skills they have acquired; for example, the operationalization of scientific knowledge or historical understanding. As such a curriculum is a statement of intent, and knowledge carried by a curriculum logically has significant effects and projects forward into anticipating and preparing for the future and educating future persons. A curriculum has wider consequences for how knowledge (carried by individual graduates) is distributed in society and has an instrumental role in making society. University students will form their understanding of society at least in part through the curriculum knowledge and narratives made available to them by university teachers and teaching.

Rather crucially, a focus on curriculum offers the possibility of more sustainable change than the more usual higher education focus on teaching and learning, where so much rests on the individual lecturers. In the case of curriculum reform, the more powerful combination of curriculum structures (which are institutionally embedded and persist over time), and individual efforts aligned with these and evaluated against them point to embedded changes over time. Thus, attention to curriculum as a university-wide project holds considerable – and sustainable – transformative potential and the possibility of inclusively mobilizing a university community through 'public reasoning' (Sen 2009) about worthwhile education, provided that a critical, human development perspective (Sen's 'impartial spectator') on higher education purposes and policy is also kept in view. Arguably, curriculum reform and change ought to be in the direction of human development if we are to have some hope for addressing the global and local challenges that confront all of us.

Walker (2012) therefore outlines a curriculum based in human development dimensions aligned with capabilities formation and functionings outcomes. Curriculum and knowledge selection principles would be determined contextually, subject by subject, but could include general ideas and approaches such as: interdisciplinarity; the study of both science and arts subjects; ethics; global processes and human interconnectedness as well as real problems and issues of the local context; inequalities; and sustainability. Indicative capabilities to be created through curriculum might include: practical reasoning, 'thick' critical thinking and reasoned analysis, respect, imagination and empathy, cosmopolitan citizenship and ethical awareness. These opportunities would be made available through appropriate pedagogical arrangements to foster participation, reflexivity, inter-culturality and so forth, and with functioning outcomes such as acting as a critical agent in one's own life, having multiple perspectives on the world, being open-minded, decent, humble, curious and tolerant towards others, and able to lead a dignified life with a fair chance of choosing among preferred alternatives. At stake in this is the claim that a curriculum grounded in human development dimensions, capabilities and functioning achievements can form rich human beings; teaching and learning and graduate formation is then one site where we might 'advance justice or reduce injustice in the world' (Sen 2009: 337). A university education provides knowledge for new ways of understanding oneself and the world beyond university. Does a university and a curriculum, we ought to ask, encourage students to develop maps for civic and social responsibility and contributions to democratic public life? Or does a university promote maps for consumerism, individualism, compliance and only private benefits?

Concluding thoughts

The UNESCO declaration, reaffirmed in 2003 at a meeting with higher education representatives from 120 countries, states that higher education has acquired an 'unprecedented' role in present day society, not least we suggest in its role in the reproduction of capital, a role which has drawn it to the attention of policy makers and governments who seek to regulate and control higher education to advance capitalist economies and to generate profit. But higher education, as UNESCO (2004) affirms, is also a vital component of cultural, social and political development, of endogenous capacity building, the consolidation of human rights, sustainable development, democracy, and peace, in a context of justice.

While many of our own colleagues are pessimistic about the possibility of change in the face of consumerist social and cultural values, recent research in the UK (Dittmar 2008) shows that materialist values are linked to lower well-being and negative effects on all dimensions of personal well-being – poorer life quality, less positive self-worth, poorer mental and physical health and dysfunctional consumer behaviour, not to mention greater anxiety and depression across all age groups. This suggests hope for the pendulum swinging back from a market society. If we add to that McMahon's (2009) detailed research in the US and Schuller *et al.*'s (2002) research on the wider benefits of higher learning, which clearly demonstrate the wider benefits of higher education, we might begin to marshal more confident arguments in favour of change and the possibility for higher education as a public good, which advances public over consumerist values. However, we also need a normative framework for equality, human development and human capabilities and in this respect policy makers and government bent on pursuing free market practices may be harder to convince, notwithstanding the evidence.

Calhoun (2006) reminds us that universities offer tremendous public benefits, not only in the field of science and technology but also in contributions from the social sciences and humanities to debates on how to live well. He urges more and better thinking about how universities can be truly public and how this debate can be pursued reflexively within universities and on national and international levels. For his part, Vernon (2011) reminds us of the continuing belief among electorates that universities are powerful engines of social mobility.

The challenge is then considerable, but not, we think, impossible.

Acknowledgements

An earlier version of the paper was presented by Melanie Walker at the annual conference of the Society for Research in Higher Education in Newport, Wales, 7–9 December 2011.

Notes

1   Available at http://www.magna-charta.org [accessed 1 December 2011].
2   Available at http://www.tufts.edu/talloiresnetwork/?pid=17 [accessed 15 December 2011].
3   Available at http://www.unesco.org/education/educprog/wche/declaration_eng.htm [accessed 15 December 2011].
4   See http://publicuniversity.org.uk/ [accessed 22 December 2011].

References

Alcoff, L. (2002) 'Does the public intellectual have intellectual integrity?', *Metaphilosophy*, 33: 521–34.

Anand, P.B. (2004) 'Financing the provision of global public goods', *World Economy*, 27: 215–37.

Boni, A. and Gasper, D. (2012) 'Rethinking the quality of universities: how can human development thinking contribute?', *Journal of Human Development and Capabilities*, 13(3): 451–70.

Boni, A. and Taylor, P. (2011) 'Higher education institutions as cosmopolitan spaces for transformative development: re-imagining learning through teaching', Occasional Paper 23, in H. Arts, T. Halvorsen and P. Taylor (eds) *Democratising Knowledge for Global Development: The Role of European Higher Education Institutions*, Amsterdam: European Association for International Education.

Boni, A., McDonald, P. and Peris, J. (2012) 'Cultivating engineers' humanity: fostering cosmopolitanism in a technical university', *International Journal of Educational Development*, 32: 179–86.

Brown, W. (2011) 'The end of educated democracy', *Representations*, 116: 19–41.

Burawoy, M. (2011) 'Redefining the public university: global and national contexts', in J. Holmwood (ed.) *A Manifesto for the Public University*, London: Bloomsbury Academic.

Calhoun, C. (2006) 'The university and the public good', *Thesis Eleven*, 84: 7–43.

Collini, S. (2010) 'Browne's gamble', *London Review of Books*, 32: 4.

Crocker, D. (2009) *Ethics of Global Development: Agency, Capability, and Deliberative Democracy*, Cambridge: Cambridge University Press.

Deneulin, S. and Townsend, N. (2007) 'Public goods, global public goods and the common good', *International Journal of Social Economics*, 34: 19–36.

Dewey, J. (1927) *The Public and Its Problems*, New York: H.Holt, republished by Ohio University Press, 1954.

Dittmar, H. (2008) *Consumer Culture, Identity, and Well-Being: The Search for the 'Good Life' and the 'Body Perfect'*, European Monographs in Social Psychology Series, London and New York: Psychology Press.

Docherty, T. (2011) 'The unseen academy', *Times Higher Education*, 37: 36–41.

Escrigas, C. (2008) 'Foreword', in GUNI (eds) *Higher Education in the World 3. Higher Education: New Challenges and Emerging Roles for Human and Social Development*, GUNI Series on the Social Commitment of Universities 3, London: Palgrave.

Folbre, N. (2010) *Saving State U*, New York: The New Press.

Gamble, A. (2010) 'After the crash', *Journal of Education Policy*, 25: 703–8.

Grafton, A. (2011) 'Our universities: why are they failing?' *The New York Review of Books*, 24 November: 38–42.

Grant, R. (2011) *Strings Attached: Untangling the Ethics of Incentives*, Princeton: Princeton University Press.

GUNI (2008) *Higher Education in the World 3. Higher Education: New Challenges and Emerging Roles for Human and Social Development*, GUNI Series on the Social Commitment of Universities 3, London: Palgrave.

Habermas, J. (1989) 'The idea of the university: learning processes', in J. Habermas, trans. S. Weber Nicholson, *The New Conservatism: Cultural Criticism and the Historians' Debate*, Cambridge: Polity Press.

Habib, A. (2011) 'A league apart', *Times Higher Education*, 13 October: 28.

Haq, Ul M. (2003) 'The human development paradigm', in S. Fukuda-Parr and A.K. Shiva (eds) *Readings in Human Development*, Oxford: Oxford University Press.

Holmwood, J. (ed.) (2011) *A Manifesto for the Public University*, London: Bloomsbury Academic.

Lakoff, G. (2011) 'The brain, the mind and the threat to public universities', *Representations*, 116: 185–8.

McLean, M., Abbas, A. and Ashwin, P. (2011) 'Pedagogic rights and human capabilities', paper presented at the annual conference of the Society for Research in Higher Education at Newport, Wales, 7–9 December 2011.

McMahon, W. (2009) *Higher Learning, Greater Good: The Private and Social Benefits of Higher Education*, Baltimore: Johns Hopkins University Press.

Marginson, S. (2010) 'Creating global public goods', opening keynote for seminar on the Global University at the University of Virginia, USA, 14 November 2010. Available at http://www.cshe.unimelb.edu.au/people/marginson [accessed 12 December 2011].

Moellendorf, D. (2009) *Global Inequality Matters*, Houndmills: Palgrave Macmillan.

Morrison, T. (1993) Nobel Lecture. Available at http://www.nobelprize.org/nobel_prizes/literature/laureates/1993/morrison-lecture.html [accessed 22 December 2011].

Nussbaum, M. (2010) *Not For Profit*, Princeton: Princeton University Press.

—— (2011) *Creating Capabilities*, Cambridge, MA: The Belknap Press.

Polanyi, K. (1944) *The Great Transformation: The Political and Economic Origins of Our Time*, 2nd edn, Massachusetts: Beacon Press.

Ranis, G., Stewart, F. and Ramirez, A. (2000) 'Economic growth and human development', *World Development*, 28: 197–219.

Saltmarsh, J. and Hartley, M. (2011) *To Serve a Larger Purpose: Engagement for Democracy and the Transformation of Higher Education*, Philadelphia: Temple University Press.

Schuller, T., Brasett-Grundy, A., Green, A., Hammond, C. and Preston, J. (2002) *Learning, Continuity and Change in Adult Life*, London: Institute of Education.

Sen, A. (1999) *Development as Freedom*, New York: Alfred A. Knopf.

—— (2009) *The Idea of Justice*, London: Allen Lane.

Stewart, F. (2010) 'Power and progress: the swing of the pendulum', *Journal of Human Development and Capabilities*, 11: 371–98.

UNESCO (2004) *General Report by Jacques Proulx, The Meeting of Higher Education Partners*, UNESCO, Paris 23–25 June 2003. Available at http://unesdoc.unesco.org/images/0013/001352/135213e.pdf [accessed 15 September 2012].

Unterhalter, E. (2011) 'What is wrong with global inequality in higher education? Public good, reciprocity and associational justice', Paper presented at the annual conference of the Society for Research in Higher Education, Newport, UK, December 2011.

Unterhalter, E. and Carpentier, V. (eds) (2010) *Whose Interests Are We Serving? Global Inequalities and Higher Education*, New York: Palgrave.

Vernon, J. (2011) 'Canary in the coalmine', *Times Higher Education*, 1 December: 42–7.

Vessuri, H. (2008) 'The role of research in higher education: implications and challenges for an active contribution to human and social development', in GUNI (eds) *Higher Education in the World 3. Higher Education: New Challenges and Emerging Roles for Human and Social Development*, GUNI Series on the Social Commitment of Universities 3, London: Palgrave.

Walker, M. (2009) 'Making a world that is worth living in', *Arts and Humanities in Higher Education*, 8: 231–46.

—— (2011) 'Operationalizing the capability approach: universities' public good contributions to reducing injustice for people living in poverty', paper presented at the Annual International Conference of the Human Development and Capability Association, Den Haag, 5–8 September 2011.

—— (2012) 'Universities and a human development ethics: a capabilities approach to curriculum', *European Educational Research Journal*, 47(3): 448–61.

Williams, R. (1977) *Marxism and Literature*, Oxford: Oxford Paperbacks.

Chapter 3

University knowledge, human development and pedagogic rights

Monica McLean, Andrea Abbas and Paul Ashwin

The British sociologist Basil Bernstein (2000) introduced the concept of 'pedagogic rights' to evaluate the extent to which processes of teaching and learning in formal educational systems reproduce or interrupt social hierarchies. The argument made in this chapter has two parts: (1) that university-level knowledge acquisition is an important element of human development and capability expansion; and (2) that combining the concepts of human capabilities and access to pedagogic rights can provide an analytical framework to evaluate pedagogic efforts aimed at human development.

First, we rehearse ideas in literature about the capability approach and education, and follow this by connecting university-level education to human development goals and to capability expansion. We turn then to explaining Bernstein's contribution to thinking about education and social equality, in particular his emphasis on knowledge and pedagogy; and then, in this context, the concept of pedagogic rights is introduced. After briefly introducing the research project on pedagogic quality and inequality in sociology-based social science degrees in four universities of different status in England,[1] which supplies some illustrative empirical material, we demonstrate how pedagogic rights and the capabilities approach are complementary – each assisting the other to deepen understanding of the possibilities of university education.

The capability approach and education

The capability approach (CA) is Amartya Sen's (1999) highly influential and productive contribution to thinking broadly about human development. The expansion of human capabilities as a social goal is conceptualized as expansion of the essential means for individuals and groups to be free to make reasonable choices about who they want to be and what they want to do. While Sen does not specify capabilities, there have been a number of lists of multiple capabilities drawn up, which vary somewhat according to focus and empirical basis. Martha Nussbaum's (2000) list of comprehensive human capabilities is probably the best known. These capabilities are 'human abilities that exert a moral claim that they should be developed'; if they are not developed, human action and expression is curtailed, and that is 'tragic' (Nussbaum 2000: 83).

Individual choice is central to the CA: individuals should be free to choose to operationalize capabilities that they have reason to value. So a distinction is made between 'capabilities' and 'functionings' (capabilities-in-action) which adult citizens choose to undertake. In this sense, capabilities are opportunities for functionings that might or might not be taken up. Yet, even when referring to 'basic' human capabilities, such as bodily health, when it comes to education, capabilities and functionings relate in complex ways. On the one hand, education itself is often viewed as a capability (to be educated); and, on the other, educationally based capabilities – any, for example, that involve reading and writing – require functioning (or practice) to develop (for both points see Walker 2006 and Walker and Unterhalter 2007).

Education is now central for organizations focusing on worldwide human development. Primary education is one of the eight Millennium Development Goals;[2] it is a key dimension of the United Nations Development Programme's (UNDP) Human Development Index (HDI)[3] measured by the mean of years of education; and the Delors Report (1996) report to the United Nations Educational, Scientific and Cultural Organization (UNESCO) of the International Commission on Education for the Twenty-first Century proposes the four pillars of learning – to be, to know, to live together and to do – as an ethical–political guide to education for human development.

Most emphasis in human development is on the spread of more basic levels of education to people who are not yet receiving it. Nonetheless, it is observable that globally the hunger for higher education is keen[4] and universities are seen both as 'guarantors of universal values and cultural heritage' (Delors *et al.* 1996) and as providing the higher and middle level education and training necessary for countries to 'escape from their present treadmills of poverty and underdevelopment' (Delors *et al.* 1996). There is, we think, a strong case to make for mass higher education beyond it use-value. Nussbaum (2000) partly touches on it when she argues that a narrow focus on literacy and other basic skills is insufficient for the development of the full range of human capabilities. We build on this point in the next section by arguing that university education plays a central role in producing reasoning citizens capable of participating in civic and political life. In this connection, we shall briefly look at the work of educationalists motivated by human development, which illuminates the tasks of university education through the lens of a CA.

Human development, capability expansion and university education

For Amartya Sen, human development is an approach to thinking about human well-being which emphasizes the 'richness of human life rather than the richness of the economy in which human beings live, which is only a part of it'.[5] In harmony with this central tenet of human development is a substantial body of scholarly work which, though not directly associated with human development, presents alternatives to policy purposes which foreground university education for individual prosperity and national wealth making, at the expense of personal growth and moral, civic purposes. From a range of perspectives, higher education is cast as a social, public good contributing to healthy, democratic societies by producing critical and responsible citizens, as well as competent professionals (e.g. Delanty 2001; Taylor *et al.* 2002; McLean 2008).

In particular, Jurgen Habermas' ideas about the (ideal) functions of universities resonate with human development. For him, universities are sites of social transformation (Habermas 1971, 1989) because there is a 'structural connection' between the 'learning processes' of universities and the processes of democratic decision making (Habermas 1989: 125). He claims that universities are unique in producing and reproducing the human lifeworld (culture, society and identity) by way of a 'bundle' of four functions: knowledge generation; professional preparation; transmission, interpretation, development of cultural knowledge; and the enlightenment of the public sphere (Habermas 1989: 118). Arguably, these four functions can be conceptualized as enhancing the capabilities of students both to make choices for themselves and to benefit society.

A number of scholars have explored the connection between capability expansion and university education. Notably, Nussbaum argues about the shape of a liberal higher education in *Cultivating Humanity* (1997), in which she proposes three core capabilities to be developed in students: 'critical self-examination' of assumptions and beliefs; the 'ideal of the world citizen', whereby the individual student feels tied to all people globally; and the development of the 'narrative imagination', that is, for a student to imagine sympathetically the lives of people different from him/herself. Others have elaborated. Melanie Walker has written a seminal book *Higher Education Pedagogies* (2006) in which she draws up a list of eight capabilities for higher education, which is both based on a normative view of what university education is for and grounded in empirical evidence about what students value. Taking a different direction in his evaluative list, Pedro Flores-Crespo (2007) highlights the functionings of university graduates, dividing seven functionings into 'personal achievements ("beings")[6] and professional achievements ("doings")'.[7] Lozano *et al.* (2012) compare and contrast the 'competencies' and CAs to higher education showing how the former is based on a functional analysis of what university education is for, while the latter's basis is ethical normative; and Andresen *et al.* (2010) relate the CA to the German notion of *Bildung*, which corresponds inasmuch as it points to the formation in the individual of autonomy and responsibility for self and others.

Individual agency and freedom is emphasized in the CA. Accordingly, the sets of capabilities and CA-inspired ideas discussed in the literature above are offered as an 'evaluative space' for pedagogic processes and social arrangements in universities directed at effective individual agency and human well-being. Yet, while the importance of a multidimensional approach to developing the individual's capacity to opt for ways of life is prioritized, special emphasis is put on critical thinking as a means of judging reasonably what courses of action are valuable (Nussbaum 2010). We can see too from, for example, Nussbaum's 'narrative imagination' and 'ideal of the global citizen' that for the higher education context, the concern is not only the individual: a properly educated university graduate is capable of participating in the construction of her/his life in ways that also contribute to society as a whole.

We have established the contribution that human development and the CA make to creating and evaluating university education for the transformation of individuals and society. We turn now to a discussion of what new and useful perspectives might be added by the sociological concept of 'pedagogic rights'.

Bernstein's theory about the equitable distribution of knowledge

The centrality of curriculum

The concept of three 'pedagogic rights' was introduced by the late Basil Bernstein, a sociologist of education, in a fifth and final volume of work entitled *Pedagogy, Symbolic Control and Identity* (2000). The rights are to individual enhancement, social inclusion and political participation and can be seen both as driving pedagogic processes and as outcomes of an educational process. We shall further define and illustrate the three rights later in the chapter.

The concept needs to be understood in the context of Bernstein's complete oeuvre, which developed theories about how unequal distribution of knowledge in formal education systems relays inequalities in society:

> Education is central to the knowledge base of society, groups and individuals. Yet, education, like health, is a public institution, central to the production and reproduction of distributive injustices. Biases in the form, content, access and opportunities of education have consequences not only for the economy; these biases can reach down to drain the very springs of affirmation, motivation and imagination. In this way such biases can become, and often are, an economic and cultural threat to democracy. Education can have a crucial role in creating tomorrow's optimism in the context of today's pessimism. But if it is to do this then we must have an analysis of the social biases in education. These biases lie deep within the very structure of the educational system's processes of transmission and acquisition and their social assumptions.
>
> (Bernstein 2000: xix)

For Bernstein, as for human development and the CA, inequities for individuals and groups are about constraints on what people can do and be. In Bernstein, though, knowledge is power and so access to knowledge is paramount in fighting inequalities. This is because constraints and enablements in life arise from the relationship between the outer world of material conditions and inner worlds of consciousness and identities. This structure/agency relationship is familiar to all sociologists who strive, as C. Wright-Mills (2000: 4) famously put it: 'to grasp the interplay of man [sic] and society, of biography and history, of self and world'. Bernstein's take on structure/agency highlights the extent to which people have the capacity to change the inner/outer relationship. The capacity to do so is the capacity to manipulate the 'discursive gap' (Bernstein 2000: 30) between knowledge about everyday life, acquired in local contexts, and specialized knowledge, usually acquired in formal education. People are shaped to perceive specific (im)possibilities by the myriad messages sent within the social hierarchies into which they are born – that is, origins and destinies are strongly connected – but the discursive gap that knowledge opens up is 'a site for alternative possibilities, for alternative realisations of the relation between material and immaterial . . . the site for the unthinkable, the site for the impossible' (Bernstein 2000: 30).

'Thinking the impossible' might be termed a 'capability' and certainly connects to Nussbaum's capability for 'senses, imagination and thought'. As a capability, it requires access to abstract, expert discourses, what Bernstein calls 'vertical discourse'; it also requires seeing relationships between everyday discourses, what Bernstein calls 'horizontal discourse', and 'vertical discourse'. Table 3.1 shows Bernstein's definitions of the two discourses.

In Bernstein, the degree of exchange between the two discourses dictates whether communities and individuals have strategies in horizontal discourse which carry the potential to transfer to new contexts. It is the interchange between the two discourses which is powerful.

So the first offering is that acquisition of knowledge or curriculum content is prioritized, while in CA-based education literature it tends to be seen as one among other capabilities, or in Sabine Alkire's (2002) term, as a 'dimension'. For example, it is in Walker's list (2006: 128), and she observes that at university 'we do not just learn mathematics, or philosophy or history; we also learn ways of being,

Table 3.1 Bernstein's two discourses

Horizontal discourse	Refers to everyday, common and 'commonsense' meanings (about life and death). It is local, context dependent, specific and 'segmentally' organized. It is a set of strategies, highly relevant to lives 'for maximizing encounters with persons and habitats, [it] is the major cultural relay [and the acquisition is usually in] face to face relations with a strongly affective loading as in family, peer, group or local community.'
Vertical discourse	'(a) is coherent, explicit, systematic, principled, abstracted from meanings embedded in everyday life (b) is found in the specialized languages of disciplines. It operates at all levels of the official educational system and produces "graded performances.'

Source: Bernstein 2000: 158.

whether to be open-minded or fair or generous spirited' (Walker 2006: 99). In Bernstein's view, though, acquiring powerful, abstract knowledge, which resides in the disciplines taught in universities, bestows confidence, a sense of place in society and the means to participate in it, in one way or another. It is noteworthy that this view chimes with that of Stanley Fish (2008: 168), who argues vociferously that the job of universities is 'to introduce students to bodies of material new to them and equip those same students with the appropriate (to the discipline) analytical and research skills'. His point is that university education should be about developing minds (as Dewey would have it) and he quotes Derrida: 'Thinking, if it is to remain open to the possibility of thought . . . must beware ends' (Fish 2008: 177–8). Michael Young (2008), too, argues for the reinstatement of the role of knowledge in the sociology of education.

Pedagogic means to acquiring knowledge

> Pedagogy is a sustained process whereby somebody(s) acquires a new form or develops existing forms of conduct, knowledge, practice and criteria from somebody(s) or something deemed to be an appropriate provider and evaluator – appropriate either from the point of view of the acquirer or by some other body(s) or both.
>
> (Bernstein 2000: 78)

Educational literature that takes a CA highlights the need for student participation and dialogue. Walker, in particular, embeds arguments for a capability list in empirical detail supplied by students about their university educational experiences. She conceptualizes 'pedagogies' as 'structurally and contextually located [and] as a matter of micro-processes of capability development, agency and learning in which we make futures' (Walker 2006: 5). What Bernstein contributes to such a conceptualization is a way of thinking about pedagogic 'micro-processes'. How pedagogy is 'framed' is the key to understanding how students best acquire knowledge. The main issue is the locus (whether with teacher or with student) and degree of control over organization, selection, sequencing, pacing and criteria for assessment, as well as teacher/student relations. Each of these aspects can be discretely strongly or weakly framed. Strong framing places control with the teacher, who makes the boundaries explicit, and weak framing places control with the student. Briefly, since it is not the main subject of this chapter, although progressive teachers lean towards weak framing, it can work to exclude from knowledge acquisition working-class students who are not familiar with academic ways of thinking and writing. Ascertaining what pattern of framing works best is a matter of pedagogical judgement and empirical investigation. But what should hold steady for all groups in society is access to 'powerful knowledge' (Young 2008), that is, it is inequitable to teach strong disciplines to some (usually the elite) and weak generic skills to others.

In this section we have contextualized the concept of 'pedagogic rights' in the broader work of Basil Bernstein, showing how he relates formal education to social hierarchy and inequity by way of curriculum and pedagogy.

The concept of pedagogic rights

Both Nussbaum (2000) and Walker (2006) discuss the connection between human rights and the CA, arguing that the latter goes further by specifying what it takes for people to benefit from their rights (for example, the right to education is not useful without the capability to be educated). It might, therefore, seem retrogressive to return to the language of rights. Yet, Nussbaum (2000: 100) herself argues that the concept of 'rights' does a good deal of rhetorical work by signalling 'justified and urgent claims to certain types of treatment' and it also suggests obligations and responsibilities on both sides. Further, we think that 'pedagogic rights', as conceived by Bernstein, bridge first-generation rights' (political and civil liberties) and 'second-generation' rights (economic and social rights) by providing educational means to 'opportunities and capacities with which to make choices about life plans' (Nussbaum 2000: 97).

Bernstein (2000) discusses pedagogic rights only briefly in his final volume, so we have had leeway to develop and empirically investigate the concept. This is what he does set out. Pedagogic rights are translated from rights in democratic societies. He establishes two conditions for democracy: (1) that people feel they have a 'stake' in society; that is, they feel they both have rights to receive and obligations to give; and (2) that people have confidence that political arrangements allow the realization of the stake. These conditions can, Bernstein argues, be translated in terms of educational institutions: students must have a stake in the education a university offers and confidence in the arrangements to realize it. He proceeds to propose that for the two conditions to be realized three interrelated rights should be institutionalized. Each right creates conditions for what might be called a 'capability' and each operates at a different level. In Table 3.2 we show: the three rights; the level at which each operates; Bernstein's outcome or capability associated with each right; and a selection of the capabilities from the literature discussed above that have helped us expand and deepen our understanding of the meaning of pedagogic rights.

It seems to us that Bernstein's pedagogic rights are fundamentally about how the construction of symbolic and real boundaries in education influences the extent to which people become free to imagine and act. The question is whether the educational process itself is differentially and unfairly enabling and constraining students to be who they want to be and do what they want to do.

In the next section, we introduce briefly the research project which set out to explore access to pedagogic rights as an alternative way of evaluating the quality of undergraduate degrees so that we can move on to a more detailed exploration of pedagogic rights, with some empirical illustration.

Table 3.2 The concept of 'pedagogic rights'

Right	Level	Capability (Bernstein's)	Human development capabilities
Enhancement	Individual	Confidence	Practical reason; senses imagination and thought[a]
Inclusion	Social	Communitas	Affiliation; social relations and networks; narrative imagination[a]
Participation	Political	Civic discussion and action	Rationality and reasonableness[b]

a Nussbaum and Walker.
b Sen.

Investigating quality and inequality in undergraduate degrees

The Quality and Inequality in University First Degrees project[8] used a theoretical framework derived from the work of Basil Bernstein to investigate the teaching of social science with a sociological basis (sociology, social policy and criminology) in four universities of different status in England as reflected in a position in the most commonly referred to national higher education UK league tables.[9] The context of the project is widespread concern about the limitations that a stratified and differentiated higher education system places on achieving social justice, despite arrangements for access and widening participation in university. Students from poorer backgrounds tend to study at lower-status and less well-resourced universities for which the social and economic value attached to the degree is likely to be less (Boliver 2011; Iftikhar *et al.* 2009). Furthermore, league table measures are unfair because they are largely based on wealth and already established status, thereby confirming the ranking of universities as if it is the natural order (Amsler and Bolsmann 2012).

Of the four research sites, 'Prestige' and 'Selective' regularly appear in the top half of these league tables, and 'Community' and 'Diversity' in the bottom quartile, and here we refer to them as 'higher status' and 'lower status' respectively. The Bernsteinian framework was used to evaluate whether and how differences in the experience of university education reproduce or disrupt social inequality by exploring what kind of university undergraduate sociology-related social science is being transmitted; how it is being acquired; to what effect on students; and whether the effects are inequitable.

Combining pedagogic rights and human capabilities

Bernstein (2000: xxi) proposed that the three pedagogic rights 'set up a model against which [to] compare what happens in various education institutions to see whether there is unequal distribution of these rights'. While we found differences in the framing of pedagogy in the different departments, we did not find systematic differences in access to pedagogic rights. Here we use pedagogic rights to organize a discussion about the capabilities that students appear to gain from studying sociology-related social science, whatever the university they attend. It should be noted immediately that sociology-based disciplines engage students – who have already demonstrated a preference by their choice – in a specific knowledge that has specific effects on student consciousness. Nonetheless, it is our view that similar outcomes can be expected in any humanities and social science subject. Of course, pedagogic rights pertain to all university disciplines and it is still an empirical question how they might play out in different disciplines.

The selection of empirical findings[10] used here for illustrative purposes are robust and drawn from the first wave of data analyses encompassing interviews, life histories, the survey, recordings of teaching, and documentary analysis. We have brought the analysed data sets into relation with each other and reflected on them through the lens of Bernstein's theory of pedagogic rights to evaluate the effects of studying a specific body of knowledge in different universities. Each right is discussed by offering: Bernstein's brief definition – pedagogic rights are discussed in two pages only in *Pedagogy, Symbolic Control and Identity*; illustrations of how a consideration of human development and capability literature can enrich an understanding of the right; and examples of how the right appears in the lives of students in our study. Throughout we draw attention to how the concepts of pedagogic rights and human capabilities might combine to illuminate university educational goals.

Pedagogic right 1: individual enhancement

The first pedagogic right is 'the means of critical understanding and to new possibilities'. Access to the right of 'individual enhancement' is the means to expanded personal horizons and results in 'confidence' (Bernstein 2000: xx). The juxtaposition of confidence with expansion of horizons brings individual enhancement close to the capability of 'practical reason', whereby individuals can plan their own 'good' life. This first right can be seen as foundational, in much the same way that for Nussbaum, among all human capabilities, practical reason is one of two (the other is affiliation) which 'stand out as of special importance', because it 'organise[s] and suffuse[s] all the others, making their pursuit truly human. To use one's senses in a way not infused by the characteristically human use of thought and planning is to use them in an incompletely human manner' (Nussbaum 2000: 82). Walker's definition is particularly apt and elaborates Bernstein's terse definition:

> Being able to make well-reasoned, informed, critical, independent, intellec-
> tually astute, socially responsible and reflective choices. Being able to construct
> a personal life project in an uncertain world. Having good judgement.
>
> (Walker 2006: 128)

What Bernstein adds to these descriptions of the basic capability of practical reason that sits so well with the transformatory goals of higher education is insight about the educational process necessary to achieving it. Access to individual enhancement requires boundaries to be 'experienced [as] tension points' and 'entails a discipline' (Bernstein 2000: xx); and our study revealed how a university social science education is an experience of boundary crossing. We found students forming a specialized social science pedagogic identity by way of the experience of 'tension points' in the boundaries between abstract disciplinary knowledge, which in Bernstein's terms is 'sacred', expressed and in vertical discourse, and previously held 'mundane' knowledge about people and everyday life, expressed in horizontal discourse.

Students repeatedly report that having their eyes and minds 'opened' about themselves, others and society by way of disciplinary knowledge has changed them forever in ways that they value. For us, the personal transformation that students report is the formation of a specialized disciplinary identity of a person who has acquired confidence and practical reason by seeing the relevance of the knowledge they have acquired to everyday life.

Pedagogic right 2: social inclusion

The second pedagogic right is 'to be included socially, intellectually, culturally and personally [including] the right [to be] autonomous' (Bernstein 2000: xx). Bernstein uses the anthropological term 'communitas' (Turner, first published in 1969) to describe what students gain from access to the second pedagogic right.[11] Communitas is characteristic of people who experience liminality or periods of transition together; and, in some interpretations, communitas denotes an unstructured community outside society, yet from which society benefits. For our purpose, communitas describes the specialized place and role in society that university social science can assist students to achieve. Developing communitas relates strongly to the personal/social facet of a specialized pedagogic identity.

The specialized place that students achieve by access to social inclusion relates closely to 'affiliation' which is Nussbaum's (2000: 82) second capability (with practical reason) to hold a special status: 'To plan for one's own life without being able to do so in complex forms of discourse, concern, and reciprocity with other human beings is, again, to behave in an incompletely human way.'

Social science knowledge illuminates the interaction between individuals and social systems or structure. In our study we revealed sociology-based social science knowledge allowing students to gain insight into why people are as they are, including themselves. Our data suggest that social science knowledge places students in two specific and related relationships to other people and to society in general: as those who empathize with, understand, are interested in and accept others, especially those who are designated 'different', and as those who question and challenge what goes on the world around them. In a rather direct way, the students were developing the capability of affiliation as defined by Nussbaum (which connects also to 'narrative imagination' and Walker's 'social relations and social networks'):

> Being able to live with and toward others, to recognise and show concern for other human beings, to engage in various forms of social interaction; to be able to imagine the situation of another and to have compassion for that situation; to have the capability for both justice and friendship.
>
> (Nussbaum 2000: 79)

By way of acquiring something sacred (a specialized knowledge and understanding), as social science graduates the students will have achieved a positional good; that is, a different and higher social position. Simultaneously, this position brings a sense of obligation; students expect to use their knowledge to enlighten others, for example, to argue with their parents about capital punishment or with their friends about the need to be sceptical about the news. The 'rite of passage' of the social science degree invests students with specialized knowledge and understanding which benefits society by way of their capability for affiliation. In this way, too, graduates have accessed the right to be included in the society at large.

Pedagogic right 3: political participation

The third pedagogic right is to participate in debate and practices that have outcomes in society: 'to participate in the construction, maintenance and transformation of social order' (Bernstein 2000: xxi). In Bernstein's view an effective democracy needs people who 'have a stake in society' by which he means they both receive (rights) and give (obligations). The evidence of the students' capability of civic discussion and action is considerably less than for the other capabilities of confidence and communitas: just a few students have joined societies or do voluntary work. Yet here, the capabilities approach provides an alternative perspective: students not choosing a functioning associated with a capability is not evidence that the capability has not been achieved. The students we studied questioned the status quo and thought about ways in which society might be differently arranged. Furthermore, when asked about future employment, most students envisage public service work in which they use their knowledge, understanding and dispositions to contribute to society.

In this respect the three pedagogic rights and associated capabilities can be seen as building one to the other: the confidence and practical reasoning that comes with individual enhancement is necessary to access social inclusion and to realize fully communitas and affiliation, and both individual enhancement and social inclusion are necessary to access political participation. Of central importance in human development terms is that students in a mass higher education system in a range of universities are being educated to be 'reasonable people'[12] of the kind Habermas (1993) proposes; that is, open-minded enough to allow the 'better argument' to sway them. And, as Sen (2009: 44) puts it in *The Idea of Justice*, 'public reasoning is quite central to democratic politics in general and to the pursuit of social justice in particular'.

In summarizing this section, we want again to focus attention on how a Bernsteinian analysis centralizes knowledge acquisition as the access to pedagogic rights. Sociology-based social science knowledge enlightened the students in our study about themselves and others (individual enhancement); it located them in a loose group of people who have specialized understanding about how individuals and society interact (social inclusion); and it will be of use – in or out of employment – to improve the social world (political participation).

Conclusion

An important aim of this chapter is to persuade the reader of the potential role of student engagement with university disciplines in interrupting social hierarchies (if powerful knowledge is equitably distributed) and in producing responsible, critical citizens, both goals central to human development. What we have not been able to do is discuss how good teaching strongly mediates students' capacity to engage in disciplinary knowledge, of which we found more instances in the lower-status universities.

The second aim is to demonstrate how the concepts of pedagogic rights and human capabilities can be combined to provide an evaluative framework in terms of educational outcomes for graduates and society. A practical point might be made in this connection. As Walker (2006) reminds us, the 'space' of capabilities is evaluative; that is, once there is a list it should be possible to find ways (often by looking at functionings as a proxy measurement) of making judgements about whether and to what extent a student has the potential and opportunity to function in terms of specific capabilities. Yet, lists tend to be long and unwieldy and, furthermore, they should ideally be negotiated locally (Alkire 2002). Rather than finding and measuring proxy indicators for a list of agreed capabilities, pedagogic rights might more feasibly be explored from the students' own perspective, either by way of qualitative data derived in interviews and focus groups or by survey. As Walker suggests, if we can combine the notion of capabilities (a list drawn up locally, discipline by discipline, to prevent 'normalization') and pedagogic rights 'we would have a demanding and ethical set of standards by which to judge accomplished university teaching' (Walker 2006: 140) which concerns itself with human development, particularly the development of minds and reason, which are essential to the achievement of freedom and justice (Sen 2004).

Notes

1. Economic and Social Research Council-funded three-year project RES-062-23-1438.
2. http://www.undp.org/content/undp/en/home/mdgoverview.html.
3. http://hdr.undp.org/en/statistics/hdi/.
4. http://www.oecd.org/dataoecd/24/48/39997378.pdf.
5. http://hdr.undp.org/en/humandev/.

6. Being able to feel confidence and self-reliance; being able to visualize life plans; being able to further abilities; being able to transform commodities into valuable functionings.
7. Being able to acquire knowledge required in a job position; being able to look for and ask for better job opportunities; being able to choose desired jobs.
8. November 2009–January 2012 funded by the ESRC: RES-062-23-1438.
9. Specifically, *The Guardian*, the *Sunday Times*, *The Times* and *Complete University Guide*.
10. Three years' intensive fieldwork in four university departments produced extensive data sets. These include: interviews with students (162) and staff (16); student life histories (96); longitudinal case studies of students (31); recordings of teaching for the three years of the degrees (12); student essays and dissertations; analyses of curriculum, departmental, institutional and national documents; a student survey (750); field notes; and statistical data. Qualitative data sets have been coded using NVivo software and our analytical process has involved research team members independently generating coding themes and using cross-validation processes and inter-coder reliability checks. The survey was analysed using SPSS.
11. The concept of communitas is not attributed, defined or elaborated, allowing us that work.
12. In the *Idea of Justice* (2009) Sen uses Rawl's term to characterize an open-minded, deliberating human being.

References

Alkire, S. (2002) 'Dimensions of human development', *World Development*, 30(2): 181–205.
Amsler, S.S. and Bolsmann,C. (2012) 'University ranking as social inclusion', *British Journal of Sociology of Education*, 33(2): 283–301.
Andresen, S., Otto, H-U. and Ziegler, H. (2010) 'Bildung as human development: an educational view on the capabilities approach', in H-U. Otto and H. Ziegler (eds) *Der Erziehungswissenscaft*, VS Verlag fur Sozialwissen.
Bernstein, B. (2000) *Pedagogy, Symbolic Control and Identity*, Oxford: Rowman and Littlefield.
Boliver, V. (2011) 'Expansion, differentiation, and the persistence of social class inequalities in British higher education', *Higher Education*, 61(3): 229–42.
Delanty, G. (2001) *Challenging Knowledges*, Buckingham: SRHE/Open University Press.
Delors, J. et al (1996) *Learning: The Treasure Within*, Report to UNESCO of the International Commission on Education for the Twenty-First Century, Paris: UNESCO Publishing. Available at http://unesdoc.unesco.org/images/0010/001095/109590 eo.pdf.
Fish, S. (2008) *Save the World on Your Own Time*, Oxford: Oxford University Press.
Flores-Crespo, P. (2007) 'Situating education in the human capabilities approach', in M. Walker M. and E. Unterhalter (eds) *Amartya Sen's Capability Approach and Social Justice in Education*, New York: Palgrave Macmillan.
Habermas, J. (1971) *Towards a Rational Society: Student Protest, Science and Politics*, trans. J.J. Shapiro. Boston: Beacon Press.
—— (1989) 'The idea of the university: learning processes', in J. Habermas, trans. S. Weber Nicholson, *The New Conservatism: Cultural Criticism and the Historians' Debate*. Cambridge: Polity Press.
—— (1993) *Justification and Application: Remarks on Discourse Ethics*, trans. C. Cronin, Cambridge, MA: MIT Press.

Iftikhar, H., McNally, S. and Telhaj, S. (2009) 'University quality and graduate wages in the UK', Discussion Paper, Bonn, Germany: Institute for the Study of Labor.

Lozano, J.F., Boni, A., Peris, J. and Hueso, A. (2012) 'Competencies in higher education: a critical analysis from the capabilities approach', *Journal of Philosophy of Education*, 46(1): 132–14.

McLean, M. (2008) *Pedagogy and the University: Critical Theory and Practice*, London: Continuum.

Nussbaum, M.C. (1997) *Cultivating Humanity: A Classical Defense of Reform in Liberal Education*. Harvard: Harvard University Press.

—— (2000) *Women and Human Development: The Capabilities Approach*, New York: Cambridge University Press.

—— (2010) *Not for Profit – Why Democracy Needs the Humanities*, Oxfordshire: Princeton University Press.

Sen, A. (1999) *Development as Freedom*. New York: Oxford University Press.

—— (2004) *Rationality and Freedom*, Cambridge, MA: The Belknap Press of Harvard University Press.

—— (2009) *The Idea of Justice*, Cambridge, MA: The Belknap Press of Harvard University Press.

Taylor, R., Barr J. and Steele, T. (2002) *For a Radical Higher Education*, Buckingham: Open University Press.

Walker, M. (2006) *Higher Education Pedagogies: A Capabilities Approach*, Maidenhead: Open University Press.

Walker, M. and Unterhalter, E. (eds) (2007) *Amartya Sen's Capability Approach and Social Justice in Education*, New York: Palgrave Macmillan.

Wright-Mills, C. (2000) *The Sociological Imagination*, Oxford: Oxford University Press.

Young, M. (2008) *Bringing Knowledge Back In*, London: Routledge.

Chapter 4

What is wrong with global inequality in higher education?

Elaine Unterhalter

Virtually all discussion of collective good associated with the increase in university tuition fees in England has been framed by national concerns to ensure Britain's universities remain 'world class'. The term denotes intrinsic achievement, but also implies rank order and attendant inequalities. The UK is not alone among university systems in an obsession with world rankings. What, then, is wrong with these assumptions about global inequality in higher education?

Global inequality in higher education is enmeshed with dimensions outside the sector often associated with poverty (Unterhalter and Carpentier 2010; Carpentier and Unterhalter 2011). Poverty may be considered an absolute line; for example, numbers living on less than $1.25 a day or it may be linked with other measures of a decent life – longevity, reasonable levels of education, and income (United Nations 2010; United Nations Development Programme 2011). Some measures look at how intense the experience of poverty is for certain countries and groups and whether people who are poor are also illiterate and malnourished (Oxford Poverty and Human Development Initiative 2010). Inequalities associated with poverty and lack of dignity are often linked with gender, racial, ethnic or age divisions which exacerbate aspects of what I have described as poverty in the guise of a net of intersecting structural inequalities, or a fuel that may propel one out into different circumstances or force one to take possibly risky action for change (Unterhalter 2012a). In all these measures of inequality, poverty is excluding and life-threatening. It undermines survival and the chance of a decent life.

Global responses to poverty outside the country in which one votes or pays taxes range from the minimal humanitarian to the maximal egalitarian but the particular role of higher education has not been specified in these discussions and has to be discerned from quite abstractly specified approaches. Minimal humanitarian responses generally concede that we must provide emergency rations to those without food for brief periods. They place enormous faith in national and local economic processes to pull people through periods of want, which tend to be deemed temporary or the result of national not international failings (Nagel 2005; World Vision 2012). Maximal egalitarians argue for a substantial provision of public goods by national and international agencies in relation to education, health and social development to establish the conditions for decent life, not just for citizens of the particular countries that pay for or administer these, but for all (Armstrong 2008; Brock 2009). They generally note the importance of state and global organizations in establishing these conditions and argue for responsive and participatory processes to allow the poor, the marginalized and the subordinated to be represented in taking decisions about public good. Some egalitarians see the market as a useful contributor to the free flow of information and job opportunities, associated with the development of public good. Others see the market as not nearly so benign, and neoliberal marketization, with its concern to assign a money value to everything and undermine the capacity of states to make social and economic provision, as a major threat to egalitarian engagements with poverty (Brock 2009; Hill 2009). Higher education institutions, staff and students position themselves on a spectrum between these positions, largely as a response to contextual processes (Unterhalter and Carpentier 2010) but there has been little critical reflection on developing a normative position for this sector.

Global inequalities

A number of features of global inequalities within or associated with the sector shape the context of any such discussion. Firstly, there are very different patterns of participation. In 2008 there were 159 million tertiary students globally, roughly a 54 per cent increase over 2000. Fifty-one per cent were women (UNESCO Institute for Statistics [UIS] 2010: 170). In low-income countries tertiary-level participation has improved only marginally, from 5 per cent in 2000 to 7 per cent in 2007. In 2008 China enrolled about 23 per cent of the university-going age cohort, and India around 13 per cent (UIS 2010: 164,168). Sub-Saharan Africa has the lowest participation rate in the world (6 per cent). But for some of the countries with the lowest levels of human development this is even lower. Thus, in Kenya and Tanzania, the participation rates in 2008 were 4 per cent and 1 per cent, respectively (UIS 2010: 170). Morley *et al.* (2008) show that in a public university in Ghana, where women comprised 29 per cent of those enrolled on commerce courses and 41 per cent of those enrolled in degrees in primary education, women who attended a deprived school were only 1 per cent of those enrolled. Thus, while there has been some expansion of opportunities for lower socio-economic groups to participate in higher education in richer countries, these chances are virtually non-existent in the poorest countries in the world, where arguably the expansion of higher education might make a difference. Some aspects of this emerge from quantitative studies in Nigeria and Tanzania (Unterhalter and Heslop 2011) and qualitative work in South Africa and Kenya (Unterhalter 2012b). In the quantitative study 129 schools with poor facilities in districts with high levels of poverty were surveyed. Girls were markedly more able to speak up about this at schools where teachers were better qualified than in schools where they had minimal or no qualifications beyond a secondary school certificate. In-depth discussion in two qualitative studies confirmed this trend. While we cannot make causal claims, it is evident that teachers qualified to a higher education level appear associated with how girls can speak out about their lives. Moreover, experiences of schooling will have considerable impact on whether or not these girls can choose to access and succeed in higher education.

Secondly, there are inequalities in resources. Nearly half of those teaching in higher education worldwide possess only a bachelor's degree. In many countries class sizes have increased and students receive little personal guidance. Academic salaries have deteriorated and many academics hold more than one job and have few opportunities to undertake research (Altbach 2010). Access to international education communities is extremely uneven. Kim and Locke (2010) show how there is staff migration *to* the most prestigious universities and departments in the UK, high levels of out-migration of academic staff to undertake doctorates in countries such as Mexico, while in many countries the academic labour market is highly localized. Academics differ markedly in how much they know or are concerned with the world beyond their locale.

Thirdly, there are inequalities in status. League tables rank universities nationally and internationally deploying some measures of esteem. For example, in 2010 the *Times Higher Education* world university ranking was based on a survey of 13,000 experienced academics from 131 countries regarding how they ranked universities and where they would recommend their top students went. All the top 200 universities were located in countries with high or very high human development, with only two exceptions: the University of Cape Town in South Africa ranked 107 and the University of Alexandria in Egypt ranked 147. Both universities are located in countries with vast inequalities and both have histories of serving small elites. Esteem seems clearly associated with income and wealth, since the qualities that make for estimations of a good university are qualities about the academic environment, the time accorded academics and the colleagues with whom they work to inquire in depth and teach with space for reflection. This is very rarely possible in mass higher education systems and thus the circle of esteem is a closed one.

These contextual inequalities have a bearing on how higher education institutions (HEIs), staff and students take up positions on the spectrum sketched above with regard to engaging with global inequality. Some may have an almost exclusive focus in curriculum and pedagogy on economic, social and political processes that heighten inequality and lack of dignity for the poorest, with some minimal provision for acute humanitarian need. Others might orient every aspect of the institutional mission to work on a very participatory view of building towards global equality. While some academic distance is useful in assessing how one makes a judgement about inequality in higher education, such discussion is inevitably routed through our experiences of existing HEIs and the ways in which they have confronted this issue.

In trying to begin an assessment of what is wrong with higher education inequalities, it is useful to think first about inequalities. Some appear neutral while others have particularly harmful effects. In the UK it does not make much difference what colour one's eyes are, but a great deal of research suggests it still does make a difference what colour one's skin is. This, often in association with socio-economic conditions, affects whether or not one gets good school leaving results, which university one attends and whether one will become a professor (Shepherd 2011). These penalties associated with parents, the history and levels of equality within the country of one's birth and with regard to the higher education opportunities between countries indicate that in understanding higher education inequalities we are not assessing a situation that is natural, but one where the inequalities that matter – for example, having access or resources – are made by human relationships. Thus, while one might respond that some inequalities are just the way things are, our response to this can be a passive acceptance or an acknowledgement of history and a range of attempts to change.

Some inequalities associated with prodigious talent appear neutral or somewhat beside the point. Huge achievement can sometimes attract immense rewards. But one cannot ignore the distribution of the recognition of that talent between particular groups or the ways in which the reward system is regulated. A male professional footballer earns much more than a female player and professional footballers earn hugely more than virtually all their fans. It is not necessarily the case that the well-paid footballer in the public eye all the time has a better life than the fan, who earns modestly but enjoys watching a match and lives in a society and community which accords her dignity. While there are inequalities, they do not matter to quality of life. However, if the modestly paid fan does not have a decent life, and if the money tied up in football as a business is implicated in that lack of a decent life, possibly because taxes are not paid by companies associated with teams or because the private sector transfers many of its costs to the state, receiving hidden subsidies, and reducing the amount the state can spend on a good life for the fan, the inequalities matter. A commodified higher education system with star professors and little public regulation or strong sense of normative direction may not operate so differently to a commercial football team.

Inequalities in one space; for example, the level of esteem given pure mathematics in different well-funded higher education communities, may not be the same as inequalities in another; for example, the numbers of well-taught primary health care workers who are able to work with the poorest. This is not to say I value health education over pure mathematics. I see the value of both. However, the forms of the kinds of inequality are different and their immediate consequences matter.

In trying to draw out what I think is wrong with global inequalities in higher education, I want to stress that the global inequalities I am concerned with are those that limit capabilities; that is, the social arrangements that constrain people's freedom to promote or achieve what they value doing or being (Sen 1992; Alkire and Deneulin 2009). I am concerned with the ways in which unequal HEIs may contribute through omission or commission to limiting the chance of lives with dignity for the poorest. Currently, global higher education does not tend to address questions of ethics very much. Here is a vignette from a report of the British Council's Going Global conference, which took place in Hong Kong on

10–12 March 2011. The conference was addressed by a range of vice chancellors, government ministers and academic entrepreneurs. Donald Tsang Yam-Kuen, Chief Executive of Hong Kong, used the powerhouse metaphor and spoke about Hong Kong having the foundations, the location, the money (25 per cent of government expenditure), strong institutions and the real vision to make its mark as a regional higher education hub (Greatrix 2011). This presentation was placed next to that of Professor Olugbemiro Jegede (2011) from Ghana, Secretary-General and Chief Executive of the Association of African Universities, who outlined the challenges for Africa. These encompassed inclusion, equity, social justice, skills development, national development, massification, uneven infrastructure, very different funding arrangements, variations in support for academic development and maldistribution of qualified staff. For him the best the power-house of higher education could generate was 'collaboration and a continent-wide academic framework including mobility and mutual recognition' (Greatrix 2011). These are quite small crumbs. If you do not generate mains supply for the powerhouse you probably cannot expect much more. What this juxtaposition highlights is that a plea from those with the least in no way enters the language or configuration of global relationships set out by those with the most.

Justifying global inequalities

Three kinds of justification for global inequalities between universities are generally offered. Firstly, the competition argument is made. This assumes that, like free trade, the free flow of ideas and expertise requires multiple producers and deregulated exchange. Supply and demand will introduce a natural balance to reward excellence. This is the argument David Willetts (2011) emphasized at Going Global, where he spoke about how he welcomed the open climate in UK higher education, pointing out that the change in the fee regime in the UK would not alter the openings and costs for international students. He was proud that 16 per cent of UK students were international and 45 per cent of research papers co-authored in the UK in 2010 were with academics from other countries.

By this analysis there is nothing morally problematic about opening up higher education to a range of providers, a range of fee structures and a range of delivery mechanisms, and encouraging every kind of exchange. In allowing the market to regulate which kinds of ideas flourish, or which pedagogies come to the fore, and which kinds of students and disciplines 'make it' (in both senses of the word) we are supporting the very lifeblood of free flows, which have always made knowledge grow. This implies inequalities between institutions do not carry harm.

Secondly, a diversity argument acknowledges that students and HEIs are different. This is the kind of argument implicit in supporting a wide range of experiences of higher education. Some students and staff, the argument goes, want intensive academic engagement in sequestered communities, some want to fit studies around work and some want a hybrid experience. Acknowledging this is both respectful and inclusive, because it does not force a particular template of what a higher education system is or should be. These inequalities are no more different than blue or brown eyes. In some countries, higher education is very well endowed and centuries old. It would be impossible to replicate this model everywhere. Expanding access must entail allowing many different kinds of unequal HEIs to flourish. As long as we respect different cultures of learning, teaching and research in higher education, and possibly mitigate some of the worst effects of untrammelled expansion, like insanitary buildings or underqualified staff, inequality is not in itself problematic.

A third justification is a version of national or community or family desert. This is exemplified in the unproblematic juxtaposition at the Going Global conference of the massively well-endowed plans for a global hub of HEIs planned for Hong Kong and the plea for collaborations made from Africa. According to this argument, if citizens of a particular country or members of a particular faith community or family work hard, save prudently and invest wisely in higher education, they deserve the benefits of that system and would be justified in saying those benefits should not be extended to other nations, communities or families that have not taken these steps, unless they are prepared to pay for them. If you have not saved, and come to the table with nothing but your problems, as the representative of the universities in Africa appeared to do, all you 'deserve' is recognition of the problems you face and some form of rather underspecified, and possibly not well-targeted, collaboration.

Rebutting global inequalities

In rebutting these arguments as to why global inequality in higher education is not problematic I want to challenge a number of presuppositions on which they rest. The first is that competition, difference and desert are neutral. They can only be understood in these terms if they are completely abstracted from the contexts that give them meaning. While the free flow of ideas, students, researchers, teachers and academic practices is an important feature of the development and worthwhile-ness of higher education, a completely deregulated market might never allow the talented natural scientist, who speaks KiSwahili at home and who struggles to pass his school leaving exams in English, to ever enter university. It might never encourage students to study arts or humanities subjects, for which job prospects are not clear, and it may favour the academic mobility of young men from affluent backgrounds, who do not have family responsibilities, while keeping young women from poorer backgrounds to struggle on their own against a parochial view of their discipline. Competition is neutral on whether it does or does not challenge inequalities. When these inequalities both within and between countries are stark, competition as the powerful motor of global higher education will not effect redress.

Similar points can be made about difference. A banal recognition of difference, without some consideration that some differences, such as lack of resources or opportunities, are harmful and militate against the production of well-informed graduates and insightful academics, is extremely blinkered. Many differences associated with deficit actually amplify each other and have long-term effects over generations of students. They also have particularly harmful effects in relation to the quality of research work linked to social development. Tolerating a wide variety of HEIs without working towards improving equity and democracy or reflecting together on processes for change, resourcing and the sustainability of organizations, actually hollows out the higher education project and only partially supports expansion. Inequality in one space, say student diversity, might be important to acknowledge but does not justify inequalities in other spaces regarding capacity, esteem, resources or endeavour.

The argument about desert is also vulnerable to rebuttal on grounds of context. A particular country, say the UK or the US, might well have amassed large amounts of intellectual and academic social capital over centuries. But we cannot discuss this wealth without also considering the extraction of surplus labour or the uneven terms of trade which generated the profits invested in higher education. A similar point could be made about the university where I did my undergraduate study, the University of the Witwatersrand, massively endowed by profits from the dangerous, ill-paid and socially dislocating work of miners, very few of whose children even now gain admission. Desert, like competition and difference, is not historically neutral.

Arguments for competition have merit, because they emphasize freedom. Arguments for difference must be acknowledged, because they recognize diversity. Arguments for desert cannot be completely ignored, because they do give credit to hard work, enterprise and risk (even if they ignore the terms on which these are sometimes conducted). But making these arguments only in relation to these abstracts and failing to contextualize them undermines their salience.

Inequality in higher education capabilities for institutions and individuals tends to undermine investigation into global public goods. For example, despite the huge numbers living in poverty, until relatively recently there has been very little research on gender, schooling and poverty, although quite extensive studies of girls' education (Lloyd 2005). A free-for-all global market that tolerates high levels of inequities and differences between institutions, staff and students does not appear the best setting to address these tricky non-glamorous subjects. But if we do not address them through scholarship as much as political or economic action, key elements of the conditions in which higher education thrives appear to be in doubt. Global inequality in higher education exacerbates inequalities in income, basic education and health. The lowest participation rates in higher education in the countries with the lowest human development scores is no coincidence. In some areas benefits of higher education take so long to trickle down, no one gets even a drop of water, never mind the semblance of being wet. Failing to engage with an aspiration to redress these injustices appears to offend, in some intrinsic way, the very nature of a higher education project.

Collini (2012: 38) points out that changes in the administration, financing and regulation of higher education are not commensurate with changes in concern among academics regarding what universities are for. A similar point may be made about inequalities. Arguments regarding attending to inequalities have tended to be made with regard to finance, and whether or not financial resources are available for expanding provision, and less with regard to normative deliberation on whether or not reflecting on inequality and injustice is a key concern of higher education. Because the arguments have tended to be made instrumentally, rather than as an intrinsic feature of expanding scientific discussion, the aspects of competition, diversity and desert have been given prominence. However, within particular disciplines, we have a very uneven record of considering how or why particular kinds of inequalities manifest themselves and what their consequences may be. We have not yet looked at the resources for thinking about global justice in relation to higher education. The question of what is wrong with global inequality in higher education is linked with the question about universities, the public good and how this is configured in a space of unequal global relations. It is this question a world class needs to deliberate on with the people who it most grievously effects.

References

Alkire, S. and Deneulin, S. (2009) 'The human development and capability approach', in S. Deneulin and L. Shahani (eds) *An Introduction to Human Development and Capability Approach*, London: Earthscan.

Altbach, P. (2010) 'Trouble with numbers', *Times Higher Education*, 23 September. Available at http://www.timeshighereducation.co.uk/story.asp?storyCode=413555&sectioncode=26 [accessed 6 June 2012].

Armstrong, C. (2008) 'Global egalitarianism', *Philosophy Compass*, 4(1): 155–71.

Brock, G. (2009) *Justice: A Cosmopolitan Account*, Oxford: Oxford University Press.

Carpentier, V. and Unterhalter, E. (2011) 'Globalization, higher education and inequalities: problems and prospects' in R. King, S. Marginson and R. Naidoo (eds) *Handbook on Globalization and Higher Education*, Cheltenham: Edward Elgar.

Collini, P. (2012) *What are Universities For?*, London: Penguin.

Greatrix, P. (2011) 'World education: the new powerhouse', *Registrarism Blog*. Available at http://registrarism.wordpress.com/2011/03/21/world-education-the-new-powerhouse-going-global-2011-%C2%A71/ [accessed 15 February 2011].

Hill, D. (ed.) (2009) *Contesting Neoliberal Education*, New York: Routledge.

Jegede, O. (2011) 'World education: the new powerhouse?', presented at Going Global 2011, Hong Kong, 10–12 March 2011. Available at http://embed.policyreview.tv/video/530/3221 [accessed 15 February 2011].

Kim, T. and Locke, W. (2010) *Transnational Academic Mobility and the Academic Profession*, London: Centre for Higher Education Research and Information, The Open University.

Lloyd, C. (2005) *Growing Up Global*, Washington: National Academies Press.

Morley, L., Leach, F. and Lugg, R. (2008) 'Democratising higher education in Ghana and Tanzania', *International Journal of Educational Development*, 29(1): 56–64.

Nagel, T. (2005) 'The problem of global justice', *Philosophy and Public Affairs*, 33(2): 113–47.

Oxford Poverty and Human Development Initiative (2010) *Multidimensional Poverty Index 2010*, Oxford: Oxford Poverty and Human Development Initiative.

Sen, A. (1992) *Inequality Re-Examined*, Oxford: Clarendon Press.

Shepherd, J. (2011) '14,000 British professors – but only 50 are black', *The Guardian*, 27 May. Available at http://www.guardian.co.uk/education/2011/may/27/only-50-black-british-professors [accessed 28 May 2012].

UNESCO Institute for Statistics (2010) *Global Education Digest*, Montreal: UIS.

United Nations (2010) *The Millennium Development Goals Report 2010*, New York: UN.

United Nations Development Programme (2011) *Human Development Report*, New York: UNDP.

Unterhalter, E. (2012a) 'Mutable meanings: gender equality in education and international rights frameworks', *Equal Rights Review*, 8: 67–84.

—— (2012b) 'Inequality, capabilities and poverty in four African countries: girls' voice, schooling, and strategies for institutional change', *Cambridge Journal of Education*, 42(3): 307–25.

Unterhalter, E. and Carpentier, V. (eds) (2010) *Global Inequalities and Higher Education. Whose Interests Are We Serving?* Basingstoke: Palgrave.

Unterhalter, E. and Heslop, J. (2011) *Transforming Education for Girls in Nigeria and Tanzania. A Cross-Country Analysis of Baseline Research*, Johannesburg: ActionAid.

Willetts, D. (2011) Opening remarks to Going Global 2011, Hong Kong, 10–12 March 2011. Available at http://www.policyreview.tv/video/530/3219 [accessed 6 June 2011].

World Vision (2012) *Minimum Standards for Protection Mainstreaming*, London: World Vision UK.

Chapter 5

Education and capabilities for a global 'great transition'

Des Gasper

What are the implications for education of the emergent global challenges of sustainability? Various studies suggest that major changes are required in predominant human values during the next two generations, to ensure politically and environmentally sustainable societies and a sustainable global order. Three required moves, according to the Earth Charter and the Great Transition study by the Stockholm Environment Institute (Earth Charter Commission 2000; Raskin *et al.* 2002), are: (1) from pursuit of human fulfilment, predominantly through consumerism, to a focus on quality of life above quantity of commercial activity; (2) from the predominance of possessive individualism towards more human solidarity; and (3) from a stance of human domination and exploitation of nature towards an ecological sensitivity. This essay considers such a neo-Stoic project – covering, broadly speaking, the cultivation of humanity's flourishing as individuals, as collectivity, and in and towards our natural environment, each of them as desirable in themselves and in order to preserve humankind.

The challenge of value transition is also a challenge for the capability approach to human development. The tension between individualist consumerist and solidarist humanist versions of liberalism is found also between some of the possible interpretations of the capability approaches of Amartya Sen and Martha Nussbaum. The capability approach in a form which lacks notions of caring, and lacks an emphasis on the paradoxes of choice whereby, in many cases, having more options can bring less satisfaction (Schwartz 2005), could become an instrument of consumerism rather than a tool in its critique and reconstruction (Gasper and Truong 2010). Similarly, doubts arise over how far an individual-centred human rights perspective alone can motivate a solidaristic global ethics. A larger vision of human be-ing may be required.

This chapter looks first at the scale of the challenge and at some possible paths of social change, using the work of the Great Transition project. Like other recent surveys (e.g. UNDP 2007; Jackson 2009a, 2009b; Stern 2010) this material underlines the extreme challenges that humankind faces, given the nature of current values and behaviour.

Second, we consider the possibilities of change at personal, societal and global levels, with reference to the roles and mutual entanglement of personal change and system change and the question of where education fits in. The Great Transition Initiative's work[1] accords a vital role to national and global citizens' movements driven by the energies of young people, and implies potential major roles for progressive education and, conversely, a negative role for anti-progressive education. We use Brown and Lauder's study *The Future of Society in a Global Economy* (2001) to identify some of the barriers to change, and elements of the required rethinking of personhood, intelligence and education. However, that study's conventional preoccupation with 'success' in the global economy partly counteracts its other insights. So we will move on to Nussbaum's *Cultivating Humanity* for a more profound discussion of the roles for liberal humanist education in our 'one world', with special reference to university education.

The final section reviews the various discussions of required roles and links them to George's work (1997 and see chapter in this book) on possible lessons from multinational postgraduate education in the field of international development studies. This illustrates a form of education that can contribute towards two of the value changes required for sustaining humankind: greater global solidarity, and a rethinking of quality of life as rooted in richness of relationships more than in volume of possessions.

The great transition that awaits us: but which one?

Long-range trajectories

Work in the Great Transition Initiative (GTI) identified three areas of critical uncertainties for humanity's future (Raskin 2006a): (1) environmental risks; (2) the economic instabilities of – to use Edward Luttwak's (1999) term – 'turbo-capitalism'; and (3) socio-political combustibility. The three areas are strongly interconnected, which brings the risk of destructive chain reactions and resultant crises. The likely triggering factors are: financial collapse; pandemics; climate change; mega-terrorism and key resource shortages. All the elements of high vulnerability are present: high exposure to shocks, due to turbo-capitalism's economic, political, and environmental imbalances and low capacity to anticipate and avert or mitigate their consequences; high sensitivity to shocks when they arrive, thanks partly to the pervasive interconnectedness; and low coping capacity, including for adaptation to the effects and for learning about and acting on the causes.

The GTI sketches six indicative scenarios of global futures (Raskin *et al.* 2002; Raskin 2006a). First are two 'Conventional Worlds' scenarios. The 'Market Forces' scenario is an optimistic story of adaptation through the operation of markets guided by an inbuilt hidden hand and the occasional light touch by market-friendly technocrats. The 'Policy Reform' scenario too embodies a 'sustainable development' belief that unending economic growth, environmental sustainability and equity can somehow be combined through better technology and (in this case) active policy intervention. The GTI studies consider that these two scenarios contain internal contradictions and extreme risks: 'They must reverse destabilizing global trends – social polarization, environmental degradation, and economic instability – even as they advance the consumerist values, [unending] economic growth, and cultural homogenization that drive such trends' (Raskin 2006a: 3).

The 'Barbarization' scenarios present the working out of these contradictions. The 'Breakdown' scenario shows a Malthusian future in which human expansion triggers cataclysmic chain reactions of pestilence, war, famine and ecosystem decline. In 'Fortress World' some groups, intra- and internationally, manage to barricade themselves off from the zones of breakdown.

The two remaining scenarios concern futures of sustainability through radical change. The 'Eco-communalism' scenario is a traditional Green utopia of 'small is beautiful', in which humankind turns away from large-scale industrialism, a globalized economy and attempted environmental engineering. The GTI studies see this variant as implausible. Their hopes rest instead on the final scenario, the 'New Sustainability Paradigm', marked by an 'alternative globalization' guided by values of human solidarity and a rethinking of the nature of human be-ing and well-being:

> It sees in globalization, not only a threat, but also an opportunity for forging new categories of consciousness – global citizenship, humanity-as-whole, the wider web of life, and sustainability and the well-being of future generations . . . a pluralistic vision that, within a shared commitment to global citizenship, celebrates diverse regional forms of development and multiple pathways to modernity.
>
> (Raskin 2006a: 3)[2]

All the scenarios can in fact be called a great transition of one sort or another, in face of the crises that likely await humankind in the twenty-first century. Which of the scenarios is more likely depends on what combination emerges of intensity of crisis and degree of coping capacity. A low intensity of crises plus high coping capacity would allow a Conventional Worlds path. That pair of scenarios appears implausible on the basis of current evidence. Given a high intensity of crises and low coping capacity we will move along a Barbarization pathway. This second pair of scenarios would be intolerable. Given a high intensity of crises yet high coping capacity we may be both driven towards and able to make a Great Transition of a profound yet favourable kind. Our need is to build coping capacity, including through value change.

The GTI judges that global coping capacity can only increase greatly if a powerful global citizens' movement emerges (or, more precisely, a 'movement of the movements'; Hintjens 2006). The project's detailed analyses show contingent pathways, each representing a different possible direction beyond each phase of crisis, depending on the presence in those phases of either a weak or a strong global citizens' movement (Raskin 2006a). But the presence and strength of a movement are not sufficient. Required for a favourable transition in face of the likely crises are elements of shared vision, a shared identity of global citizen, and a realistic change strategy. Only with a powerful *and* well-oriented global citizens' movement can even the modest Policy Reform scenario become plausible, as opposed to the pattern we have seen during the past generation: recurrent, fine-sounding global commitments which then remain largely unimplemented.

History shows that people's and sometimes even societies' choices can be affected through envisioning alternative stories about the future and responding to the perceived threats and opportunities. Human values and the resulting social movements form key sets of variables that have influence and are themselves influenced and influenceable (Raskin 2006a, 2006b).

Value change?

For major societal reform people must perceive that they face real choices and must feel deeply motivated to take the reform choice. Processes of societal reform thus require values as drivers that help to motivate and reconfigure patterns of action. Humankind, especially its high-impact consumers clustered mostly in high-income countries, must become motivated towards choices which are compatible with global sustainability.

The Great Transition work presents three major types of value change required in response to the emerging and foreseeable crises and for a move to a sustainable global society: (1) from consumerism, and an ideology of life-fulfilment through buying, to a focus instead on quality of living; (2) from individualism to human solidarity, including concern for the 'external effects' one imposes on others; and (3) from domination of nature to ecological sensitivity. This formulation is inspired by the work that led to the Earth Charter (Raskin 2006b: 3). Even Nicholas Stern, former Chief Economist of the World Bank and an apostle of unending growth, argues that basic value changes will be needed to motivate the types of lifestyle reorientation, long-term-oriented investments and international cooperation that are essential for preventing dangerous global warming (Stern 2010).

A study by Robert Kates *et al.* (2006) takes a hard look at the scale of required value change.[3] It summarizes eight multinational surveys of stated values, such as the World Values Survey, which has been run since 1981 by Ronald Inglehart and others (Kates *et al.* use the 2002 World Values Survey, conducted in 79 countries). Here are the surveys' main findings in the three key areas:

- *Quality of life:* Strong orientation to pleasure through purchases predominated around the world (Kates *et al.* 2006: 5). We seem, in the majority, presently to embrace an ongoing, never-ending quest for fulfilment through purchase of ever-growing volumes of commodities.
- *Human solidarity:* Large majorities were concerned about the weak (children and elderly, sick or disabled people). But views were divided about poverty; for example, large majorities in Pacific Rim countries, including China and the USA, blamed poverty on laziness and lack of willpower, while majorities

elsewhere stressed instead lack of fair opportunities as the main cause. Despite this division, large majorities everywhere were reportedly willing to pay 1 per cent more of their income as taxes to help the world's poor; vastly more than nearly all governments actually give. Tolerance of other groups was supported in the abstract, but a third of the respondents wanted to not live next to specified other groups. Increased global interconnection was seen as having been good overall so far, but at the same time majorities were worried at the prospect of having any more of it.

- *Ecological sustainability:* Large majorities rejected an ethic of human domination of nature, when they considered the issue directly.[4] But strong tensions existed between the different values that people espoused. While most people 'think that less emphasis on material possessions would be a good thing' (Kates *et al.* 2006: 8), at the same time meaning and fulfilment are pursued to a large extent through acquisition of commodities.

Kates *et al.* (2006: 11) conclude that there is much stated support for values of solidarity and ecological sustainability, but our behaviour does not yet match this well. They state: 'Regarding quality of life values . . . much more fundamental value change is required', away from a preoccupation with unending, ever-growing commodity acquisition and to better balance material consumption in relation to other values.

Major and surprising value changes can occur. Kates *et al.* contrasted the world of 2006 with the world of the late 1920s, which lies as far back from their time of writing as 2084, the end date in GTI scenarios, lies in the future. Compared to the early twenty-first century, in value terms the 1920s represent in many respects another mental universe, thanks partly to the unexpected extent of growth from the 1940s onwards of values of universal human rights, including of women's rights and racial equality.

How can fundamental changes in values and practices arise? What roles does or can education play? Is it just a dependent variable within society, with no fundamental system-altering impacts? We will focus here on attitudes towards consumption and ideas about sources of well-being, which Kates *et al.* identified as the biggest challenge. We will give attention also to value change for global solidarity, which involves a rethinking of personhood and identity and perhaps an awareness that richness lies especially in relationships, and connects to the rejection of consumerism.

Values and change at the level of the person

Individualization and the lack of subjective security

According to Brown and Lauder (2001: 54), individualist consumerism is one of several forms of individualism and individualization which grew in mass industrial society as types of 'answer to the threat to personal identity posed by the factory

model of Fordist and bureaucratic work'. With mass fashion, individuals can experiment with 'personal statements' that yet use a given, society-wide or subgroup-
specific, visual language, so that the individual remains safely a group member.
We see also increasing negotiation of roles in various life-spaces, including regarding marriage, roles of parent and son/daughter, and so on. Several of these forms
of individualism may reinforce the preoccupation with purchasing.

In Brown and Lauder's (2001: 281) judgement, the society of self-concern 'is
ultimately self-defeating as many are finding to their material and psychological
cost'. Well-being research confirms this argument for at least a large proportion
of people in high-income countries (e.g. Easterlin 2002; Seligman 2002; Schwartz
2005; Barber 2007; Bruni and Porta 2007). The argument criticizes consumerism,
in terms of how to promote self-interest; it is not yet an evolved critique of non-
solidarity and it may not move those people who have the luck to achieve fulfilment
through self-concern and consumerism, perhaps in part thanks to ability to exploit
others. To deepen the critique of consumerism as well as to open out to solidarity,
we require some rethinking of 'self'.

Consumerism provides for a form of identity in mass society, and identity in
turn provides subjective security. Seeking that security through consumption
requires constant reinforcement through new expenditures. Objective security in
terms of health and physical and economic security does not guarantee subjective
security. Indeed, the more that people have, sometimes the more fearful they
become that they will lose it. In the absence of subjective security, wants are
insatiable. Modern capitalism consciously fuels subjective insecurities, as a basis of
new demand (see also Hamilton 2010).

Historically, religion has figured as a major source of subjective security, though
not a very reliable one. It can also become a source of fear and discontent – as
when other people are considered to be not following the good road – and a
justification for seeking domination. External sources for internal subjective
security, whether religious guarantees or consumer expenditures, are in general at
risk of failure. A subjective security that does not rest on some profounder reasoned
accommodation with life, not simply on authority or constant material reassurance,
is liable to recurrent destabilization or decay (Gasper 2007).

Change: personal change or system change?

Consumerism offers an apparent path for assuaging long-term dissatisfactions that
it cannot in reality address. But it does provide short-term gratifications, so while
it may not profoundly or sustainedly satisfy, how far can it be changed? Many social
scientists are sceptical regarding what to expect from change by individuals – even
if financially motivated by new incentives or full-cost accounting – if the required
change runs against predominant meaning systems.

Tim Jackson, director of the Economic and Social Research Council Research
Group on Lifestyles, Values and Environment at the University of Surrey, concluded as follows from a multiyear research programme on personal motivation

and systems of consumption. First, people's major motivations include a need for meaning and identity: 'Material artefacts embody symbolic meanings' (Jackson 2006: 378). The consumption of the already well-off is mainly a pursuit of symbolic meanings and identity through acquisition and possession of goods. The relative emptiness of the purchase and consumption themselves allows their endless repetition. Meaning giving comes more through the process than the product: meanings arise within social living. The individual is not simply bound into a social fabric, but created therein: 'Self is a social construct' (Jackson 2006: 374).

Second, in particular, 'consumer society is a cultural defence against *anomie*' (Jackson 2006: 384), and one or other such defence is required now that people live long and, in most countries, face fewer direct threats yet still face the certainty of death. Attempts to change individual consumers' behaviour towards sustainability, through information and financial incentives and disincentives, will typically have little impact, given people's other motivations, their social lock-in to a set of roles, institutions and infrastructures, and the massive resources of capitalist business that pull in the other direction. Instead, to a large extent, change must come through changing the perceptions and norms in their peer groups and communities.

Third, can education contribute? The conundrum that 'we can't change persons unless we change systems' and 'we can't change systems unless we change persons' partly arises out of the crudity of our concepts, as a sort of Zeno's paradox of social movement. Social change does happen and it happens through actions of persons. This is the premise of scenario analyses. Jackson was talking about moves towards sustainable consumption, a field where little progress has been made so far in rich countries, despite forty years of knowledge of the directions required. But in terms of value systems more widely we do see changes, such as the growth of belief in and commitment to human rights and racial equality, and the gradual change of norms about gender relations. Important historic examples of value change that have contributed to eventual social change can inform and inspire us: such as the removal of slavery and the decline of colonialism (Crawford 2002), and the largely peaceful displacement of the British Raj in India, the colour-bar in the USA and apartheid in South Africa (Sinha and Gasper 2009).

Values and change at the level of society

Education can contribute better to rethinking in and of society, suggest Brown and Lauder, if it itself exemplifies an inspiring social alternative. They propose a stress on collective intelligence, as a counterbalance to the language of individualism. Robert Bellah's (1985) famous study *Habits of the Heart*, for example, while it did not find a purely 'me'-generation in the USA, found 'that the language of individualism, as the primary language of self-understanding, limited the ways in which people think' (Brown and Lauder 2001: 209). So, first, consistent with Jackson's observations, we should understand people as social beings, marked by mutual dependence and sociability, between whom informal learning and trust are vital for much complex cooperation. Second, individual intelligence is thus for nearly everyone not fixed but capable of increase, given intelligence's strong cultural and social determination. Third, intelligence must be recognized as also a property at the group level. We must correspondingly recognize the central importance of maintaining a social fabric, for allowing good quality of life and good socio-economic performance. So the idea of what is work must expand to cover also care activities and periodic retraining. Fourth, intelligences are plural (Gardner 1983); in particular, emotional intelligence, which covers knowledge and skills in self-management and in managing one's relations with others, is very important for well-being and in complex cooperative flexible work and living. Flexible cooperation in a complex world calls for skills in communication, understanding others, and negotiating roles and relationships. 'Yet many of the trends [in the past generation] have served to stunt these abilities', argued Brown and Lauder (2001: 174). They outline how isolation in social life brings a lack of feelings of commonality, which contributes to increased self-interested behaviour and to a lack of the interactions that can generate both informal learning and a picture of well-being that is different from 'the struggle for money, power and status' (Brown and Lauder 2001: 223).

This rethinking, of intelligence and of persons as social beings, leads into a rethinking of education around a wider set of capabilities:

> [A] Collective Intelligence [perspective] . . . suggests that all are capable rather than a few; that intelligence is multiple rather than [exclusively] a matter of solving puzzles with only one right answer; and that our human qualities for imagination and emotional engagement are as important as our ability to become technical experts.
>
> (Brown and Lauder 2001: 8)

In the terms of the United Nations Educational, Scientific and Cultural Organization, education must cover four types of learning – to know, to do, to be, and to live together.

Brown and Lauder's book thus indicates some steps that are useful for the moves required beyond consumerism and towards greater human solidarity, by acknow-ledgement of persons as social beings and by corresponding recognition of collective intelligence and of multiple dimensions in individual intelligence. Yet, the book retains a mindset that hinders both those essential moves. It remains parochial, and unfortunately representative, in its national-level focus and preoccupation with contributing to national economic product and its growth. Rich country governments continue to take economic growth rates as their lead performance criterion. This perspective has become archaic in a twenty-first century of stagnant rich country levels of subjective satisfaction, melting polar ice-caps and dangerous pockets of desperation in the South and indeed in the North too. Even in terms of self-interest, there can be no human security for the rich without an empathetic global vision.

Some authors think that to change society we must change individuals, while others think that we cannot change individuals unless we change society, including the driving forces in polity, culture and economy. But, in either case, who are the 'we' who would take action? Some discussions of social change assume that elite-determined strategies can be implemented by pulling the switches in a societal control room, including those on the education control panels. What can we achieve via education, though, if education is merely talk delivered in isolated, socially marginal situations? Asking such questions makes us become more explicit about our hypotheses concerning social change, education's roles in it, and the capabilities required in processes of change.

In one family of hypotheses, education can lead to value change that can generate pressures on power holders that can lead to reform. In a more specific subset of the hypotheses, such processes require incubators and carriers within suitable civil society organizations. More specifically still, in the GTI, the most dynamic group in civil society is posited as young people, who in the optimistic scenarios eventually join and lead successful movements of value reorientation (Raskin *et al.* 2002).

Young people are no automatic source of reform, and every age group must play a part, but to bank on youth as the key force of energy, impatience and potential is indeed what many educators and educationists typically do. Let us look at how higher education in particular might contribute to the progress required on the rethinking of quality of life and a move to greater global solidarity.

The global level: cultivating humanity

Liberal education, in the view of Seneca (c. 4 BC–AD 65), is such education as 'makes its pupils free, able to take charge of their own thought and to conduct a critical examination of their society's norms and traditions' (Nussbaum 1997: 30). It promotes what some modern authors call critical autonomy. The Stoic ideal of education went further: it aimed to produce people who can function with sensitivity and alertness as citizens of the whole world. This is what Seneca means by 'the cultivation of humanity' (Nussbaum 1997: 8). It matches the calls for extension of human solidarity.

Three capacities, says Nussbaum, are required. First is 'the narrative imagination. This means the ability to think what it might be like to be in the shoes of a person different from oneself' (Nussbaum 1997: 10–1); and, more fully, 'a capacity for sympathetic imagination that will enable us to comprehend the motives and choices of people different from ourselves, seeing them not as forbiddingly alien and other, but as sharing many problems and possibilities with us' (Nussbaum 1997: 85). We could also call this empathy. We require empathetic imagination concerning both those with whom we are in direct contact and others anywhere else, in our socio-political community and in the world. The Stoics saw this as the basis for a stance of world citizenship. This stance is not the same as an assertion of insignificance of the local and of local ties and commitments, and there remain many good reasons for strong such ties.

Required secondly is 'the capacity for critical examination of oneself and one's traditions' (Nussbaum 1997: 9). The 'capacities to be a good reflective citizen' (Nussbaum 1997: 26) include these first two capacities: narrative imagination and critical self-examination.

Third, her picture of requirements for global citizens goes further: 'an ability to see [ourselves] not simply as citizens of some local region or group, but above all, as human beings bound to all other human beings by ties of recognition and concern' (Nussbaum 1997: 10). The three features are interconnected: empathy or the narrative imagination supports the capacities for solidarity and being self-critical.

Let us similarly then distinguish aspects in Nussbaum's formulation of the Stoic ideal of the formation of 'people who can function with sensitivity and alertness as citizens of the whole world' at three levels: personal and interpersonal or face to face; the citizen within a wider society; and the citizen of the world.

Requirements at the first level, of face-to-face interactions and interaction with oneself, include cultivation of self-control. This requires support from appealing narratives of well-being that provide alternatives to the narratives of consumerism, and corresponding alternative channels for improving well-being. Two generations of experiments with 'alternatives' force us though to think hard about how and when such shifts are feasible on a large scale, given that, as Jackson noted, we are social beings, largely confined and driven within a social system and culture. Encouraging examples of innovation do exist but system change requires more than only efforts directed at better quality in immediate individual life-worlds.

Beyond the face-to-face level, other citizenship qualities are required, including deliberative capacities and respect for others. Respect, Nussbaum argues, depends on the images that we use to characterize ourselves and others (Nussbaum 1997: 65). Here again, besides change at individual level we need changes in the categories and power systems which structure our societies.

At the third level, objectives for creating, strengthening and nurturing a global community vary, from high cosmopolitan ambitions to make obligations to all people both considerable and identical, to more modest variants that will ensure that all people are considered and are given weight (Nussbaum 1997: 9). Cosmopolitanism in the sense of treating people everywhere the same is not itself enough, and includes variants that differ utterly from global solidarity. Market cosmopolitanism in particular is not encumbered by what it considers parochial local solidarities: it treats people worldwide according to a universal principle that their wishes are weighted according to their purchasing power, and those without purchasing power are ignored (Gasper 2005). A cosmopolitanism that incorporates global solidarity is utterly different. To try to counter and redirect market forces, solidaristic cosmopolitanism needs to be incorporated in an education guided by something like the Stoic ideals that Nussbaum enunciates.

Nussbaum's *Cultivating Humanity* reviewed a range of relevant initiatives in university education in the USA in the 1990s. It recounts eloquently their rationales and islands of success. Similar studies are required in every country, to identify and share possibilities of advance. In another chapter in this book, George (see also 1997, 2002, forthcoming) presents an example from the Netherlands of a type of international education that can contribute positively, which I will refer to in my conclusion. She noted also some other types of international education that can be a handmaiden of economistic and often egoistic Conventional Worlds, and that carry the risk of leading into Barbarization scenarios.

Conclusion: global challenges and the possible role of international graduate education

We have asked what roles should and can higher education, in particular, play in responding to the global challenges of sustainability and in contributing to required moves in values. We looked in particular at the necessary moves from consumerism to a focus instead on quality of living, and from normative individualism to human solidarity. We suggested that these moves involve promoting and using the following capacities, which Nussbaum highlights as required for sensitive global citizenship: the ability to place oneself mentally in the position of other persons; the capacity for critical examination of oneself and one's society; and ability to see oneself as, besides an individual and group member, also a human being connected to fellow human beings by heritage, similarity and intensive mutual dependence.

Let us review a number of warnings and suggestions regarding value change that emerged in the essay, and briefly refer to how some forms of international graduate education might helpfully contribute.

First, we saw that consumerism will not be moderated merely through distributing information and changing financial incentives; change must involve evolution of the perceptions and norms in consumers' peer groups and communities. One insight from consumption studies is that contemporary consumerism is grounded in part in subjective insecurity, and reinforces it, and in needs for meaning and identity in the face of our now much longer but still foreseeably finite lives. Alternative sources of security, meaning and identity must be advanced. How?

Building solidarity can be one important way to reduce subjective insecurity and to change perceptions of identity and norms of behaviour. Fostering of empathy through modalities such as shared postgraduate education for future senior professionals and leaders can, if well designed, make a valuable contribution. We know that scenarios thinking, as exemplified in the Great Transition work, is an important tool for focusing attention on fundamental issues about sustainable and unsustainable futures, provided that the groups who prepare or consider the scenarios contain sufficient variety of experience. Insight about future possibilities can grow out of, and in turn strengthen, empathy and mutual concern; these qualities are important for making realistic projections as well as for subsequent cooperation. The required types of sustained mutual exposure and serious shared exercises in imagining are feasible within suitably designed postgraduate international education. This form of education can involve substantial mixed groups, each of which lives and works together for a substantial period, and within which junior and mid-career professionals mature who will later assume influential positions within their societies and in many sorts of international organization and social movement.

Next, we noted how understanding of present-day consumerism, education and potential paths of societal change must involve seeing people as social beings, who are marked by mutual dependence and sociability and between whom informal learning and trust are vital for complex cooperation. Such understanding can be promoted particularly well by residential education, which provides time and spaces for people to interact face to face over sustained periods, especially in informal forums.

The emphasis on persons as social beings, and a corresponding recognition of the multiple dimensions in individual intelligence and of collective intelligence, are relevant to making progress beyond consumerism and towards greater human solidarity. Among the multiple aspects of intelligence, the knowledge and skills involved in self-management and managing one's relations with others are important for well-being and flexible complex cooperative work and living. Further, for a group to show collective intelligence it must possess sufficient relevant variety and overlaps in backgrounds and information sources, otherwise it is liable to group-think or conflict when it is later forced to attempt to respond to events (Kahane 2010). Co-residential education is again an important potential contributor in strengthening such awareness and skills, including awareness of the multiple valuable types of background, perspective and intelligence, and recognition of how different contributions are brought by different sorts of people.

The form of international development studies education that George documents and analyses (1997 and see chapter in this book) can be a particularly intensive and effective 'pressure cooker' for these sorts of knowledge, skills and awareness, especially when it has good geographical balances both among students and among staff, with inclusion of a good number of students from rich countries but without their predominating numerically; and provided that it maintains the core emphases that she highlights: a wide-ranging and systematic analysis of poverty, marginalization and exclusion, and a cosmopolitanism that is interested in all levels, from the local through the national and regional to the global.

Many of the important principles that are embodied in such an educational format can be included also to a worthwhile degree in other, more conventional, formats. For responding sufficiently to growing worldwide pressures and likely crises, however, the world would be well served by the creation of more such pressure cookers of international higher education, which can contribute to the future leadership and energy that will be needed in major processes of intentional social change. J.S. Mill's observation,[5] 150 years ago, of 'the value, in the present low state of human improvement, of placing human beings in contact with persons dissimilar to themselves, and with modes of thought and action unlike those with which they are familiar' takes on additional relevance in the present era.

Notes

1 See http://www.gtinitiative.org.
2 For more details, see materials at http://www.gtinitiative.org.
3 See also Leiserowitz, Kates and Parris, 2005.
4 In many cases there was greater environmental concern in developing countries than in rich countries.
5 Mill 1848: Vol.2, Book 3, Ch.17, Section 5.

References

Barber, B.R. (2007) *Consumed*, New York: W.W. Norton.
Bellah, R. Madsen, R., Sullivan, W.M., Swidler, A. and Tipton, S.M. (1985) *Habits of the Heart*, Berkeley, CA: University of California Press.
Brown, P. and Lauder, H. (2001) *Capitalism and Social Progress: The Future of Society in a Global Economy*, Basingstoke: Palgrave.
Bruni, L. and Porta, P.L. (eds) (2007) *Handbook on the Economics of Happiness*, Cheltenham: Edward Elgar.
Crawford, N.C. (2002) *Argument and Change in World Politics*, Cambridge: Cambridge University Press.
Earth Charter Commission (2000) 'The Earth Charter'. Available at http://www.earthcharterinaction.org/content/ [accessed 23 May 2012].
Easterlin, R. (ed.) (2002) *Happiness in Economics*, Cheltenham: Edward Elgar.
Gardner, H. (1983) *Frames of Mind: The Theory of Multiple Intelligences*, New York: Basic Books.
Gasper, D. (2005) 'Beyond the inter-national relations framework: an essay in descriptive global ethics', *Journal of Global Ethics*, 1(1): 5–23.
—— (2007) 'Uncounted or illusory blessings? Competing responses to the Easterlin, Easterbrook and Schwartz paradoxes of well-being', *Journal of International Development*, 19(4): 473–92.
Gasper, D. and Truong, T-D. (2010) 'Development ethics through the lenses of caring, gender and human security', in S. Esquith and F. Gifford (eds) *Capabilities, Power and Institutions*, University Park, PA: Pennsylvania State University Press.
George, S. (1997) *Third World Professionals and Development Education in Europe: Personal Narratives, Global Conversations*, New Delhi, London, and Thousand Oaks, CA: Sage.
—— (2002) 'Technocrats and humanist intellectuals in the Third World: cases from a school of development studies in Europe', Working Paper No. 364, The Hague: Institute of Social Studies.
—— (forthcoming) *Reimagined Universities for Global Citizen Professionals: International Education, Cosmopolitan Pedagogies and Global Friendships*.
Hamilton, C. (2010) *Requiem for a Species: Why We Resist the Truth About Climate Change*, London: Earthscan.
Hintjens, H. (2006) 'Appreciating the movement of the movements', *Development in Practice*, 16(6): 628–43.
Jackson, T. (2006) 'Consuming paradise: towards a social and cultural psychology of sustainable consumption', in T. Jackson (ed.) *The Earthscan Reader in Sustainable Consumption*, London: Earthscan.

—— (2009a) *Prosperity Without Growth? The Transition to a Sustainable Economy*, London: Sustainable Development Commission.

—— (2009b) *Prosperity Without Growth: Economics for a Finite Planet*, London: Earthscan.

Kahane, A. (2010) *Power and Love: A Theory and Practice of Social Change*, San Francisco: Berrett-Koehler.

Kates, R.W., Leiserowitz, A.A. and Parris, T.M. (2006) 'Great Transition values: present attitudes, future changes', GTI Paper 9, Boston: Tellus Institute and Great Transition Initiative. Available at http://www.gtinitiative.org/documents/PDFFINALS/9Values.pdf [accessed 23 May 2012].

Leiserowitz, A.A., Kates, R.W. and Parris, T.M. (2005) 'Do global attitudes and behaviors support sustainable development?', *Environment*, 47(9): 23–39.

Luttwak, E. (1999) *Turbo-Capitalism: Winners and Losers in the Global Economy*, New York: Harper Collins.

Mill, J.S. (1848) *Principles of Political Economy*, London: J.W. Parker.

Nussbaum, M.C. (1997) *Cultivating Humanity: A Classical Defence of Reform in Liberal Education*, Cambridge, MA: Harvard University Press.

Raskin, P. (2006a) 'World lines: pathways, pivots and the global future', GTI Paper 16, Boston: Tellus Institute and Great Transition Initiative. Available at http://www.gtinitiative.org/documents/PDFFINALS/16WorldLines.pdf [accessed 23 May 2012].

—— (2006b) 'The Great Transition today: a report from the future', GTI Paper 2, Boston: Tellus Institute and Great Transition Initiative. Available at http://www.gtinitiative.org/documents/PDFFINALS/2GTToday.pdf [accessed 23 May 2012].

Raskin, P., Banuri, T., Gallopin, G., Gutman, P., Hammond, A., Kates, R. and Swart, R. (2002) *Great Transition*, Boston: Stockholm Environment Institute. Available at http://www.gtinitiative.org/documents/Great_Transitions.pdf [accessed 23 May 2012].

Schwartz, B. (2005) *The Paradox of Choice: Why More is Less*, New York: Harper Perennial.

Seligman, M. (2002) *Authentic Happiness*, New York: Free Press.

Sinha, M. and Gasper, D. (2009) 'How can power discourses be changed?', *Critical Policy Studies*, 3(3&4): 290–308.

Stern, N. (2010). *A Blueprint for a Safer Planet: How We Can Save the World and Create Prosperity*, London: Vintage Books.

UNDP, 2007. *2007/2008 Human Development Report. Fighting Climate Change: Human Solidarity in a Divided World*, New York: Human Development Report Office, United Nations Development Programme.

Part II

Policy implications

Chapter 6

Equity and graduate attributes

Vivienne Bozalek

While the notions of graduate attributes and human capabilities share many common conceptions, they do also differ in significant ways. This chapter examines the similarities and differences of graduate attributes and the human capabilities approaches and contends that the human capabilities approach has the potential to offer a different and enhanced conception of higher education when considered in relation to a graduate attribute approach. The chapter critiques a reductionist focus on employability and argues for a broader view of higher education, which the human capabilities approach provides. The approach offers three alternative dimensions to traditional approaches to graduate attributes which focus on employability. The first dimension is a normative framework incorporating human flourishing as an ultimate goal of social justice and higher education. Secondly an emphasis on social good and citizenship rather than employability per se, and thirdly a focus on students' needs and the resources that they would require to achieve the human capabilities or graduate attributes envisaged, rather than an assumption that students are a homogeneous group, and similarly prepared for higher education.

The first part of the chapter examines graduate attributes from a critical perspective. This section focuses on how graduate attributes have been defined and operationalized, and examines the conceptual logics which underpin such processes. The second part of the chapter considers how the human capabilities and graduate attributes approaches cohere and differ, and proposes ways in which the human capabilities approach (CA) can offer an enlarged view of higher education. The third part of the chapter uses a case study of the University of the Western Cape to illustrate ways in which the human CA can be used to develop alternative conceptions graduate attributes based on an idea of human flourishing, the social good and students' and lecturers' needs.

Graduate attributes

Since the 1990s policies on higher education from Europe, the USA and Australia have showed an increasing preoccupation with employability rather than education for its own sake; for example, the Bologna process in Europe (European Ministers of Education 2009). This concern with equating success in higher education with employability has subsequently become a global concern, influencing both Northern and Southern contexts (there was, for example, a conference in Accra, Ghana, focusing specifically on employability in African higher education organized by the British Council and the Association of Commonwealth Universities [2011]).

From the perspective of employability, discipline-specific knowledge in itself became considered to be insufficient for the job market, with concentration instead on generic skills and knowledge pertinent to all employment situations, which have come to be regarded as a legitimate focus in higher education. In addition to this, there has been an increasing focus on the disparity between the knowledge, skills, abilities and values with which students are leaving universities and what employers are seeking from students (see research by Griesel and Parker 2009 for South Africa; and Barrie 2007 and Treleaven and Voola 2008 for reference to international studies).

Simon Barrie (2005, 2007), one of the more prolific writers in the field of graduate attributes in higher education, defines graduate attributes as core, generic and employability qualities. He sees them as being infused in university learning and knowledge in a wide variety of contexts – beyond the content knowledge of disciplines, and as qualities that every graduate from every degree will possess. From this perspective, graduate attributes are generally seen to be the agreed-upon abilities, skills, knowledge and values that a given university agrees that each student should develop during the course of study and with which they should leave the university.

Barrie (2004) identifies four key features pertaining to the definition of graduate attributes:

1   They are generic, in that they transcend disciplinary boundaries, but may be developed within the context of a discipline.
2   They are developed at the end of a degree and are not expected of entry-level students.
3   They are referred to as generic attributes rather than skills or knowledge, in that they encompass new forms of wisdom and knowledge.
4   They are not extra- or co-curricular but developed within the curriculum through the usual process or experience of higher education embedded in course assessment activities.

However, according to Barrie (2004), graduate attributes lack the support of a conceptual framework but are supported by plurality of viewpoints and approaches. He notes that the variety of terms used for graduate attributes is a signifier of the lack of a coherent theoretical model (Barrie 2005). The concern is that there is no widely shared conception of the theory underpinning graduate attributes or even the processes involved in teaching and learning to achieve these attributes. In order to address these concerns, Barrie (2005) developed a two-tiered approach to graduate attributes at the University of Sydney. The first tier consists of the 'attitudes or stances that allow a graduate to prosper in a postmodern world' (Barnett 2004 cited in Barrie 2005: 3). These are complex conceptualizations of attributes such as lifelong learning, scholarship and citizenship – the three which the University of Sydney has identified as their first-tier attributes – which are not easily assessable in teaching and learning. The second tier of graduate attributes, on the other hand, are seen as clusters of personal skills and abilities, which are more explicit ways of translating the first-tier general attributes into disciplinary fields and which lend themselves more to being integrated into an aligned curriculum through teaching and learning activities and assessment tasks.

There are five identified second-tier graduate attributes at the University of Sydney – research and inquiry; information literacy; personal and intellectual autonomy; ethical, social and professional understanding; and communication Although the two-tiered approach makes it easier to identify broader attributes from skills and abilities which are contextual and can be embedded into the curriculum, it still does not provide an adequate theoretical framework to guide the implementation of graduate attributes in higher education. Barrie's assertions that graduate attributes are not located within a theoretical or conceptual framework obscure the fact that the overarching frame for the construction of graduate attributes is a market-driven neoliberal one, eulogizing a work ethic directed towards money and profit.

What is the problem represented to be?

A useful approach to deconstructing higher education policies such as the turn to graduate attributes is that of Carol Bacchi's (2009) *What's the Problem Represented To Be?*, which can be used to identify and analyse the conceptual logics that underpin specific problem representations. By conceptual logics she means 'the assumptions, values, presuppositions and accompanying signs' (Bacchi 2009: 7) which shape the understanding of an issue. Using this approach, the current emphasis on graduate attributes presupposes a particular understanding of what is considered to be problematic in higher education, and this understanding determines what the response should be to address the problem. From this perspective, a concern with graduate attributes is focused on the employability (or lack thereof) of university graduates. The focus for higher education would therefore be on preparing graduates for the world of work, rather than any other purpose.

A South African study on graduate attributes conducted by Griesel and Parker (2009), for example, looked specifically at what employers expected of graduates and how far their expectations were being met or not. The general purpose of foregrounding graduate attributes in higher education would be to make the system run more smoothly and be more compliant and attractive to the corporate world. From this study, the implied response from higher education institutions (HEIs) in South Africa is that they should pay attention to the gaps or deficits in knowledge, skills and values which have been identified by employers. The graduate attributes approach to higher education assumes a generally well-functioning higher education system and society, and does not problematize existing power relations and inequities within the sector. However, the idea that curriculum alignment alone can be used to embed graduate attributes and ensure that students leave with the required attributes is assuming that students are equally positioned in the first place to acquire these graduate attributes. There is also the assumption that HEIs are similarly situated to be able to provide students with the necessary resources, including teaching and learning, to acquire the desired attributes. Thus, what fails to be problematized in these notions embedding graduate attributes is firstly that students are differently positioned from the outset and would need different resources to be able to achieve graduate attributes and secondly that HEIs are similarly differently able to accommodate diverse students' social and learning needs. In fact, there is a silence regarding student needs and any reference to resources in the language of graduate attributes.

There is no reference in the literature on graduate attributes about how students are conceptualized. One can assume from the focus on employability, however, that students may be regarded from this conceptual logic which is implicit in the graduate attribute approach. As the American political scientist Joan Tronto points out, 'market assumptions of the consumers [students in this case] are that they are rational, autonomous, capable of making [academic] choices and possessed of adequate information to do so' (Tronto 2010: 159). I would add that there are more assumptions in this market-driven model of higher education which graduate attributes subscribes to. Since there is no acknowledgement in the approach of students being differently prepared for higher education, and that they have different social, economic and cultural needs, the assumption is that this is a middle-class student who is adequately prepared and enculturated into higher education expectations, with good economic opportunities. The focus on the alignment of the curriculum rather than on the students' needs assumes that as long as the learning activities, assessment tasks and learning outcomes are aligned, students will acquire the necessary attributes needed for the job market.

What alternatives does the human CA offer to students and institutions in the higher education sector regarding graduate attributes? In the next section I will consider ways in which the human CA can address some of the effects produced by how problems are representation by the graduate attribute approach.

Human capabilities and graduate attributes

The human CA offers a substantial contribution to higher education primarily because it is derived from a normative framework which places human flourishing rather than employability as its primary goal. The approach is similar to the graduate attributes approach in its focus on what students would be able to do and to be at the end of their degrees. 'What valuable beings and doings would students need to achieve by the end of their study at a higher education institution?' is the sort of question that one could ask from a human capability perspective. However, the ultimate purpose of higher education according to the human CA is to enable students to flourish as human beings rather than to focus only on how to make students employable in particular jobs – thus it is a broader conception which has the students' needs as the emphasis. The approach is one that treats each and every person as a worthy human being, as an end rather than a means to an end, and as a source of agency (Nussbaum 2006). The 'good life', according to Amartya Sen (1999) and Martha Nussbaum (1995, 2006, 2011), is the ability to achieve capabilities or to do valuable things and achieve valuable states, as well as being able to choose from different livings and meaningful affiliations, and not to be constrained into living a particular form of life. Participation, which means being able to do something for oneself and for others, is also considered to be an important aspect of quality of life in the human CA (Dreze and Sen 1989).

Nussbaum has foregrounded education as being an essential human capability for human flourishing and for being a citizen who is loyal to other human beings. She has built on her original three capacities for cultivating humanity (1997) – firstly the critical examination of oneself and one's traditions, secondly to see oneself as a global citizen bound to other people through ties of recognition and concern, and thirdly the narrative imagination – the ability to empathize with others and to intelligently understand another's story. She has recently expanded on these three capacities and identified the following list of what schools need to do to produce citizens for a healthy democracy – the list is just as appropriate for higher education:

- Develop students' capacity to see the world from the viewpoint of other people, particularly those whom their society tends to portray as lesser, as 'mere objects'.
- Teach attitudes towards human weakness and helplessness that suggest that weakness is not shameful and the need for others not unmanly; teach [students] not to be ashamed of need and incompleteness but to see these as occasions for cooperation and reciprocity.
- Develop the capacity for genuine concern for others, both near and distant.
- Undermine the tendency to shrink from minorities of various kinds in disgust, thinking of them as 'lower' and 'contaminating'.
- Teach real and true things about other groups (racial, religious, and sexual minorities; people with disabilities), so as to counter stereotypes and the disgust that often goes with them.
- Promote accountability by treating each [student] as a responsible agent.
- Vigorously promote critical thinking, the skill and courage it requires to raise a dissenting voice.

(Nussbaum 2010: 45–6; author's additions in parentheses)

As can be seen in the above list, qualities such as critical thinking and communication skills are part of some universities' graduate attributes, but empathy and anti-discriminatory practices, which are considered important in Nussbaum's list, are rarely mentioned as important for employability. Nussbaum's major concern, of course, is to educate citizens rather than students who will be employable.

A second difference between the human capabilities and the graduate attributes approaches is the differential emphasis on the social good. Some definitions of graduate attributes are entirely focused on employability, while others do make reference also to the social good. Bowden *et al.* (2000), for example, do incorporate the social good into their definition of graduate attributes:

> The qualities, skills and understandings a university community agrees its students should develop during their time with the institution. These attributes include but go beyond the disciplinary expertise or technical knowledge that has traditionally formed the core of most university courses. They are qualities that also prepare graduates as agents of social good in an unknown future.
>
> (Bowden *et al.* 2000 cited in Barrie 2007: 440)

With the exception of this definition, however, employability remains the foregrounded area of emphasis in conceptualizations of graduateness and graduate attributes (e.g. Scott and Yates 2002; Kember and Leung 2005; Vescio 2005; Treleaven and Voola 2008). On the other hand, academics (e.g. Unterhalter 2003, 2005; Walker 2006a, 2006b, 2008, 2010a, 2010b; Walker and Unterhalter 2007; Walker *et al.* 2008, 2009; Walker and McLean 2010; Boni and Gasper 2012) have highlighted the social good as a focus for higher education, focusing specifically on the contribution that the human CA can provide for reconceptualizing the social good in higher education. Melanie Walker, in particular, has thought about alternatives to graduate attributes from a human capability perspective. She has, for example, with a research team in South Africa, investigated the sorts of attributes which would be needed to develop professionals to deal with a world of injustices – what are termed 'pro-poor professionals' or 'public good' professionals committed to working for social transformation (Walker *et al.* 2009). This research project endeavoured to collaboratively develop a set of dimensions for such a transformative professional by building on Nussbaum's list of comprehensive capabilities to inform local conceptions of professional capabilities.

The human CA offers a way of taking into account where students and institutions are positioned and what they are able to do with personal, material and social resources, rather than merely looking at what resources people have and assuming that people are equally placed in relation to these resources. Resources in themselves are not a meaningful way of assessing human flourishing and well-being. Without considering the particularity of who needs the resources and in what context these resources are needed, it is difficult to assess how effective the resources will be in allowing different individuals to flourish. The liberal ideal of equality predicated upon equal agents is challenged in this approach, which acknowledges how people are differently positioned in terms of social markers.

This means that students' social positioning (such as the social markers of race, gender, generation, sexuality, social class) determines what sort of resources they will need in order to be able to flourish as human beings or, in this case, to attain the necessary graduate attributes. The human CA thus offers an enlarged view of higher education in that it focuses attention also on the particularities of student needs, which would require varying resources in order for the students to achieve graduate attributes or valuable beings and doings at the end of their degree. For instance, impoverished rural students who are first-generation literate persons among their kin would need more and different resources to be able to attain the same graduate attributes as middle-class urban students whose kin are all literate. A disabled person would need more and different resources to attain graduate attributes than an able-bodied person. Similarly, a person who has dependents would require more and different resources to participate at university and achieve graduate attributes than somebody who has no dependents. The human CA thus requires an examination of students' vulnerabilities in their life circumstances and their learning needs in order to be able to understand what resources would be required to successfully achieve graduate attributes or valuable beings and doings at the end of university study.

In the next section, a case study of a South African university is presented as an example of how a human CA to graduate attributes has informed the teaching and learning project at the institution.

The University of the Western Cape as a case study

The University of the Western Cape (UWC), situated in Cape Town, South Africa, is a historically black university or, as it is more currently known, a historically disadvantaged institution. This reflects its history as an apartheid-state creation, as it was specifically designed to be a university for those categorized as 'the coloured[1] population' of South Africa.

By the 1980s, however, UWC had become a respected institution, which attracted into its employ progressive anti-apartheid academics under the leadership of Professor Jakes Gerwel. By 1997 UWC's mission statement stated the aims of the University as to:

- assist educationally disadvantaged students to gain access to higher education and succeed in their studies;
- seek racial and gender equality and contribute to helping the historically marginalized participate fully in the life of the nation.

During the 1980s an affirmative action admissions policy was introduced to encourage students from the 'disadvantaged majority' to study at the university. This disadvantaged majority includes African language-speaking students from all over South Africa, particularly women from poor rural backgrounds. In 2009 the student population comprised 48 per cent coloured, 39 per cent African, 7 per cent Asian/Indian and 4 per cent white students. According to a Human Sciences Research Council study conducted by Breier (2010), which examined throughput of graduates in seven HEIs in South Africa, UWC had the highest proportion of graduates in the lowest socio-economic category (75 per cent), compared with an average of 56 per cent across all seven institutions studied.

Furthermore, in South Africa, there is a distinctive and continuing disparity between those who have access to quality education at a primary and secondary school level, and a small minority of largely white middle-class population being adequately prepared for higher education. This racially skewed access to quality education has resulted in a situation where only 5 per cent of the 20–24-year-old black age group are succeeding in higher education (Scott *et al.* 2007). Most of the students who go to historically white or advantaged HEIs have had access to high-quality schools which were in the apartheid era the preserve of white children, but now have a smattering of middle-class black children. Historically black or disadvantaged HEIs such as UWC generally accommodate or attract students who have not had access to these schools and who are therefore academically under-prepared for higher education.

Developing graduate attributes at UWC

In 2008, I was seconded from the Department of Social Work to assist the university to develop a strategic plan for teaching and learning at UWC. In order to develop such a plan, in keeping with the human CA, institution-wide research across all faculties was conducted in 2008, surveying both student and staff needs relating to teaching and learning. These findings were used to inform the strategic plan on teaching and learning as well as the development of the UWC Charter of Graduate Attributes.

Establishing staff and student needs

As Director of Teaching and Learning, I devised a questionnaire and administered this to all academic staff at faculty board meetings to ascertain how academic staff were experiencing teaching and learning, how in touch they were with existing assessment and teaching and learning policies, what they thought about staff development, e-learning, the scholarship of teaching and learning, and what their own needs were in relation to these. The questionnaire worked best where deans allowed their faculty staff members to complete it there and then.

In addition to finding out about the needs of academic staff members, an institution-wide project, funded by the Council on Higher Education in South Africa, was initiated in 2008 to establish student needs in relation to teaching and learning. The study was motivated by the impetus to improve the learning environment at UWC and to bring about an improved culture of learning among its students.

The study was intended to probe deeply into students' subjective experiences of the university, their own perceptions of and attitudes towards tertiary study, and the nature of their relationships with the teaching staff. The research examined issues such as:

- Student perceptions and attitudes towards learning.
- Orientation experiences; the communication they received from the university and lecturers.
- Experiences of admission processes.
- Experiences of classroom/lectures.
- Their own forms of resistance to university study, as manifested in phenomena such as non-participation in lectures and other learning opportunities.
- Identification and misidentification with the university; what they think/ imagine is required of them.
- Policies (teaching and learning, assessment, e-learning): do student behaviours and experiences reflect what is in these policies?
- (Mis)recognition: the degree of alienation and/or inclusion felt by students in relation to the institution.

A questionnaire was designed and administered to a sample of 696 students from all seven faculties in the institution. Data were also collected from a participatory workshop held in October 2008. The workshop addressed students' experiences of factors impacting on student learning at UWC. Facilitators were trained to lead focus groups and use certain participatory learning and action (PLA) techniques in a workshop on PLA techniques run by an expert from an non-governmental organization in the field. The workshop was attended by 20 students from community and health sciences, natural sciences, economic and management science, and arts faculties. The workshop was digitally recorded and students' drawings and pictures of their participation were uploaded onto a virtual e-learning platform site that students could access after the workshop.

The quantitative and qualitative results from the survey and the PLA discussions, as well as the audit on staff needs and the recommendations from the Council on Higher Education audit, were used to develop the Charter of Graduate Attributes and a strategic plan for teaching and learning at UWC. The UWC charter defined graduate attributes as:

the qualities, values, attitudes, skills and understandings that a particular university sets out as being important for students to develop by the end of their studies. These attributes are both intended to equip them for future employment and as critical and responsible citizens, contributing to the social and economic well being of society.

More specifically the attributes were elaborated in the following way. They are based on the Sydney first- and second-tier attributes, but reconfigured for the UWC context from the perspective of social justice.

Graduate attribute 1

Scholarship: a critical attitude towards knowledge

UWC graduates should be able to demonstrate a scholarly attitude to knowledge and understanding within the context of a rapidly changing environment. UWC graduates should have the ability to actively engage in the generation of innovative and relevant knowledge and understanding through inquiry, critique and synthesis. They should be able to apply their knowledge to solve diverse problems and communicate their knowledge confidently and effectively.

Graduate attribute 2

Critical citizenship and the social good: a relationship and interaction with local and global communities and the environment

UWC graduates should be engaged, committed and accountable agents of social good. They must aspire to contribute to social justice and care, appreciative of the complexity of historical contexts and societal conditions through their roles as professionals and members of local and global communities. They should demonstrate leadership and responsibility with regard to environmental sustainability.

Graduate attribute 3

Lifelong learning: an attitude or stance towards themselves

UWC graduates should be confident lifelong learners, committed to and capable of continuous collaborative and individual learning and critical reflection for the purpose of furthering their understanding of the world and their place in it.

Overarching skills and abilities

- *Inquiry-focused and knowledgeable:* UWC graduates will be able to create new knowledge and understanding through the process of research and inquiry.
- *Critically and relevantly literate:* UWC graduates will be able to seek, discern, use and apply information effectively in a range of contexts.
- *Autonomous and collaborative:* UWC graduates will be able to work independently and in collaboration with others, in a way that is informed by openness, curiosity and a desire to meet new challenges.
- *Ethically, environmentally and socially aware and active:* UWC graduates should be critical and responsible members of local, national, international and professional communities. They should also demonstrate a thorough

knowledge of ethical, social, cultural and environmental issues relating to their disciplines and make professional and leadership decisions in accordance with these principles.

- *Skilled communicators:* UWC graduates should recognize and value communication as a tool for negotiating and creating new understanding, interacting with diverse others, and furthering their own learning. They should use effective communication as a tool to engage with new forms of complexity in social and working life.
- *Interpersonal flexibility and confidence to engage across difference:* UWC graduates should be able to interact with people from a variety of backgrounds and have the emotional insight and imagination to understand the viewpoints of others. They should be able to work in a productive team, to lead where necessary and to contribute their skills as required to solving complex problems.

In addition to developing the Charter of Graduate Attributes, the strategic plan for teaching and learning at UWC (which was developed in tandem) emphasized, among other things, enhancing epistemological access for students through responsive teaching and learning programmes that adequately address students' learning needs.

Conclusion

UWC was able to use the human CA to develop relevant graduate attributes which resonated with the ethos of the university. This was made possible through a focus on human flourishing, a concern for the social good, an investigation of the needs of students and staff and a collaborative deliberation on what would be appropriate graduate attributes for the institution.

In addition to this the importance of identifying of students' needs has become an important aspect of teaching and learning at UWC. Ways of identifying student needs have been incorporated into professional development sessions with staff to challenge the assumption that students are equally positioned in relation to graduate attributes – therefore signalling that they would need different and more resources depending on their learning, social and economic needs.

This chapter has put forward the idea that a single-minded focus on graduate attributes is problematic in that it does not take into account where students are situated when they come in to university, what they are able to be and to do when they come in, and that they would need to be able to achieve success in relation to the graduate attributes. In other words, graduate attributes tell us nothing about the means to determine what it would take for each student to be able to achieve the desired ends. The human CA is able to assist by identifying and investigating how students are differentially positioned in relation to the desired outcomes of a university education. This is an institutional task as it requires us to look at institutional arrangements to address barriers to students' achieving the graduate attributes. We thus need to examine the institutional arrangements of an HEI such as UWC to see what differentially positioned students would need in order to achieve the desired graduate attributes. This would require knowledge of where each student is positioned in relation to the graduate attributes when they enter the institution and what resources and opportunities it would take to get them to achieve the graduate attributes. In the institutional arrangements we need to find the best ways of reducing the social, cultural, educational and environmental barriers to achieving graduate attributes.

Note

1   Under the apartheid state, the Population Registration Act No. 30 of 1955 categorized people differently by race. Every South African citizen had to be classified and registered as White, Coloured, Indian or African, and Africans had to be further classified into the ethnic groups to which they belonged. In this chapter I make use of these terms, as they are still referred to in post-apartheid South Africa to indicate discriminations, present and past. They are used, however, with the proviso that they are socially constructed and politically imposed terms which have been used to socially mark people for a variety of purposes.

References

Bacchi, C. (2009) *Analysing Policy: What's the Problem Represented to Be?*, New South Wales: Pearson.

Barnett, R. (2004) 'Learning for an unknown future', *Higher Education Research and Development*, 23(3): 247–60.

Barrie, S. (2004) 'A research-based approach to generic graduate attributes policy', *Higher Education Research and Development*, 23(3): 261–75.

—— (2005) 'Rethinking generic graduate attributes', *HERDSA News*, 5(March): 1–6.

—— (2007) 'A conceptual framework for teaching and learning of generic graduate attributes', *Studies in Higher Education*, 32(4): 439–58.

Boni, A. and Gasper, D. (2012) 'Rethinking the quality of universities: how can human development thinking contribute?', *Journal of Human Development and Capabilities*, 13(3): 451–70.

Bowden, J., Hart, G., King, B., Trigwell, K. and Watts, O. (2000) Generic Capabilities of ATN University Graduates. Canberra: Australian Government Department of Education, Training and Youth Affairs. Available at http://www.gradskills.anu.edu.au/generic-capabilities-framework [accessed 29 February 2012].

Breier, M. (2010) 'Dropout or stop out at the University of the Western Cape?', in M. Letseka, M. Cosser, M. Breier and M. Visser (eds) *Student Retention and Graduate Destination: Higher Education and Labour Market Access and Success*, Cape Town: HSRC Press.

British Council and Association of Commonwealth Universities (2011) 'Making the best use of Africa's graduates and the role of international partnerships', Accra, Ghana, 16–18 January 2011. Available at http://accra2011.acu.ac.uk/ [accessed 8 December 2011].

Dreze, J. and Sen, A.K. (1989) *Hunger and Public Action*. Oxford: Clarendon Press.

European Ministers of Education (2009) 'The Bologna Declaration'. European Commission. Available at http://ec.europa.eu/education/higher-education/doc12 90_en.htm [accessed 8 December 2011].

Griesel, H. and Parker, B. (2009) *Graduate Attributes: A Baseline Study on Graduates from the Perspective of Employers*, Pretoria: Higher Education South Africa and the South African Qualifications Authority.

Kember, D. and Leung, D.Y.P. (2005) 'The influence of active learning experiences on the development of graduate capabilities', *Studies in Higher Education*, 30(2): 155–70.

Nussbaum, M. (1995) 'Human capabilities, female human beings', in M. Nussbaum and J. Glover (Eds.) *Women, Culture and Development. A Study of Human Capabilities*, Oxford: Clarendon Press.

—— (1997) *Cultivating Humanity: A Classical Defense of Reform in Liberal Education*, Cambridge, MA: Harvard University Press.

—— (2006) *Frontiers of Justice: Disability, Nationality, Species Membership*. Cambridge and London: The Belknap Press.

—— (2010) *Not for Profit: Why Democracy Needs the Humanities*, Princeton: Princeton University Press.

—— (2011) *Creating Capabilities: The Human Development Approach*. Cambridge and London: The Belknap Press.

Scott, G. and Yates, W. (2002) 'Using successful graduates to improve the quality of undergraduate engineering programs', *European Journal of Engineering Education*, 27(4): 363–78.

Scott, I.R., Yeld, N. and Hendry, J. (2007) 'A case for improving teaching and learning in South African higher education', *Higher Education Monitor*, 6: iii–v.

Sen, A. (1999) *Development as Freedom*, New York: Knopf.

Treleaven, L. and Voola, J. (2008) 'Integrating the development of graduate attributes through constructive alignment', *Journal of Marketing Education*, 30(2): 160–73.

Tronto, J. (2010) 'Creating caring institutions: politics, plurality, and purpose', *Ethics and Social Welfare*, 4(2): 158–71.

Unterhalter, E. (2003) 'The capabilities approach and gendered education: an examination of South African complexities', *Theory and Research in Education*, 1(1): 7–22.

—— (2005) 'Global inequality, capabilities, social justice and the Millennium Development Goal for gender equality in education', *International Journal of Educational Development*, 25(2): 111–22.

Vescio, J. (2005) *An Investigation into Successful Graduates in the Early Stages of Their Career Across a Wide Range of Professions*, Final Report, Sydney: University of Technology.

Walker, M. (2006a) *Higher Education Pedagogies*, Maidenhead: Open University Press.

—— (2006b) 'Towards a capability-based theory of social justice in education', *Journal of Education Policy*, 21(2): 163–85.

—— (2008) *Ontology, Identity Formation and Lifelong Learning Outcomes: Theorising the Relationship Between Discipline-Based Research and Teaching*. York: Higher Education Academy.

—— (2010a) 'Critical capability pedagogies and university education', *Educational Philosophy and Theory*, 42(8): 898–917.

—— (2010b) 'A human development and capabilities "prospective analysis" of global higher education policy', *Journal of Education Policy*, 25(4): 485–501.

Walker, M. and McLean, M. (2010) 'Making lives go better: university education and professional capabilities', *South African Journal of Higher Education*, 24(5): 847–69.

Walker, M. and Unterhalter, E. (eds) (2007) *Sen's Capability Approach and Social Justice in Education*, London: Palgrave.

Walker, M., McLean, M., Dison, A. and Vaughan, R. (2009) 'South African universities and human development: towards a theorization and operationalization of professional capabilities for poverty reduction', *International Journal of Educational Development*, 29: 565–72.

Walker, M., McLean, M., Vaughan, R. and Dison, A. (2008) 'Choosing dimensions of human development', *Development Discourses: Higher Education and Poverty Reduction in South Africa*, ESRC Award number RES-167-25-0302. Available at http://www.nottingham.ac.uk/educationresearchprojects/documents/developmentdiscourses/rpg2008walkermclean7.pdf [accessed 29 February 2012].

Chapter 7

Employability
A capability approach

Geoffrey Hinchliffe

The concept of graduate identity

The idea of graduate identity has been explored by Len Holmes (2001). Holmes' starting point is a dissatisfaction with the prevailing concept of graduate employability in terms of skills acquisition. The skills approach simply cannot do justice to the complexity of graduateness because of the assumption that skills performance must be measurable and observable. Performance, Holmes suggests, depends upon interpretation of a situation but this ability to interpret cannot be measured in any straightforward sense. Interpretation itself is a complex activity depending on both understanding a situation in terms of a practice and on understanding agents in terms of their identity in the context of that practice. Thus, a practice provides the site within which identity is constructed. This identity itself is not fixed since a practice itself may legitimize a series of related identities depending upon context. Furthermore, a practice also provides the site in which identities can be modified, revised and developed.

What Holmes' analysis does is to take us beyond the skills agenda to an examination of the *conditions* of performance. It is not a naive condemnation of performativity as such; rather, it provides us with an analysis of the conditions of performativity. In order to perform in the appropriate manner, a person needs to be able to do at least two things: first, understand how a particular practice is enacted (the language and vocabulary, the goals and purposes and the broader environment in which a practice takes place) and second, a person must be able to construct for herself a legitimate identity. Therefore, when we examine graduate employability we should not think so much in terms of skills and performance but more in terms of practice and identity as forming the basis of that performance. This, however, presents a problem as far as the recruitment of agents into a particular practice is concerned since, to varying degrees, those agents will not be sufficiently aware of either the practice or the identity required. What is required is that those agents have the *potential* to become cognizant of both practice and identity, based on their current identity. In addition (and this is the peculiarity of employment-based practices) agents also require the potential to perform. This potential cannot always be based on actual performance or current cognizance of a practice. Holmes' suggestion, then, is that graduate recruitment is an exploration of current identity, in terms of graduateness, with a view to judging whether a person is capable of assuming a role in respect of practice, identity and performance.

It therefore follows that graduate identity, of its very nature, is something that is malleable and plastic. It cannot be something that is merely a series of attributes that can be enumerated and ticked off. In an elaboration of his ideas, Holmes (2006: 9) observes that identity is to be taken 'non-essentially, as relational, the emergent outcome of situated social processes. . . identity is thus socially constructed and negotiated, always subject to possible contestation and so fragile'. Thus, it may be that the identity claimed by an individual is also one which is affirmed by others, as recognizable; in this way convergence occurs. But of course, it may be that the identity a graduate presents is not recognized, or at least not wholly recognized by an employer. Prior to taking on a graduate identity, an agent has a student identity primarily formed through subject discipline and a range of student experiences. It may well be that the students experiment with their identity during the course of study – this being one of the great benefits of being an undergraduate. But once the students emerge out of university, their identity is no longer under their control. Emerging at last into the public domain, their identity as a graduate is shaped by social and economic processes that are not under their control. And the chief agent in shaping this identity – by virtue of economic power – is the employer.

What we were particularly concerned to do in this research was to probe behind the standard employability discourse comprising skills-talk and personal attributes in an attempt to discover the extent to which this discourse exhausted employer thinking. Criticism of skills-led approaches to employability supports earlier theoretical criticisms (e.g. Norris 1991; Hyland 1997) of skills and competence-led learning and assessment. A modified, contextualized approach to skills development was defended by Bridges (1993) and Hinchliffe (2002) but, more recently, Papastephanou and Angeli (2007) have argued that even the modified approach does not fully address the need for critical thinking and judgement. However, all of these theoretical approaches, however valid, are not backed up by appropriate qualitative evidence, making them more easy to dismiss. Our research provides evidence supporting the theoretically based critique of skills development and, in particular, of equating skills with employability.

Investigating graduate identity

The research project, which was conducted over six months from March to September 2009, aimed at probing beneath the conventional employability discourse of skills, competencies and attributes by speaking directly to employers. Moreover, we wanted to hear the employer's voice, differentiated across size and sector. In this way we would test the feasibility of the concept of graduate identity and find out if employers worked with a tacit or explicit concept of graduate identity. Thus, we could provide both the data and theoretical framework for evaluating the skills-led approach to employability by higher education institutions.

Participants were drawn from small- and medium-sized enterprises (SMEs), large organizations and public sector bodies predominantly in the county of Norfolk, UK. However, national and multinational organizations comprised 12 per cent of the respondents. A total of 105 online surveys were received from a variety of employers; 35 per cent in the public sector. SMEs comprised 66.7 per cent of the responses. Sectors included finance, local government, creative industries, IT, energy, construction, marine engineering and business support. In order to elaborate the responses in the survey, we followed this up with 20 in-depth interviews. Respondents came from a range of roles within organizations, including but not predominantly HR professionals. This reflected the number of smaller businesses with owner–managers and small teams responsible for recruitment.

Since employers naturally use skills-talk in graduate recruitment we asked a series of questions relating to skills and competencies and then broadened this out to ask about broader attributes relating to values and engagement. The aim was to find out what employer expectations were of graduates and to see if these expectations reached beyond customary talk about skills and employability attributes. Inevitably, we were also told of where graduates fell short of these expectations, but it was not our primary aim to elicit this.

In particular, in the online survey we used three separate but related instruments in eliciting expectations of graduates. The first of these instruments tested expectations in accordance with well-established recruitment criteria. The second instrument then took a limited number of employability skills (elicited from the first instrument) and obliged the respondent to make a forced ranking. The third then explored the extent to which employers recognized broader, social values typically associated with a university experience.

Evaluating employer expectations of graduate potential

In the first of these instruments, a total of 47 statements of graduate potential were explored. These statements incorporated a range of accepted employability skills, competencies, attributes and personal qualities based on a survey of recruitment literature. Table 7.1 ranks each statement according to the percentage of respondents who expected the statement to be evidenced on appointment.

The first thing that is noticeable here is that the majority of employers require graduates to perform to expectation by the end of the first year, with many attributes required on appointment. This judgement is not confined to smaller businesses, but applies across all sectors and sizes of organization. There are other interesting results as well. To begin with, it is clearly those personal ethical qualities of honesty, integrity and trust that are expected at appointment, ahead of any other skill or competence. Moreover, technical skills are not expected to be as highly developed as so-called soft skills (e.g. listening skills, ability to integrate). For many

Table 7.1 Employer expectations ranked by preference

Expectation	On appointment (%)	At 1 year (%)	At 3 years (%)
Demonstrates honesty and integrity	98.10	0.90	0.90
Is someone I can trust	94.40	5.60	0.00
Is able to listen to others	93.50	6.50	0.00
Is able to integrate quickly into a team or department	92.60	7.40	0.00
Is able to present ideas clearly, both verbally and in writing	86.10	11.10	2.80
Can assimilate information quickly	84.10	15.90	0.00
Works safely	83.20	15.90	0.90
Demonstrates good time-management	82.20	17.80	0.00
Can plan and manage their time	79.60	20.40	0.00
Can demonstrate attention to detail and thoroughness	79.60	19.40	0.90
Has a mature attitude	79.20	17.90	2.80
Is willing to take responsibility for their work	78.30	19.80	1.90
Is interested in learning and development	78.30	20.80	0.90
Can share ideas with others	77.80	22.20	0.00
Can demonstrate tact	76.90	20.40	2.80
Demonstrates cultural/social awareness	75.70	20.40	3.90
Has confidence in their own abilities	71.70	25.50	2.80
Is able to take the initiative	71.30	25.90	2.80
Can be relied upon by other members of the team/department	67.30	31.80	0.90
Is capable of learning new IT products and systems quickly	65.10	34.90	0.00
Is willing to take on new challenges and responsibilities	64.50	34.60	0.90
Has relevant technical skills	63.60	29.00	7.50
Thinks critically about their work	63.60	34.60	1.90
Shares the goals and objectives of my organization	61.70	35.50	2.80
Can report progress to colleagues and managers	61.70	37.40	0.90
Is able to learn about my product/service thoroughly and quickly	59.30	39.80	0.90
Is able to recognize the limits of their responsibilities	58.30	39.80	1.90
Can take responsibility for a piece of work and see it through	57.40	41.70	0.90
Is capable of working without close supervision	57.00	39.30	3.70
Is willing to take on a range of tasks to achieve team goals	54.60	42.60	2.80
Is capable of understanding the structure of the organization	53.30	45.80	0.90
Is able to communicate ideas about the service/business/product	51.90	47.20	0.90
Can communicate appropriately and effectively with clients/other agencies	50.50	45.80	3.70
Can represent my business well to others	48.10	44.40	7.40

Table 7.1 Continued

Expectation	On appointment (%)	At 1 year (%)	At 3 years (%)
Is able to work unsupervised	46.20	47.20	6.60
Is capable of taking on a broad range of tasks	45.80	44.90	9.30
Quickly gains an understanding of policy and procedure	45.80	54.20	0.00
Can break elements of a job/project down and plan accordingly	43.00	52.30	4.70
Is able to reflect on their own development and identify strengths and weaknesses	42.50	50.90	6.60
Is able to see how my business fits into the wider sector/market place	41.70	56.50	1.90
Can identify the appropriate tools (physical/virtual/administrative)	40.60	53.80	5.70
Can negotiate with others	36.40	53.30	10.30
Can be asked to undertake independent research	29.90	59.80	10.30
Is capable of identifying some strengths and weaknesses of my business	21.50	69.20	9.30
Is able to identify areas of weakness and suggest strategies to change	17.60	66.70	15.70
Is able to identify areas for change or improvement	7.50	85.80	6.60

employers, less is expected regarding technical skills than the one thing that all graduates are presumably good at: the ability to present ideas clearly, both verbally and in writing. Indeed, the ability to demonstrate cultural and social awareness, on appointment, comes ahead of IT skills. This does not demonstrate, of course, that employers think that technical skills are less important than soft skills. But they *may* be less important when deciding whether a graduate should be offered a job. The graduate must be able to fit quickly into a team, and if this attribute is lacking they may not get appointed even if their technical skills are highly developed.

Forced ranking of employability skills

The second instrument takes a selection of skills related to the above statements in order to find out just how much employers are committed to them. In order to achieve this, we asked the employers to indicate their rankings, which were, in effect, forced. The results are shown in Table 7.2.

Respondents were asked to rank these skills in order of importance, on a scale of 1–7. The ranking confirms much of what employers told us about what their expectations were on appointment. Interpersonal skills come out far ahead of any other skill and, again, written communication comes ahead of IT skills. Note the low priority given to presentation skills – possibly suggesting that academics would

Table 7.2 Employer rankings of employability skills

Employability skill	1 (%)	2 (%)	3 (%)	4 (%)	5 (%)	6 (%)	7 (%)
Interpersonal skills	57.80	18.90	8.90	8.90	4.40	1.10	0.00
Written communication skills	14.40	28.90	13.40	16.50	17.50	6.20	3.10
IT skills	9.00	15.70	19.10	18.00	14.60	9.00	14.60
Experience of the work environment	8.40	8.40	14.70	13.70	13.70	20.00	21.10
Commercial/ business awareness	7.50	16.10	14.00	9.70	16.10	12.90	23.70
Numeracy skills	5.50	9.90	19.80	16.50	16.50	18.70	13.20
Presentation skills	1.10	9.70	16.10	17.20	14.00	25.80	16.10

be better employed in improving their students' written communication rather than spending hours helping them to hone skills using PowerPoint. Of course, the fact that an employer ranks IT skills lower than interpersonal skills does not mean that the former are thought to be unimportant. But comments in the online interview, confirmed in the interview stage, emphasized the importance of written communication skills and teamwork ahead of IT skills.

Recognition of broader values

Here, we tried to adopt a different perspective by focusing less on employer requirements and more on the kind of values associated with the university experience. We wanted to find out the extent to which employers recognized the kinds of activities that universities themselves typically value and encourage their undergraduates to develop. The results are shown in Figure 7.1.

These findings contain a few surprises. For example, we had not expected such a strong endorsement of diversity awareness, although the importance of this had already been flagged up by the first instrument: 75 per cent of respondents indicated that they expected diversity awareness on appointment. At the interview stage, employers told us that this ranking flowed from the diversity of their customers and clients: the importance of diversity awareness was business driven and was not determined by expectations related to political correctness.

Constructing graduate identity

In constructing graduate identity, it is not enough simply to read off employer requirements, for this merely gives us the 'attribute list' approach to employability whereby skills needed for employment can be duly 'ticked off'. Yet, if anything emerges from our findings it is that employers do indeed think beyond conventional skills discourse and attempt to probe a broader range of graduate experience in order to assess their potential. How, then, should we conceptualize this experience? A heuristic method instantly presents itself: instead of reading off from

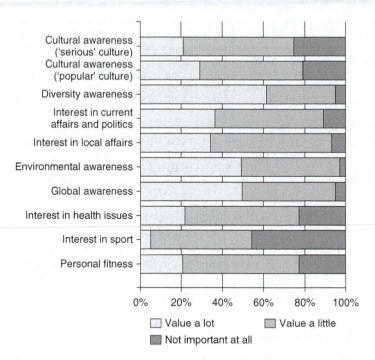

Figure 7.1 The value to employers of broader attributes gained through university experience.

employer requirements a list of skills, we use these requirements to identify the kinds of graduate *experience* that employers are interested in. And given our findings, four types of experience suggest themselves. First, it is clear from the employer concern with diversity and personal ethics that values are a key component of graduate identity; that is, the extent to which the graduate has engaged with values. Second, it became clear (especially in the longer interviews) that employers value the role of intellect, which they see as delivered through discipline-related study. Thirdly, all employers are looking for performance – the ability to deliver results. And finally, it goes without saying (from the persistent high ranking given to interpersonal skills) that employers are looking for evidence of experience of engagement with others across a variety of contexts. Graduate identity, we suggest, is made up of the four strands of values, intellect, performance and engagement. The precise mix will vary by employer, size and sector, reflecting the distinct nature of each organization, its structure, 'product' and ethos. The implication of this is that graduates need to be aware of their own identity (or profile) across these four sets of experience. But before discussing how graduate identity might be developed we shall first explore the four strands in a little more detail.

Values

Values include personal ethics, social values and contextual, organizational values, including the value of entrepreneurship. The world of work is sometimes mistakenly seen as a value-free, technocratic domain. Thus, the emphasis placed on personal ethics is not something which is merely a given:

> The trust thing is really important because without it we can't have confidence in someone – even leaving someone to lock up if they are last one out is an important sign of trust in them.
>
> (IT manager, international company)

Thus, graduates need to be able to demonstrate they have held positions of trust; it is not assumed that everybody is equally trustworthy.

By social values we refer to diversity awareness, cultural awareness, interest in the environment and the other values indicated in Figure 7.1. As we have already mentioned, the importance placed on these is primarily business driven. But an engagement in social values not only indicates that a person has a more heightened sense of social responsibility; it indicates to the employer that the graduate who has demonstrated awareness is more likely to be aware of, and respond to, the normative environment in which the business operates. Partly this is a question of a willingness to espouse all the issues across diversity and equal opportunities that employers have to address. But the normative dimension is also an aspect of the business environment: an employee who is diversity aware is less likely to miss or neglect real business opportunities.

Thus, the awareness of different cultures, races and religions developed at university was important to respondents, recognizing that such awareness may bring benefits to the client/customer relationship. Testing these findings at interview, it was also noticeable that diversity awareness was appreciated for and of itself, rather than to fulfil or comply with legislative requirements in the workplace. Such social values were also expressed in terms of respect for others and, more subtly, a respect of status (individuals recognizing their need to learn and develop and not to impose ideas and opinions on colleagues or clients).

> It's less because we have to tick [the box], yes we are a diverse organisation, but for me it says more about their mind. If you are culturally aware and aware of diversity you are probably a more rounded person. In our organisation we probably don't have a huge number of external clients, we've got lots of internal clients and being able to meet someone for the first time and assess how you can then develop a rapport with them; it's quite important. I think that if you have that awareness, it helps, because you are able to adapt your style . . . to get the results you want, the answers that you need.
>
> (Finance sector, multinational)

Intellect

Intellectual rigour is central to the graduate 'offer' and, at its core, this means the graduate's ability to think critically, analyse and communicate information, reflect on all aspects of their work and bring challenge and ideas to an organization. Again, intellect can take many forms in the mind of the employer, but may be best defined as creative, situational or applied and reflective.

Intellectual curiosity and a creative approach (particularly to problem solving) are elements of the graduate identity that are especially valued by medium-sized organizations and those with a structured graduate route. These respondents (at interview) viewed the graduate development process as an opportunity for trainees to apply their recent experience of learning, questioning and testing to a new environment. Therefore, the need for proactive, enthusiastic individuals who offer fresh ideas was paramount, and reflected this desire for intellectual curiosity:

> I want people who can think, who can paint pictures and communicate that – and be prepared to have discussion and debate and dialogue and argument.
> (Departmental manager, construction sector)

Employers recognized the central role that university plays in developing intellect, but inherent in this is also the ability to broaden thinking and reflect on learning and development:

> In a nutshell – wouldn't it be great if unis [sic] could develop a person's self-knowledge, not just here's a piece of paper that says that I can do PR but what do you mean by that? How much do you know yourself? How much have you put that into practice, how much have you tested that? Just something that shows I have stripes on my sleeve doesn't mean that I am a leader.
> (Director, creative industries sector)

The capacity to reflect is one of the fundamental requirements of employers, influencing, as it does, the graduate's ability to make choices about and develop their own careers, operate well in a team and with clients, identify development and training needs and assess the efficacy of their own work.

Performance

Performance may be usefully defined as the application of skills and intellect in the workplace and, for the graduate, this equates to the ability to learn quickly and effectively and to develop skills appropriate to the role. Performance is therefore most closely aligned to the established employability skills matrix that dominates current definitions of graduate identity. Performance is about delivery and results. In this respect, the survey interrogated employability skills both implicitly (embedded in competency statements in Table 7.1 of the survey) and explicitly (requiring respondents to rank commonly accepted employability skills).

Consistent in both survey responses and at interview, employers combined their sector/business-specific requirements with a desire for strong communication skills:

> When I think about it, it all boils to the ability to communicate. I think that's really the key for me when I recruit. You've got to have a 2:1, get through the numeric tests, through the telephone interview which tests your commercial awareness. But even when we get people at the assessment centre you know that they are not going to get through, because they don't have the ability to communicate.
>
> (UK graduate recruitment manager, multinational)

Employers generally expressed confidence in the graduates' ability to take a foundation of skills gained at university and apply them in a new setting; for example, the knowledge of IT languages could be applied in order to learn new programmes. However, there were notable concerns about core skills. For example, attention to detail and thoroughness was required by 80 per cent of employers on appointment. Yet, both those surveyed and those interviewed expressed grave concern over the ability of graduates to check and revise their work, and considered this to be one of the most lacking of competencies in graduates. Employers expressed similar concerns with regard to written communication:

> An enormous amount of my time is spent supervising the written work of those who are otherwise very intelligent and able people.
>
> (HR manager, public sector)

This is a particularly trenchantly expressed view and although other employers did not express themselves so strongly all of them recognized the concerns expressed in this quote.

Engagement

From an employer's perspective, engagement could be defined as a willingness to meet personal, employment and social challenges head on and to be 'outward looking'. For some employers, this involves having a wider perspective:

> Those who have had the largest variety of summer jobs are far more flexible, far more likely to adapt.
>
> (Manager, education sector)

For others it involves making the best use of student life:

> I am interested in seeing a range of interests, showing that the candidate has fully exploited the university experience.
>
> (Third sector arts organization)

Whereas for some it's all a question of attitude:

> A positive, can-do attitude is a real selling point for graduates. This doesn't have to be loud and gregarious, more a quiet confidence, willing to work hard to achieve goals which accord with the company's objectives. Pride in your own work and a desire to give of your best will also go along way.
>
> (Civil engineering, SME)

What came across strongly at the interview stage was a desire by employers to see some kind of evidence that graduates have engaged in work experience, in volunteering, in making the most of the student experience and have shown a preparedness to step outside the familiar and the comfortable. However, what employers also want to see is that this has been done over a sustained period and has not been merely haphazard. They are looking, in other words, for engagement in communities of practice, whether these are work-based communities, virtual communities or social communities. In this way, the graduate will have had to learn a different kind of discourse through the very act of participation itself.

This is the kind of situated learning that Lave and Wenger (1991) and Wenger (1998) have shown involves systematic participation and engagement:

- Often much of what is to be learnt is not written down.
- Learning affects and transforms attitudinal and behavioural response.
- Learning often requires the development of relatively sophisticated inter-personal skills.
- There is always a co-dependency on others so that learning never belongs solely to the individual but of its nature is sharable.
- Respect and recognition arise through sustained participation.
- Awareness of context (which itself may shift and change) is vital if successful learning and interaction are to take place.

While graduates are not expected to demonstrate a sustained engagement with a community of practice over several years, employers do indeed expect some limited engagement with such a community and to demonstrate an awareness that learning not only arises through traditional disciplinary engagement. It is the experience, albeit limited, of a community of practice that enables an employer to assess those all-important interpersonal skills.

The development of graduate capabilities

A useful way of interpreting the idea of graduate identity that has been elaborated is through the concept of capability, drawing on the work of Amartya Sen (1993). When he first theorized the concept of capability Sen suggested (in the context of asking questions about social redistribution) that perhaps we should focus not so much on goods and resources as what people could actually *do*.[1] This idea was further theorized by Sen in terms of 'functionings' or modes of being and doing. The idea is that a capability can enable a range of possible functionings.[2] A 'capability set' is therefore, according to Sen, a combination of functionings. The key point here is that there is no one-to-one correlation between capability and functions – capabilities enable a range of functionings. It follows that the development of capabilities has an empowering dimension: capabilities enable persons to do more with their lives in terms of potential functionings. For Sen, the concept of capability therefore includes a normative dimension that goes beyond standard human capital theories: a capability set becomes an index of freedom and well-being.

For graduates, then, there is a complex capability set that encompasses values, social engagement, intellect and performance. It enables, potentially, a range of functionings. What this research suggests is that underpinning the employability specifics – writing CVs, undergoing recruitment assessment, interview performance – is the need to construct an identity through combining the four dimensions that have been identified. As already emphasized, the precise mix and balance depends on the individual's experience, aims and preferences. What Sen's thoughts on capability suggest is this: that the development of employability needn't be thought of in terms of developing a set of instrumental skills and attitudes aligned to human capital requirements but entirely divorced from questions of well-being. For Sen, the development of a capability set is central to human well-being and so the development of the graduate capability set can be seen as central to graduate well-being. To live a satisfactory life (leaving aside for the moment the critical question of finding employment), graduates need to think about their own values, engagement, intellect and performance.

It might be useful at this point to think about the capabilities students and graduates need to develop their employability. But rather than suggest a long list I am inclined to identify two capabilities in particular:

Capability for voice

We might think of the capability for voice as being the ability to express one's opinions and thoughts and to make them count in the course of a public discussion (Bonvin and Thelen 2003: 3). This is more than the skill of self-assertion, which is primarily directed to ensuring recognition of the self by others. Capability for voice implies an ability to make effective interventions at both the valuational and strategic level. It is more than the ability for getting oneself heard; it implies also a capability for dialogue as well. This capability therefore includes the capacity for self-disclosure through speech. Moreover, since self-disclosure need not be confined to speech, the capability for voice may also be a surrogate for self-expression through visual and auditory signs. It should be noted that the capability for voice is not simply a self-regarding capability: for it suggests that the ability to make one's voice count depends in part on the recognition of the voice of others. Crucially, therefore, the capability for voice implies that other voices are heard and understood; it is a capability that is exercised in the context of recognition of others.

Capability for deliberation

It is being suggested that deliberation is of ends and not only means. This implies that at least sometimes we deliberate over values. For example, graduates may deliberate on the kind of occupation they wish to pursue. What is being suggested is that the framework provided by graduate identity enables these individuals to reflect on their values and intellect in the light of what a particular occupation requires. It may be that some kind of revision as to one's values may be necessary and that this revision is best conducted through experiential engagement. So someone considering entering the teaching profession, for example, may be uncertain as to whether they could fully care for children and young adults and whether 'care' is a motivating factor in their value set. Engagement with young people (e.g. on a voluntary basis) could help settle this question. Deliberation could therefore be conducted over an extended period in which values are reflected on in the light of experience.

The role of deliberation may therefore be provided by the VIPE framework (Values/Intellect/Performance/Engagement) in which what is being reflected upon is the agent herself. The assumption is that the framework is a heuristic device that helps an agent reflect on a fluid situation. And what is 'fluid' is not only a particular situation an agent is engaged in but also the self-perception of the agent as mediated through the VIPE framework. Values that at one time were assumed to be salient may now be revised in the light of engagement. Deliverances of the intellect which at one time were confidently deployed may now, in the light of difficulties with some performance, be less certain. Deliberation may lead to a loss of confidence, at least initially, but in the longer term the VIPE framework permits a revised self-identity in which confidence may be regained through pursuing new directions.

A final word regarding deliberation in the context of employability may be in order. It is important to differentiate an occupation from a job. An occupation implies a whole practice incorporating a set of skills, theoretical knowledge, technical know-how and an appropriate value set. It also involves finding out about an occupation, how it is organized, what are the qualifications, how and which employers support which occupations and so on. But a job is much less than any of that.

The example from occupational practice in Germany may be instructive, where occupation = *Beruf*. Jobs are transitory but *Beruf* gives you a place and an identity, over a lifetime. *Beruf* makes you into a someone. But a person who just does jobs has no real sense of commitment or responsibility. That, at any rate, is a popular view expressed in the Federal Republic (see Winch 2010: 72).

The difficulty in the UK (in England, certainly) is that universities are pressurized to publish graduate destination of employment figures within six months of graduation. In addition, graduates themselves are under personal economic pressure to find employment as soon as possible after graduation. In other words, all the motivation is to find a *job*, not an occupation. The long-term process of investigation, engagement and reflection is simply not encouraged to anything like the degree that is needed if graduates are to seek a suitable occupation. Yet, it is within an occupational setting that the four dimensions of employability (as illustrated through the VIPE framework) are more likely to be developed. Thus, the short-term focus on 'getting a job' not only means that graduates may go through many jobs before finding a suitable occupation; it also implies that their well-being may be less well served since they are unable to engage in reflection and different types of engagement. For the focus on jobs is essentially about performance – about results. Yet, as the small research study suggests, even employers are not solely interested in performance as such since they recognize that achieving results is a complex product of many factors.

Acknowledgement

The research cited in this article was conducted by myself and Adrienne Jolly (University of East Anglia, UK).

Notes

1   See Sen's article *Equality of What?*, originally delivered as a Tanner Lecture on Human Values in 1979, to be found in Sen (1982: 353–69, particularly 365–7).
2   See Sen (1999: 74–5).

References

Bonvin, J.M. and Thelen, L. (2003) 'Deliberative democracy and capabilities: the impact and significance of capability for voice', draft paper presented to the Third Conference on Capability Approach: From Sustainable Development to Sustainable Freedom, Pavia, Italy, 7–9 September 2003.

Bridges, D. (1993) 'Transferable skills: a philosophical perspective', *Studies in Higher Education*, 18(1): 43–51.

Hinchliffe, G. (2002) 'Situating skills', *Journal of Philosophy of Education*, 36(2): 187–205.

Holmes, L. (2001) 'Reconsidering graduate employability: the "graduate identity" approach', *Quality in Higher Education*, 7(2): 111–19.

—— (2006) 'Reconsidering graduate employability: Beyond possessive-individualism', presented at 7th International Conference on HRD Research and Practice Across Europe, University of Tilburg, 22–24 May 2006.

Hyland, T. (1997) 'Reconsidering competence', *Journal of Philosophy of Education*, 31(3): 491–503.

Lave, J. and Wenger, E. (1991) *Situated Learning*, Cambridge: Cambridge University Press.

Norris, N. (1991) 'The trouble with competence', *Cambridge Journal of Education*, 21(3): 331–41.

Papastephanou, M. and Angeli, C. (2007) 'Critical thinking beyond skill', *Educational Philosophy and Theory*, 39(6): 604–21.

Sen, A. (1982) *Choice, Welfare and Measurement*, Oxford: Oxford University Press.

—— (1993) 'Capability and well-being', in M. Nussbaum and A. Sen (eds.) *The Quality of Life*, Oxford: Oxford University Press.
—— (1999) *Development as Freedom*, Oxford: Oxford University Press.
Wenger, E. (1998) *Communities of Practice*, Cambridge: Cambridge University Press.
Winch, C. (2010) *Dimensions of Expertise*, London: Continuum.

Chapter 8

Capabilities and widening access to higher education

A case study of social exclusion and inequality in China

Li Wang

This chapter adopts a capability perspective and draws on related social exclusion theory to examine widening access to higher education. It uses China as a case study to consider educational inequality in higher education (HE) admissions, but argues that the framing of the issue is more widely relevant and applicable. The chapter commences with an introduction of social exclusion theory in general and the key features of Sen's capability deprivation approach. The importance of the capability approach (CA) is that it allows one to recognize different needs and choices confronting different social groups by distinguishing between different types of social exclusion. The chapter operationalizes Sen's ideas to appraise the process of exclusion operating in enrolment. Finally, this information is used to evaluate responses to existing issues within current Chinese HE enrolment, showing that the process is fundamentally flawed and risks reducing, rather than enhancing, capability by excluding certain groups of students from fair competition in terms of access.

The context for the argument is grounded in the last three decades of tremendous social, political and economic change in China since the adoption of the open-door policy in the late 1970s. A market economy has been implemented as a replacement to the planned economy which had previously allocated resources. Since then, attention has been drawn to social inequality due to the emergence of disparities across China. These inequities are particularly noticeable between urban and rural areas, between regions and between different social groups (United Nations Development Programme 2005). Education has been transformed from a public good to a mixed good in the transition from a planned economy to a market economy; research has focused on reviewing the problems associated with educational inequality mainly within the context of social equity and equality (Devaney and Weber 2003).

Social exclusion and educational inequality

There is a growing body of work examining social exclusion, triggered by the rise of the concept in the 1970s. However, it is a vague concept, and there are different approaches to social exclusion. Sen's (1992) CA offers a robust understanding, motivated by his dissatisfaction with utilitarianism, libertarianism and Rawlsianism, rooted 'in the failure of standard theories to take adequate account of forms of deprivation and inequality' (Vizard and Burchardt 2007: 15). Sen disputes Rawls' resources-based concept of justice and argues instead that the focus of social justice should be on the distribution of capabilities. This includes both process equity – the achievement of capabilities (such as respect, participation in social life, access to education, health care and other public services) and opportunity equity – the freedom to do so (Sen 2005). From this perspective, Sen (1992, 2000) developed the CA to illustrate how social exclusion is caused by various deprivations which prevent people from living 'a minimally decent life' (Sen 2000: 10). He employs two pairs of separate but not mutually exclusive criteria to unlock the connection between social exclusion and capability deprivation (Table 8.1). The importance of the typology is to allow us to recognize different needs and choices confronting different social groups by distinguishing between different types of exclusion. If we look at the effect of deprivation, 'Social exclusion can . . . be constitutively a part of capability deprivation as well as instrumentally a cause of diverse capability failures' (Sen 2000: 11), and thus two types of social exclusion can be identified:

- *Constitutive deprivation:* Refers to social exclusion that is intrinsically part of deprivation. For instance, being excluded from social relations is in itself capability deprivation. Exclusion from community life is also a type of direct deprivation. Social exclusion then has constitutive relevance for capability deprivation. The core of analysis on this kind of social exclusion lies in its intrinsic nature.
- *Instrumental deprivation:* Means that being excluded from some other things is not capability deprivation on its own but, rather, this type of exclusion may further result in deprivation. Sen uses credit markets as an example and points out that being excluded from credit markets is not necessarily part of deprivation itself; however, lack of access to credit markets may lead to other deprivations which are connected with the use of credit. In this case, social exclusion is instrumentally relevant to capability deprivation (Sen 2000).

In terms of the intention of deprivation it is possible to distinguish two further types of social exclusion:

- *Active deprivation:* Occurs when a group of people are deliberately excluded. It is usually a direct result of policies or regulations; active exclusion is usually caused by authorities.
- *Passive deprivation:* 'comes about through social processes in which there is no deliberate attempt to exclude' (Sen 2000: 21). Unlike active deprivation, passive deprivation is not caused by a particular policy or a government department. Instead, it is more likely a consequence of a series of social circumstances.

Table 8.1 Typology of social exclusion

Criterion	Type	Feature
Inherence	Constitutive deprivation	Constitutive importance; direct deprivation.
	Instrumental deprivation	Instrumental relevance; results in other deprivation.
Intention	Active deprivation	Deliberate exclusion; usually a result of a particular policy.
	Passive deprivation	Non-deliberate exclusion; usually a result of the overall situation.

Source: Adapted from Sen (2000).

There are both normative and evaluative dimensions embedded in Sen's approach. The former aims to answer the question: 'What is justice and equity?', and the latter concerns an evaluation of the position of individuals, groups and society (Vizard and Burchardt 2007). This chapter focuses on the normative dimension, which has particular implications for understanding inequality. Firstly, the categorization of deprivations illustrates the different cause and effect of social exclusion. It captures the key features of the process of exclusion by highlighting: (1) the context (in the case of passive deprivation); (2) the direct cause (in the case of active deprivation) (3) capabilities under deprivation (in the case of constitutive deprivation); and (4) further possible deprivation (in the case of instrumental deprivation), which is vital for social inclusion remedies. Secondly, it acknowledges individual differences and constraints which would affect what people can *actually* do and be, even if they are confronted with the same set of goods, because conversion of goods to capabilities varies from person to person (Sen 2000). This leads to a critical question, whether institutional design, and in this case, the mechanism of HE enrolment, enables people to enhance capability in their realm of autonomy or confines them to specific states or actions. Finally, the CA is sensitive to context, which is achieved through establishment of links between individuals' positions and underlying social, political, economic, and cultural conditions (Vizard and Burchardt 2007). Significantly, education can be adversely affected by social inequality and, in turn, reinforces the social exclusion it is often trying to overcome.

Sensitivity to context and individual difference assures the applicability of Sen's CA to different settings, in this case to China, without confinement to national boundaries. China, like many other countries, is experiencing social stratification and even polarization (Li and Bray 2006) which exacerbates problems associated with social exclusion. The growing Gini coefficient has ranked China far behind all developed countries and only ahead of some countries in Africa and Latin America in terms of income distribution (World Bank 2007). In addition, it is noted that the urban poor and rural poor are being excluded from markets, urban society and welfare services while the process encourages swift urbanization and social transformation in China (Liu *et al.* 2008).

The following section turns to examine inequalities caused by the HE enrolment system in China. Though inequality is not necessarily equivalent to social exclusion, it is recognized that some groups suffering from inequality are more likely to be excluded. Indeed, groups being discriminated against are often simultaneously experiencing social exclusion (Stewart 2004; Jayaraj and Subramanian 2006). In light of Sen's theoretical framework, several cases will be discussed to illustrate how access to HE is reinforcing social exclusion.

Admission to higher education in China

The HE sector in China has undergone significant reforms in past decades. Yet, for many, access to HE is still a matter beyond the individual and is instead one of family. This is due to the influence of traditional Confucian values (Cummings 1996). Given the special importance attached to HE by Chinese people, access is at the centre of far-reaching debates on further market reforms. Most students are admitted into universities through taking the College Entrance Examination (CEE). Although the CEE was only established in the 1950s, there is a long tradition of standardized national examinations in China which dates back to the 1400-year history of the civil service examination in the imperial era. Until recently the CEE has been a national examination taken by high-school graduates in China. Since 2000 it has been decentralized to promote diversity across regions. But despite attempts to provide more flexibility, approximately one-third of student are currently sitting standardized entrance examinations developed by the Ministry of Education (MOE) (Yuan and Yang 2008).

However, it has been realized that the growing demand for HE generated by economic success and associated social developments since market reform may threaten the merit-based admission system as the state is not able to respond to the growing demand for HE. Therefore, policies of decentralization, marketization and privatization have been adopted by the Chinese government to cope with the financial commitment to the expansion of HE. Consequently, the responsibility for HE funding has been reallocated between central and local governments, as well as between the public and the private sectors. Meanwhile, changes in the financing system, such as adoption of the user-pay principle and localization of public funding, are challenging the merit-based admission system and education equity in many aspects (Wang 2008).

Inequality in higher education access in China

Constitutive deprivation – economic handicaps: merit-based or money talks?

HE in China was free until the mid 1980s. The state subsidized students' living costs so HE was affordable to all qualified students and few were denied access due to financial constraints (Qu 2008). Starting from admitting a small portion of self-funded students into universities, market principles have been gradually adopted in tertiary education since market reform. In 1985, the Central Committee of CCP (CCCCP) allowed a small number of students to be admitted into HE, exceeding the quota of the state plan on condition that they paid a portion of the cost. Meanwhile, the majority of students still enjoyed free education. A shift in 1994 led to wholesale reforms of tuition fees. Consequently, double standards on the tuition fees for students within and outside the state plan were abandoned and students were charged against the same criterion, except for particular academic disciplines. In 1996, about half of higher education institutions (HEIs) in the country adopted a unified admission system (*Bing Gui Zhao Sheng*) (MOE 1996). Therefore, the user-pay principle has been widely adopted and tuition fees have increased significantly since 1997.

While the central government devolved the financing responsibility to governments at lower levels and individuals, government expenditure on HE shrank sharply from 93.5 per cent of all HE income in 1990 to 42.6 per cent in 2006 (National Bureau of Statistics of China [NBSC] 2008). Meanwhile, encouragement of multiple methods and multiple channels of provision and funding strategies directly led to the increase of tuition fees (Mok 1997). The growing prominence of 'privateness' since the adoption of the open-door policy and market economy has generated tension between merit-based selection mechanisms and financial criteria within the context of commodification of education. China Youth and Children Research Centre (2007) reported that tuition fees increased by 25 times from ¥200 (US$30) in 1989 to over ¥5,000 (US$700) in 2007, while during the same period of time, income for urban and rural residents increased only by nine and six times, respectively (NBSC 2008). Moreover, a report by the National Development and Reform Commission (2007) recently estimated that in the last decade, each student needed to spend over ¥10,000 (US$1,400), for their undergraduate study in public universities every year, and much more in private institutions. By contrast, the disposable income (per capita annual) of urban households and rural households in 2007 was ¥13,785.8 (US$1969.4) and ¥4,140.4 (US$591.5), respectively (NBSC 2008). Due to the limited access to the existing student loan/grant system, family support has been the primary source for funding university cost (Liu and Xia 2007). This means that HE has become unaffordable to many low- and middle-income families in China (Wang 2008; Zhou 2008). In absolute terms, tuition fees in China are much lower than in many other countries. However, these fees account for approximately 60 per cent of average annual household disposable income in China, compared with 22 per cent in the UK (Office for National Statistics 2010). Therefore, the soaring cost of HE disproportionate to household income has become an important cause for educational inequality in China; students are deprived of the opportunity if they cannot afford the cost of going to university, even if they are qualified.

This case exemplifies constitutive deprivation of access to HE for students from poor families. The essential cause for the exclusion is financial hardship, and the vulnerable group here is students from poorer families. Affordability is an indicator of poverty and thus a deprivation on its own. It further deprives students who cannot afford the tuition fees of the opportunity to go to universities. Thus, students from poorer families are deprived of the freedom to pursue a valued choice because of the exclusive effects of high tuition fees and lack of an inclusive support mechanism such as student loans.

Active deprivation – regional disparities: unequal admission system

China adopted an expansion policy for HE in the late 1990s. As a result of the decentralized funding policy, the amount of funding a university can generate is closely related to the economic development of the region in which it is located. In general terms, governments, social organizations and individuals in the prosperous coastal areas are more generous in funding universities than their inland counterparts. For example, in 2006 the educational income from public and non-public resources of three highly developed provinces in China (Guangdong, Jiangsu and Zhejiang) accounted for 25 per cent of national educational funding, while the three least developed provinces (Qinghai, Tibet and Ningxia) only gained 1 per cent of the national figure. Apart from the inequality in allocation of funding, the distribution of quality universities among regions is also highly uneven. Good universities are concentrated in the developed coastal areas, with seven out of the top ten universities located there (cuaa.net *et al.* 2009).

In addition to growing regional disparities in economic prosperity, inequality is simultaneously and deliberately widened by a differentiated policy for university admission. Although most students are admitted into HE through taking the CEE, the requirements for admission vary from province to province. Among all provinces, students from five minority autonomous regions, including Guangxi, Inner Mongolia, Ningxia, Tibet, Xinjiang and two municipalities at province level, namely Beijing and Shanghai, have the privilege of being enrolled by top universities with lower requirements. Admission requirements are much lower, not only in underdeveloped areas such as Tibet and Qinghai but also in well-developed regions such as Beijing and Shanghai. In 2009, the *yibenxian* (minimum requirements for admission into key universities in China) for examinees in the area of science in Shanghai was 455, while in Shandong and Hebei it was 586 and 569, respectively.

To solve this problem, the CEE system was reformed in 2002. Decentralization practices were adopted for a better fit of the CEE into local situations. Accordingly, some provinces were allowed to decide parts of, or even the whole set, of the CEE papers. However, this reform has had limited effects in overcoming regional disparity in admissions because it does not touch on the key factor leading to the different requirements – the uneven allocation of university places (Zhou 2006). The annual number of degree places in the country is decided by the central ministry and places are assigned to provinces. After this, provincial education bureaus are responsible for allocating admission quotas to individual HEIs in the territory. Based on the number of degree places assigned, individual institutions develop their own admission plan and decide how many students they will recruit from different provinces. For example, Peking University and Tsinghua University, two prestigious universities in China, recruited 286 and 270 students in Beijing in 2009. These numbers were approximately five times the number in Henan province, whereas the population in Henan was six times as large as that in Beijing (Higher Education Enrolment 2004, 2009; Zhou 2006). This, however, does not suggest students from big cities are much more talented than elsewhere. Instead, localization of enrolment is regarded as a return for the financial input of regional governments. Under the arrangement of joint development (*gong jian*), provincial governments share the funding responsibility with the central government in financing universities affiliated with the latter located in their territories (Mok 2005). Therefore, in addition to local universities which mainly serve local residents, universities affiliated with the central government also favour local students. Consequently, due to the large number of good universities in the cities, the admission requirements for students in Beijing and Shanghai are much lower than in other provinces (Higher Education Enrolment 2004, 2009; Zhou 2006).

There is no doubt that chances for access to HE varies between regions because of differentiated recruitment plans. However, given that most universities are located in developed regions such as the eastern coastal area and the top universities are concentrated in big cities, the disproportionate allocation of university places is criticized in disadvantaged regions. In addition, the *Hukou* (household registration) system in China has made the situation even worse. Controlled by the rigid *Hukou* system, people in China are not allowed to move freely among regions. Students are only allowed to be processed in university admission in the province where their *Hukou* is registered (which is usually where they are born). Thus, the vast majority of students are born with an unequal opportunity to access quality HEIs. Disparity in HE resource allocation has enforced regional discrimination in education. Therefore, in this case of active deprivation, the vulnerable group is students in provinces with less HE resources, where resources are defined not just as HEIs but also high-quality HEIs, and the direct cause for exclusion is the quota allocation mechanism.

Passive exclusion: urban–rural disparities in quality education

There is a huge gap in the HE admission rates between urban and rural students. The HE enrolment rate for rural students in 2002 was 2.37 per cent, contrasting with 19.89 per cent for urban students. Moreover, in the decade from 1990 to 1999, HE admission rates in rural areas increased by 4.33 per cent, whereas the figure soared by 147.13 per cent in urban areas (Guo 2005). The urban–rural disparity is evidence that passive exclusion exists in China. Unlike regional disparity, however, rural students are not intentionally excluded or discriminated against by educational policies. Instead, it is the poor living and learning circumstances that appear to be the primary cause of urban–rural disparities.

Passive exclusion is embedded in the sharp urban rural divide in China. Historical reasons, together with the current political and economic arrangement, have divided the urban and rural regions into two economies and two societies. Urban residents enjoy a clear advantage on income, social services and social security (Knight and Song 1999). Even though people prefer to live in cities, choices are limited for rural dwellers to move to cities and enjoy the same social welfare as their urban counterparts, restricted as they are by the *Hukou* system. The threefold higher income of urban households attracts people to cities when they have more choice, especially when they are educated and seeking to better themselves. This, however, is a vicious cycle – well-educated people go to cities leaving no one behind who can follow through good education in rural areas; the divide has sharpened the urban–rural disparity in education. Moreover, education for urban students is better than for rural students in terms of funding, quality (including quality of teachers), access to private tutoring and opportunity for further studies (Bao 2006; NBSC 2008). The underdevelopment of school education in rural areas seriously undermines successful progress from school to university and therefore challenges equal access to HE for rural students.

Instrumental deprivation: alternatives to the normal admission system

Confronted with the fierce competition in the CEE, students and families try every means to take advantage of the admission system to increase their chances of going to a good university (Waters 2006). Several alternatives to the normal admission competition are introduced below, with a discussion of their unintended consequences.

- *'CEE migrants'*: Differentiated admission requirements have resulted in the emergence of 'CEE migrants' (*gao kao yi min*), who originally study in provinces with high admission requirements but seek student registration in places with lower admission criteria (Yin 2006). The migrants usually move to the provinces with low requirements in their final year of high school and take the CEE there. In doing so, they take advantage of the differences in admission requirements between provinces. Realizing that there is much less competition to be admitted to top universities for overseas students, some Chinese families even try to get their children a passport from another country to obtain the status of overseas student. Having obtained their new passport they come back to China to apply for the best universities as overseas students (Xinhua 2009). This CEE migration poses a severe challenge to education equity, because families with less advantageous backgrounds, such as financial ability and social networks, are not able to migrate.

- *The 'extra score' system*: Another policy that intensifies educational inequality is the 'extra score' system (*jia fen zhi du*), because it is also closely related to students' socio-economic background. The extra score policy was originally designed to complement the CEE by adding extra CEE scores to students with special traits, with the hope of overcoming the weaknesses of the standardized CEE. Theoretically, two types of students are eligible for the extra scores: those with great talent in a sport, activity, subject or other interest; and those from disadvantaged backgrounds, measured by merit-based and need-based criteria, respectively. In practice, however, the policy has been manipulated by privileged families. Many unqualified students, most of whom were from prominent families, managed to gain eligibility unfairly or even illegally (He 2007).
- *The 'recommendation' system*: Similarly, the 'recommendation' system (*bao song zhi du*), which was designed to diversify the admission channel to HE by offering gifted students a direct pathway to universities, has been abused to favour advantaged groups. Students from well-off families are more likely to be identified as talented students, even if they are not academically excellent, and cases of corruption have been reported (Li and Kong 2002). Waters (2006) thus suggests that it is a common practice for affluent families in Asia to actively exclude their children from normal selection in education to circumvent local academic competition.

This analysis shows that families in China also try their best to utilize all possible resources to help their children to get around the fierce competition in HE admission. In this process, policies are manipulated by well-off families. As corrupt practices in policy implementation have translated the policies into a shortcut to HE for students from advantaged backgrounds (Yi 2000; Li and Kong 2002; He 2007), social stratification is perpetuated in the HE selection mechanisms which, in return, reinforce the privilege of advantaged groups. In this sense, students without a prominent background become the vulnerable group facing unfair competition in HE admission, and these alternatives have instrumental effects on social exclusion, despite not being intrinsically part of the problem.

Implications for policy evaluation

Having distinguished and categorized social exclusion in HE access, the second aim of this chapter is to explore the implications of the CA for tackling education inequality. This section attempts to measure the effectiveness of recent policy responses to the inequalities within Sen's construct.

The importance of Sen's typology is that it allows one to distinguish between different types of exclusion in terms of causes and effects and thus can be used as a framework to evaluate policy responses. Given the complexity of social exclusion, three grades are introduced here to assess remedies or policy initiatives:

1   *Fundamental actions*: tackle the fundamental causes of social exclusion; usually involve macro-level reforms beyond a particular system.
2   *Remedial actions*: tackle the direct cause of social exclusion; usually involve structural changes at system level.
3   *Supportive actions*: alleviate social exclusion but cannot get to the root of a problem; temporary strategies to improve the situation.

These three grades of action can interlock with Sen's framework to illustrate the extent to which recent policy responses alleviate the deprivations (Table 8.2).

In the case of constitutive deprivation, the rise of tuition fees has put students from poorer families at risk. Recognizing the tension between high education costs and low financial affordability, Chinese authorities have introduced a variety of strategies to help students in financial hardship. For example, a comprehensive student loan and grant project was launched in 2007 (The State Council of China 2007). Market mechanisms are brought in by the project, as commercial banks are providing publicly subsidized loans to college students. However, the scheme has so far had limited effects, because the available grants are limited, and the application procedure is complicated, thus discouraging students from applying

Table 8.2 Implications of Sen's approach for higher education (HE) enrolment in China

Framework adapted from Sen			HE enrolment and admissions in China	
Criterion	Type	Feature	Findings	Possible proposed solutions
Effect	Constitutive deprivation	Constitutive importance; direct deprivation	Economic handicaps	Remedial: financial aids to eligible students; Fundamental: poverty alleviation
	Instrumental deprivation	Instrumental relevance; results in other deprivation	Alternatives to the normal admission system	Supportive: closely monitor the admission alternatives; Remedial: reform of the admission system
Intention	Active deprivation	Deliberate exclusion; usually a result of a particular policy	Regional disparities	Supportive: delocalization of enrolment; Remedial: reform of the quota system
	Passive deprivation	Non-deliberate exclusion; usually a result of the overall situation	Urban-rural divide	Remedial: direct help for rural students; Fundamental: removal of the urban-rural dichotomy

Source: Adapted from Sen (2000).

(Liu and Xia 2007). Consequently, informal resources have become the primary financing channel, since more than 90 per cent of tertiary students rely on their families for education cost, as shown by a survey of over 5,000 students across China (Liu and Xia 2007).

Another apparent attempt to help students with financial difficulties as a response to high tuition fees is free normal education. Tuition fees and accommodation fees have been waived in six normal universities affiliated with the MOE since 2007 (China National Centre for Student Assistance Administration 2007). Nevertheless, the places provided by the six universities are very limited, only 12,112 quota places were available for 10 million students sitting the CEE in 2009 (China Education and Research Network 2009). Despite the limitations, however, the state initiatives provide a good example of remedial actions, as they attempt to target the direct cause of the exclusion – financial handicaps posed by the high tuition fee. However, since the strategies focus exclusively on the tuition fee they have ignored the problem of poverty deprivation, which is at the core of the exclusion. Therefore, a fundamental solution to constitutive deprivation would rely more broadly on poverty alleviation, which could only be achieved by joint efforts from the state, markets and civil society.

The cause for regional disparity, on the other hand, is apparent. Within the context of uneven development of HE and a decentralized financing system, the allocation mechanism of the HE quota has actively excluded students in some provinces by setting higher admission requirements. In this sense, remedial action would be sufficient and the strategy would be straightforward – a fair allocation system could solve the problem. In 2006, China University of Political Science and Law made a first attempt to improve the current unequal system (Zheng 2008). It allocated its enrolment quota in proportion to the population in different regions. This bottom-up reform demonstrates a successful remedial action initiated by a social organization. Seen as an essential change to overcome the regional disparity, it is nevertheless difficult to adopt quickly nationwide due to the vested interests of local authorities in the universities in their territory.

The fact that being born in a province with sufficient HE recourses would give local students much better chance to access HE, particularly good national universities, has sparked a huge debate on regional discrimination in HE admission. Facing increasing pressure, the state issued a number of administrative orders prohibiting localized HE enrolment (*Daizhong Daily* 2009). However, the orders have been criticized for their lack of effective implementation. To address these problems, the MOE passed specific policies and quantified goals in 2009 to improve policy implementation. For example, universities affiliated with the MOE were required to delocalize their enrolment by 2 per cent. In addition, 60,000 extra quotas were allocated to the western and central areas (MOE 2009). Despite the effects of these ad hoc decisions in reducing regional disparity in HE enrolment, without touching the core cause of the active deprivation they are at most a supportive action alleviating the problem temporarily.

As for the urban–rural disparity in accessing HE, there is unlikely to be a single, readily available solution. As a demonstration of passive exclusion, inequality between urban and rural students is a result of the wider urban–rural dichotomy which has emerged since the adoption of a market economy. Therefore, a fundamental solution to the urban–rural disparity in HE admission rests more on an overall development of the rural economy. Given that this would be a long process, supportive actions are necessary for disadvantaged rural students. Responding to the sharp disparities between urban and rural education, since 2005 the central government has been subsidizing rural students throughout the compulsory education stage. As supportive actions, the policies have reduced financial burdens on rural families and may counterbalance the growing urban–rural disparity to a certain extent.

Turning to instrumental deprivation, policies and regulations were issued to counter the manipulation of alternative admission channels. For example, in a recent famous case, a 'migrant student', who scored the highest in the CEE among all the examinees in the province, was deprived of eligibility for applying to key universities because of his 'migrant' status (Qiu 2005). In addition, as a response to the abuse of 'recommendations' and the 'extra score' system, the government is now imposing restricted and quantified criteria to check candidates' eligibility (Zhang *et al.* 2002). This is despite the fact that the new measures could serve to undermine the value of the two mechanisms in terms of enhancing diversity and flexibility in HE enrolment. However, given the instrumental effects of the exclusion, the key solution to the situation is not to punish the groups taking advantage of the current systems. Instead, a solution would be to correct the flawed mechanisms. Privileged groups manipulating the policies are not by themselves a kind of exclusion; rather, it is the problematic design of HE enrolment that destroys equal access to HE for students in the country. Therefore, remedial action that can systematically improve the admission system is needed.

To summarize, the analysis of responses to social exclusion demonstrates that solutions to different types of deprivation vary (Table 8.2). For constitutive deprivation, a fundamental action is needed as the cause is intrinsically a kind of deprivation. At the same time, remedial action providing direct solutions to the problem may quickly improve the situation. In the case of passive exclusion, a fundamental action is also a necessity because factors to be blamed usually include a series of social circumstances. While an ultimate solution may take a great deal of time and effort, supportive actions are useful endeavours to alleviate exclusion on an ongoing basis. On the other hand, causes and effects of active and instrumental deprivation are more straightforward compared with the former two types, so remedial actions which can systematically improve the relevant mechanism are likely to be the proper solution.

Conclusion

While the positive role of education in social inclusion is undeniable, this analysis shows the dark side of education – the reinforcing effects of the HE admission system in China on social exclusion by means of constitutive, instrumental, passive and active deprivation. Sen's CA has demonstrated its value by distinguishing different types of exclusion, illustrating mechanisms that produce education inequality and mapping a socially constructed process of exclusion in China. The CA shows an enlarged analytical space by investigating different needs and choices confronting different social groups in the same process, as exemplified by HE enrolment in China. It therefore suggests that evaluation of education inequality is not limited to the analysis of educational inputs and learning outcomes, which tend to overlook inequalities in the conversion from input to output. Related to the difference in converting resources to functions is the question whether current institutional design confines people to specific states or provides a platform to enhance capability in terms of their real freedom. A review of the HE enrolment mechanism in China has demonstrated that education does not necessarily enhance capability. Instead, the freedom to choose to enter HE is undermined by a flawed mechanism and socially constructed factors such as family background.

In addition to testing the theoretical proposition, the typology of deprivation provides a framework to evaluate existing policies and explore possible solutions not only in China but also elsewhere where there are inequalities in admission to HE. Depending on different cause and effect of the deprivations, responses to the problems may include a combination of short-term and long-term efforts ranging from supportive, remedial efforts to fundamental actions. Analysis of responses to the current situation reveals that social exclusion related to HE enrolment in China is not adequately addressed. The inadequacy derives partly from limitations of the solutions themselves, such as the restrictions of the student loans mentioned above. More importantly, there is no effective reaction tackling the real cause of certain kinds of exclusion, as shown in the case of instrumental deprivation. Among the responses to the current situation, it is apparent that the state has taken a dominant role in combating social exclusion, while the influence of civil society is limited and actions of markets can hardly be found.

Under the tide of neoliberal globalization, it is likely that inequalities will be worsened. Neoliberalism has been widely accepted in different parts of the world, including China. This is shown by the adoption of various neoliberal policies, such as privatization and marketization in China's education sector and elsewhere. Also, the knowledge-based economy requires individual countries to take HE as an important means to enhance national competitiveness. As a consequence, education has become more like an investment than a public good. Due to the changing social context and a shift in dominating ideologies and political beliefs, the state alone is unlikely to be capable of addressing all aspects of social exclusion. In addition to the state's top-down initiatives for social inclusion, a bottom-up process is equally important, with families, associations and other social networks contributing to combat social exclusion. An action package comprising joint efforts from the state, markets and civil society is probably more desirable to combat social exclusion in China.

Acknowledgement

This research is funded in part by Chinese Ministry of Education Humanities and Social Sciences Fund for Young Scholars (No. 11YJC880113). An expanded version of this chapter appears in 'Social exclusion and inequality in higher education in China: a capability perspective', *International Journal of Educational Development*, 2011, 31(3): 277–286.

References

Bao, C. (2006) 'Policies for compulsory education disparity between urban and rural areas in China', *Frontier of Education in China*, 1: 40–55.

China Education and Research Network (2009) '12112 Places were offered for free normal education in 2009'. Available at http://www.eol.cn/kuai_xun_3075/2009 0907/t20090907_405104.shtml [accessed 2 June 2010].

China National Centre for Student Assistance Administration (2007) 'Direction of financial assistance'. Available at http://www.xszz.cee.edu.cn/show_class.jsp?rootid =107&id=158 [accessed 11 November 2008].

China Youth and Children Research Centre (2007) *Report on the Situation of Youth Development in China in the 10th Five-Year Period and the Trend of Youth Development in China in the 11th Five-Year Period*, Beijing: China Youth and Children Research Centre.

cuaa.net, Da Xue Journal, and 21 Shi Ji Ren Cai Bao (2009) *2009 Report on Evaluation of Universities in China*.

Cummings, W. (1996) 'Asian values, education and development', *Compare*, 26(3): 287–304.

Daizhong Daily (2009) 'Localization of higher education admission must be solved by "hard measures"', *Daizhong Daily*, 18 May.

Devaney, M. and Weber, W. (2003) 'Abandoning the public good: how universities have helped privatize higher education', *Journal of Academic Ethics*, 1: 175–9.

Guo, R. (2005) 'Cong chengxiang ruxue jihui kan gaodeng jiaoyu gongping' [Equality in access to higher education being assessed from the opportunities between urban and rural students], *Educational Development Research*, 5: 29–31.

He, Y.H. (2007) 'Institutional analysis on extra score policy', *Journal of Xiangtan Normal University (Social Science Edition)*, 29(2): 39–42.

Higher Education Enrolment (2009). *Nationwide Admission Requirements for Higher Education by Major*, Beijing: China Higher Education Enrolment Press.

—— (2009). *Nationwide Admission Requirements for Higher Education by Major*, Beijing: China Higher Education Enrolment Press.

Jayaraj, D. and Subramanian, S. (2006) 'Horizontal and vertical inequality: some interconnections and indicators', *Social Indicators Research* 75(1): 123–39.

Knight, J. and Song, L. (1999) *The Rural–Urban Divide: Economic Disparities and Interactions in China*, New York: Oxford University Press.

Li, J.F. and Kong, S.H. (2002) 'Why recommendation system must be reformed?', *Continued Engineering Education*, 1: 1–3.

Li, M. and Bray, M. (2006) 'Social class and cross-border higher education: mainland Chinese students in Hong Kong and Macau', *Journal of International Migration and Integration*, 7(4): 407–24.

Liu, M. and Xia, C.Z. (2007) 'Wo guo zhu xue dai kuan xian zhuang diao chao ji dui ce jian yi)' [Current situation of student loans in China and suggestions], *China Finance*, 19: 73–4.

Liu, Y., He, S. and Wu, F. (2008) 'Urban pauperization under China's social exclusion: a case study of Nanjing', *Journal of Urban Affairs*, 30(1): 21–36.

Ministry of Education [MOE] (1996) 'Big issues in 1996 in education'. Available at http://www.moe.edu.cn/edoas/website18/info5006.htm [accessed 18 June 2007].

—— (2009) 'Six changes in higher education enrollment this year'. Available at http://www.edu.cn/09gaozhao_8100/20090603/t20090603_381716.shtml [accessed 11 June 2012].

Mok, H.K. (2005) 'Globalization and educational restructuring: university merging and changing governance in China', *Higher Education*, 50(1): 57–88.

Mok, K. (1997). 'Privatization or marketization: educational development in Post-Mao China'. *International Review of Education* 43 (5): 547–67.

National Bureau of Statistics of China [NBSC] (2008) *China Statistic Yearbook 2008*, Beijing: China Statistics Press.

National Development and Reform Commission (2007) 'Guan yu gong bu zhong yang bu shu gao xiao xue fei biao zhun de tong zhi' [Notice on tuition standard for HEIs affiliated with ministries]. Available at http://www.ndrc.gov.cn/zcfb/zcfbtz/2007 tongzhi/t20070706_146668.htm [accessed 17 October 2008].

Office for National Statistics (2010) *Statistical Bulletin: Regional GDHI*. Newport, UK: Office for National Statistics.

Qiu, M. (2005) 'The "CEE migrant" champion in Hainan can't be admitted into Tsinghua University?', *Guangzhou Daily*, 14 July. Available at http://edu.people.com.cn/GB/1053/3541475.html [accessed 12 July 2007].

Qu, Y. (2008) 'Reflections on the issue of students from extremely poor families in higher education', *Heilongjiang Science and Technology Information*, 23: 182.

Sen, A. (1992) *Inequality Re-examined*, Oxford: Oxford University Press.

—— (2000) *Social Exclusion: Concept, Application and Scrutiny*, Manila: Asian Development Bank.

—— (2005). 'Human rights and capabilities'. *Journal of Human Development and Capabilities*, 6(2): 151–66.

Stewart, F. (2004) 'The relationship between horizontal and vertical inequalities and social exclusion', *CRISE Newsletter*, Winter. Available at http://www.dfid.gov.uk/r4d/Output/174496/Default.aspx.

The State Council of China (2007) 'The opinion of the state council on building and perfecting the subsidization policy system for the students from poor families in universities, higher vocational colleges and secondary vocational schools', *China Vocational Education*, 22.

United Nations Development Programme (2005) *China's Human Development Report 2005*, Washington DC: United Nations Development Programme.

Vizard, P. and Burchardt, T. (2007) *Developing a Capability List: Final Recommendations of the Equalities Review Steering Group on Measurement*. London: The London School of Economics and Political Science.

Wang, L. (2008) 'Education inequality in China: problems of policies on access to higher education', *Journal of Asian Public Policy*, 1(1): 115–23.

Waters, J.L. (2006) 'Emergent geographies of international education and social exclusion', *Antipode*, 38(5): 1046–68.

World Bank (2007) *World Development Indicators 2007* (CD-ROM), Washington, DC: World Bank.

Xinhua, H. (2009) '115 Gui hua gang yao' [The 11th Five-Year Plan]. Available at http://news.xinhuanet.com/ziliao/2006-01/16/content_4057926.htm [accessed 12 March 2010].

Yi, Y. (2000) 'Recommendation system: continue? Or stop?', *Outlook*, 42: 20–2.

Yin, L. (2006) 'Cong gao kao yi min tou shi jiao yu gong ping' [Education equity from the perspective of "CEE Migrant"], *Journal of Xi'an Institute of Posts and Telecommunications*, 11(1), 137–41.

Yuan, X.W. and Yang, M.F. (2008) '16 provinces can decide the CEE system on their own', *People's Daily*, 5 June. Available at http://www.jyb.cn/zs/gxzs/ptgxzs/zszx/t20080605_168374.htm [accessed 11 October 2009].

Zhang, Y.B., Wang, L.Y. and Yue, H. (2002) 'Shi hua shi shuo bao song sheng' [The reality of recommendation system], *College and University Education*, (3): 12–3.

Zheng, Y.W. (2008) 'Analysis about the potential ideology factors of the higher education in our country to obtain the region difference of opportunity', *Meitan Higher Education*, 26(2): 76–9.

Zhou, H.Y. (2006) 'Suggestions on improving the allocation method of admission quota of key universities', China Education and Research Network. Available at http://www.edu.cn/20060306/3176686.shtml [accessed 09 July 2007].

Zhou, Z.W. (2008) 'On the industrialization of China's education industry lost in direction', *Theoretical Observation*, 50(2): 94–7.

Chapter 9

Universities and social responsibility for human and sustainable development

José-Félix Lozano and Alejandra Boni

The idea of corporate social responsibility (CSR) has gained prominence in recent years due to two main factors: the increasing demand from civil society and the need for companies to legitimize their actions to their clients and consumers (Werther and Chandler 2006; Hopkins 2007; Crane and Matten 2010; Utting and Marques 2010). Institutions like the United Nations (UN), the Organization for the Economic Cooperation and Development (OECD), the International Labour Organization (ILO) and the European Union (EU) are increasingly demanding that companies take into account the social and environmental consequences of their actions and decisions in a form that goes beyond meeting formal legal requirements. The philosophy of CSR has also expanded in recent years to include the public sector, as well as non-governmental organizations (Eade and Sayer 2006; Yaziji and Doh 2009). The university, as a social institution, has also joined this trend, with at least some universities preparing social responsibility reports (the University of Turku in Finland; and in Spain the University of Barcelona and public universities in Andalusia, among others) and sustainability reports (University of California, Berkeley; Leuphana University in Lüneburg, Germany; University of Edinburgh, UK etc.).

But, in addition to the production of reports, in our view, a policy of social responsibility should question the university's purpose, the type of professionals that are being trained, and the type of research that is considered socially responsible. And, especially in the current context of world economic and political crisis, a rigorous reflection is needed about the role played by all the institutions and main actors. Everyone involved – companies, public administrations, universities, unions, and consumers – should make a critical examination of which decisions are wrongly made and which decisions are not taken at all. Universities and business schools have an important role to play in this process of examination. As Angel Cabrera (2009), senior advisor on academic affairs at the UN Global Compact Office and president of the Thunderbird School of Global Management recently said:

> It would be presumptuous to put all of the blame for the current economic catastrophe on business schools. But it would be even worse not to make a

critical reflection and recognize how business schools have contributed to the disaster by perpetuating a mistaken vision that has damaged businesses.

We agree with this statement and consider that reflection on social responsibility in universities is particularly relevant at this time for at least three reasons. Firstly, in the information society, knowledge has become a key factor for economic wealth and well-being and, consequently, reflection over what knowledge is being generated, how it is transmitted and who it reaches is a supremely important question of justice. Secondly, the increased mercantilization of higher education (Slaughter and Leslie 1997) and its rapid privatization throughout the world is limiting many people's access to a public asset. And thirdly, the university's immense power to change people's lives, and the important service it offers society (knowledge and education), obliges us to develop a sense of responsibility worthy of that power.

This chapter therefore aims to contribute to reflections on the social responsibility of higher education institutions. In particular, we focus on the institutional level in order to reflect on university policies that favour the development of university social responsibility (USR). In order to reach that point, we begin by defining CSR and examining its essential characteristics and the extent to which it is applicable to universities. Then, we present a definition of USR and identify three trends in the different approaches to USR at universities. We go on to examine some public policy implications of assuming a USR model based on the human development approach and, finally, we present some conclusions.

Corporate social responsibility and social responsibility of universities: commonalities and differences

The relationship between business and society and reflections on the contribution of business to society has a long history (Werther and Chandler 2006), but its present form took shape mainly in the twentieth century. According to one of the most commonly accepted and influential definitions of CSR from the EU's 2001 Green Paper: '[CSR is] a concept whereby companies integrate social and environmental concerns in their business operations and in their interaction with their stakeholders on a voluntary basis' (European Commission 2001: 4). In short, the aim is the advancement of economic growth, social cohesion and environmental protection. It is important to highlight the voluntary nature of this definition and its claim to supplement the legislation in force. These initiatives do not replace the legal regulations on environmental and social matters, but supplement them. In areas where there are no minimum conditions efforts must be directed at establishing them.

The EU has recently published a new communication entitled *A Renewed EU Strategy 2011–14 for Corporate Social Responsibility*, which offers a more comprehensive definition:

To fully meet their corporate social responsibility, enterprises should have in place a process to integrate social, environmental, ethical, human rights and consumer concerns into their business operations and core strategy in close collaboration with their Stakeholders, with the aim of: maximizing the creation of shared value for their owners/shareholders and for their other stakeholders and society at large; and identifying, preventing and mitigating their possible adverse impacts.

(European Commission 2011: 6)

This definition contains four essential characteristics of CSR and how it should be carried out:

1 *Voluntary basis:* CSR is behaviour by businesses over and above legal requirements. The state can use public policies to promote and regulate information processes but cannot impose responsibility practices.
2 *Integration:* CSR initiatives must be integrated into the company's day-to-day operations in all areas and fields of business. CSR is not an optional 'add-on' to core business activities but concerns the way businesses are managed.
3 *Transparency and accountability:* Organizations must report diligently and truthfully on their actions and decisions in key aspects for various groups of stakeholders. They must be ready to listen to the demands of stakeholder groups, respond objectively and clearly and allow themselves to be evaluated by their stakeholders not only in economic but also in social and environmental matters ('triple bottom line').
4 *Dialogue and participation:* The essence of CSR is to view the company as an actor in society and as an institution that must communicatively legitimate itself (Ulrich 1997). In contrast to the conception of business as independent and even opposed to and struggling against society, a responsible company must be willing to participate in rational dialogues with affected groups.
These are the essential features of CSR that any business, regardless of size, field or industry, should make efforts to develop. The promotion of CSR requires a holistic approach which contemplates all these aspects and uses all the necessary mechanisms for its development.

Now we turn to the universities domain. These institutions are increasingly closer to the world of enterprise and business, and although this is positive and necessary it becomes a problem when there is a shift from 'being close' to being 'at the service of' (Axelrod 2002). It is normal and reasonable for universities to copy and adapt best business management practices; and for that reason we consider it positive for universities to adopt the philosophy of CSR. But adoption of that philosophy cannot be a mere copy, it must be an integration (Ulrich 1997) that respects and promotes the university's essential mission and its defining characteristics. As the Magna Charta of European Universities[1] highlights:

> The university is an autonomous institution at the heart of societies differently organised because of geography and historical heritage; it produces, examines, appraises and hands down culture by research and teaching. To meet the needs of the world around it, its research and teaching must be morally and intellectually independent of all political authority and economic power.

Taking into account the differences between a university and a company, we suggest USR shares the same purpose as CSR (integrating social and environmental impacts in the management of organizations) and the basic characteristics (voluntary basis, integration, transparency and accountability, dialogue and participation), but that it differs in other very important aspects.

The first is the mission or *telos* of business and university as social institutions. An organization's mission gives meaning and social legitimacy and is therefore a basic criterion for identifying its social responsibility. For business, the mission or *telos* of its activity is the maximization of shared value, where the main agent is the owner of the company. The university's mission has always been the search for knowledge and truth, sometimes for a practical purpose but always as a valuable end in itself (Reed 2004).

The second parameter is to ask about the key stakeholders. For a private company to be successful, management must first of all respond to the demands of clients and consumers. Secondly, company management must take into consideration the demands of other stakeholders; and if possible align the interests of other important stakeholders (employees, investors, suppliers) in order to satisfy customer demands. The university's relationship with its stakeholders differs in two fundamental aspects. Firstly, there is no clear priority or reference group of stakeholders; here the key groups are students and society in general that benefit from the knowledge created and the transfer of culture and knowledge. Secondly, the university's attitude is not only to 'respond to the demands' of these groups, but also 'to propose and offer new knowledge' and pursue the search for knowledge beyond any explicit demand from one group. Teaching and research are not simply oriented at satisfying demand from students, companies or any other stakeholders but at reaching beyond that to propose knowledge that contributes to the advancement of culture, science and technology and makes a positive contribution to a fair society (including critical reflection over what constitutes a fair society).

The third parameter is that of the criteria used to measure the success of an organization's social responsibility. Even though economic criteria have currently been imposed in almost all areas, in the case of the university note should be taken of what the most appropriate measure is for evaluating the success of higher education (Axelrod 2002; Boni and Gasper 2012). In the world of business, success is measured by the amount of profit and the economic sustainability of the activity. The relevant criteria for measuring the success or quality of university activity cannot be profitability, economic sustainability or any other economic indicators. Following the terminology of the human development approach, which frames this book and the university's traditional mission, the success criteria for higher education can be said to be its contribution to the expansion of people's real freedoms and the formation of autonomous citizens with the ability to be the protagonists of their lives in the private sphere (family and affective relations), in the employment and professional sphere, and in the public sphere (politics and culture).

The fourth parameter concerns the principles that guide governance and the management of an organization. As we have stated above, the management and government of private companies is directed at maximizing value for the different stakeholders, among whom customers and shareholders are a priority. The values that orient management towards this objective are efficiency, efficacy and financial profit and, due to that, these values normally impose on other values such as participation, communications and solidarity, which are only put into action and promoted when they contribute to efficiency, efficacy and profit. The opportunity for universities to fulfil their mission requires management and governance with real autonomy, not subject to the power of the state, the market or any other institution. Autonomy has been essential for higher education institutions since they first came into being and involves developing two basic values: participation and transparency. Transparency is intimately associated with participation (without precise information there can be no genuine participation), and it involves the exercise of impartiality and accountability. In this context, impartiality means equal opportunities to participate in dialogues on issues that affect the stakeholders and the predominance of the best argument rather than any other type of force or coercion. And accountability in the broad sense involves rigorously informing on the data and relevant information for participation and the reasons and criteria on which university government and management are based.

The fifth and final parameter for comparison refers to the impacts the institution generates. The aim of CSR is to integrate its social and environmental impacts in business decision making, but the impacts considered are mainly material impacts both on the people in the company and on the environment where its activity takes place. An essential part of university responsibility is to take into consideration educational and cognitive impacts. Educational and cognitive impacts are difficult to measure and manage, but they are an essential part of university responsibility and creative ways of addressing them should be sought.

These five significant differences highlight the importance of providing a precise definition of USR and of the policies to promote it. If these differences and the specific nature of higher education institutions are not taken into account, and we simply apply CSR criteria mechanically to the university, we run the risk of being ineffective and even losing social legitimacy by forgetting the university's mission and its inherent characteristics.

University social responsibility: different approaches and definitions

One of the earliest reflections on USR can be found in Derek Bok's (1982) *Beyond the Ivory Tower: Social Responsibility of the Modern University*, in which he analyses basic academic values with particular emphasis on university autonomy. It should be noted, however, that Bok did not use the concept of USR in the sense we are considering it here because dialogue with stakeholders, transparency and the impacts the university generates are not considered. Thus for richer understanding we need to turn to François Vallaeys' definition:

> A policy of ethical quality in the activities of the university community (students, lecturers, and administrative staff), through responsible management of the educational, cognitive, labour and environmental impact of the university, in a participative dialogue with society to promote sustainable human development.
>
> (Vallaeys *et al.* 2009: 7)

For its part, the Universidad Construye País initiative, which has been taking place in Chile since 2001, defines USR as 'a university way of being' which materializes in 'the university's ability as an institution to disseminate and put into practice a set of principles and values through four key processes: management, teaching, research and extension' (Universidad Construye País 2006: 10). The values and principles that are put into practice are: (1) on a personal level – individual dignity, freedom and integrity; (2) at the level of society – the public interest, social equity, sustainable development, sociability, solidarity for peaceful coexistence, the acceptance and appreciation of diversity, civic responsibility, democracy and participation; and (3) at university level – commitment to truth, excellence, interdependence and transdisciplinarity. Thus, the Universidad Construye País initiative views a responsible university as one that puts these values into practice in its management, teaching, research and extension.

On similar lines, but with different nuances, the Association of Jesuit Universities in Latin America (AUSJAL) says that USR:

> must be understood as the ability and effectiveness of the university to respond to the need to transform the society in which it is immersed, by exercising its substantive functions: teaching, research, extension and internal management. These functions should be driven by the search to promote justice, solidarity and social equity by constructing successful responses to attend the challenges involved in promoting sustainable human development.
>
> (AUSJAL 2009: 18)

And finally, the definition offered by the University of Lüneburg from the perspective of sustainable human development views USR:

as the integration of the impacts the university generates on its surrounding environment so that they contribute to human development. Thus defined, the social responsibility of a (public or private) university involves pursuing the goal of human development and assessing how its essential activities (research, teaching, knowledge transfer and management of the organisation) contribute to that goal.

(University of Lüneburg 2010)

Taking into account these different theoretical approaches and practical developments, and despite the newness of the topic, three trends are noticeable in the approaches to USR.

The first approach is what we could call the 'management of indicators' model, in which fundamentally CSR criteria are applied to the university and USR reports are produced following the indicators proposed by the Global Reporting Initiative for businesses. In this model, rather than rigorous reflection on the university's mission or the specific nature of its impacts, the focus is on presenting indicators for the economic, social and environmental impacts of the university on in its surrounding environment. Furthermore, management of these impacts is seen fundamentally in the form of threats and risks to the university's reputation. An example of this approach can be found in the University of Barcelona (2010), which in 2009 set up an Administrative Unit of Internal Control, Risks and Corporate Social Responsibility.

The special feature of the second model, that we will call the 'liberal USR model' is that it proposes recovering the essence of the university as a liberal education institution whose essential features are institutional autonomy, the education of cosmopolitan citizens and the quest for knowledge because of its intrinsic value. This approach has been defended by Nussbaum (1997, 2010) and developed in detail by Reed (2004) and Axelrod (2002). This model offers normative reflection on the university's mission and tasks and is based on the conception of education as a public asset at the service of human beings, rather than the market; it also reflects deeply on the university's political dimension. The major criticism of this model is that it is not operational. That is, it is a good legitimating and inspiring discourse but it lacks practical management tools and procedures.

And the third model we have identified is 'USR as sustainable human development', a model we consider to be a synthesis that overcomes the pragmatic moment (management of indicators model) and the abstract moment (liberal model). As presented in Chapter 1, human development is understood as the set of basic freedoms human beings should all enjoy (Sen 2010). Thus, USR must be defined and evaluated according to its contribution to the expansion of these basic capabilities for all citizens. This approach represents a rigorous reflection on the institution's purpose and the legitimate means for achieving that purpose. Some social responsibility reports from universities such as Leuphana University (Lüneburg, Germany) and Turku University of Applied Science (Finland), Jesuit universities in Latin America and the Universidad Construye País initiative (Chile) come under this approach as they have reflected deeply on the university's mission and purpose and have developed specific proposals to effectively perform and assess that mission. The frame of reference for this approach is sustainable human development with the core elements of empowerment, equity and participation.

Implications for university social responsibility from a sustainable human development approach

Based on the third approach we have presented, we want to explore further the policy implications of developing this model for a responsible university. According to the proposal from Vallaeys *et al.* (2009), USR's policies can be organized into four areas according to the type of impact they have: educational, cognitive, social and organizational operation.

Educational impacts

Educational impacts refer to the training students receive and include general training in values, attitudes and knowledge and training for professional development: 'the responsible university asks about the type of professionals, citizens and people it trains and about the appropriate organization of teaching to guarantee responsible training for its students' (Vallaeys *et al.* 2009: 9). On this point, it is worth emphasizing that critical pedagogy should orient the university's educational action. In contrast to the temptation to see higher education as 'training human capital', the university must educate to expand people's freedoms (Walker 2006). These educational impacts materialize mainly in two important dimensions: the theories that are explained and the teaching methodology. In particular, in the area of economics and business, the theories that are explained have a very direct impact on the responsible or irresponsible practices used by future professionals. As Ghosal (2005) correctly pointed out, in recent decades some theories (such as agency theory and rational choice) explained uncritically in business schools and departments have led to some very negative practical results.

And finally, the university's educational impact is also transmitted in the pedagogy and educational strategies it uses. Appropriate pedagogy is that which views the student as an active citizen who has critical ability and is committed to changing reality; and it views the learning process as cooperation between people motivated by the quest for knowledge; as '*Bildung*' rather than mere 'training' (Reed 2004; Walker 2006). From this point of view, the educational process must be conceived of as a process of supporting the construction of a standpoint and own criteria that enables students to critically understand, interpret and give meaning to key issues in their lives and society; or in Socrates' words: 'to live an examined life'. This involves opening up to interdisciplinarity, creativity and criticism of the knowledge acquired. Many pedagogical actions are available, but we coincide with Nussbaum when she states that:

As a starting point, critical thinking should be infused into the pedagogy of classes of many types, as students learn to probe, to evaluate evidence, to write papers with well-structured arguments, and to analyse the arguments presented to them in other texts.

(Nussbaum 2010: 55)

Cognitive impacts

Cognitive impacts concern the knowledge that is produced and how it is disseminated so that the responsible university 'asks about the type of knowledge being produced, its social relevance and who it is intended for' (Vallaeys *et al.* 2009: 9). The topics chosen for research are then a very significant indicator of university responsibility. A responsible university should promote research as something that is valuable in itself, and not simply as merchandise for those who can afford it. In our opinion, seeing research as an activity oriented to satisfying market demands is a problem because it has deviated research from the quest for knowledge for its own sake, to the quest for profit (Newman *et al.* 2004). This pressure for profit is expressed on three levels: research topics, the integrity of research procedures and the transfer of results. Firstly, the responsible university must be able to limit and control the influence and power of the market and corporations over the basic areas of research. For that reason it is important for a responsible university to ensure that research funds are distributed on the basis of discursive processes and not only according to the interests of the funding institutions (Reed 2004). Secondly, with regard to the integrity of research processes, a responsible university must have strict guidelines and appropriate enforcement procedures to prevent academic fraud and bad research practice such as plagiarism. And thirdly, the dissemination of scientific knowledge should be as fast and as extensive as possible and should not be solely or mainly guided by economic profitability. A responsible university should fight against monopolies of knowledge and offer knowledge and technologies not only to those who can pay, but to society as a whole.

Organizational operation impacts

According to Vallaeys *et al.* (2009), organizational operation impacts refer to the impact on workers and the environmental impact of the university's daily activity (energy use, waste, etc.). That is, a responsible university must offer its workers quality of life and decent working conditions; it must also make efforts to reduce its ecological impact. On this point we dare to propose the inclusion of university governance as a key element in USR. As Reed (2004) recognizes (and as we have dealt with elsewhere, Lozano *et al.* 2006), the way the university itself is structured and functions can reflect specific norms and serve different interests. A responsible university must maintain autonomy at all times in relation to economic, political, religious and any other type of power. The university must be perceived as a self-governing community of scholars that can only function with a high degree of autonomy if the processes of government are legitimated discursively and if communicative control mechanisms are developed. The discursive legitimation of university government involves developing mechanisms for dialogue and creating effective conditions for participation from all stakeholders; and in giving academics a central role in decision-making processes rather than managers, public officials or politicians. This legitimation is only possible by creating effective conditions for participation, and developing a culture of transparency and accountability that enables real participation and decision making based on reasons and not interests. Dialogue and participation must not be understood simply as a means for management decision making, but as an essential part of the way the institution and its actors behave, so that public dialogue and rational debate are promoted by university management in all areas.

Responsible university governance also includes extending ethical criteria to the other institutions involved. Thus, for example, a responsible university must require its suppliers and collaborating institutions to have the highest standards of respect for human rights and environmental protection. An essential aspect of this point would be to ensure that financial and commercial relations are consistent with the goal of expanding people's real freedoms.

Social impacts

Social impacts refer not only to material impacts (the wealth the university generates; the resources it consumes; the social action it carries out, etc.), but also to the general intangible and indirect impacts the university has on the development of society and in resolving its fundamental problems. Thus, the university's social impact is closely linked to its educational impact and to how the theories, models and aesthetic standards it generates contribute to building a fairer society. The social commitment of a responsible university should be expressed by active participation in the discussion and solution of global problems. The guiding question on this point is: 'how can the university effectively interact with society to promote more human and sustainable development?' (Vallaeys *et al.* 2009: 15). The initial response to this question is by contributing to the enlightenment of public opinion (Habermas 1962), to the strengthening of democracy (Dewey 1916) and to the configuration of sustainable preferences and lifestyles (Crocker and Linden 1998; Cortina 2002). That is, the responsible university must become actively involved in the discussion of public matters and offer information, training and reasoned opinion. Social criticism and rational questioning of social standards, habits and structures of power are tasks for which the university is particularly capable and legitimated. In particular, the university should be involved in improving democracy in both the rational criticism of the political processes and in the training of cosmopolitan citizens (Nussbaum 1997). Another activity of social commitment for a responsible university is to facilitate access to knowledge for the most vulnerable and disadvantaged groups by facilitating access to higher education for such groups and listening to their demands and needs.

Conclusion

In this chapter we have attempted to argue the importance of USR oriented towards human development principles and values. We have seen that not all university initiatives under the umbrella of USR respond to this model, because some USR practices are more or less copies of CSR and do not contemplate the elements that differentiate USR from CSR. As we have argued, the main differences lie in the mission, in the key stakeholders, in the impacts, the measurement and the principles that guide governance and management of business on the one hand and the university on the other.

We have also seen that human development can be a very relevant approach for inspiring USR if the intention is to generate and transmit knowledge that increases people's real freedoms and to educate autonomous citizens who are able to contribute to the construction of a fair society.

Finally, we have presented the possible implications of a human development-based social responsibility policy in four different areas: in relation to educational impacts, cognitive impacts, social impacts and organizational operation impacts. As the model of Vallaeys *et al.* (2009) correctly shows, these impacts produce four focuses for responsibility: responsible campus, social management of knowledge, social participation and professional training and citizenship. Seeking indicators that enable us to evaluate these impacts and design models to improve the university's results in these four areas is the next step to progressing towards the expansion, consolidation and effectiveness of a USR model based on the human development approach.

Note

1 Magna Charta Universitatum (1988). Available at http://www.magna-charta.org/library/userfiles/file/mc_english.pdf [accessed 28 February 2012].

References

Asociación de Universidades Jesuitas de América Latina [AUSJAL] (2009) *Políticas y Sistema de Autoevaluación y Gestión de la Responsabilidad Social Universitaria en AUSJAL*, Córdoba, Argentina: Alejandría Editorial.

Axelrod, P. (2002) *Values in Conflict. The University, the Marketplace, and the Trials of Liberal Education*, London: McGill-Queen's University Press.

Bok, D. (1982) *Beyond the Ivory Tower. Social Responsibility of the Modern University*, Cambridge, MA: Harvard University Press.

Boni, A. and Gasper, D. (2012) 'Rethinking the quality of universities: how can human development thinking contribute?', *Journal of Human Development and Capabilities*, 13(3): 451–70.

Cabrera, A. (2009) 'Un nuevo código ético para el capitalismo', *EL PAÍS*, 2 de marzo. Available at http://elpais.com/diario/2009/03/02/opinion/1235948410_850215. html [accessed 15 January 2012].

Cortina, A. (2002) *Por una Ética del Consumo*, Madrid: Editorial Taurus.

Crane, A. and Matten, D. (2010) *Business Ethics: Managing Corporate Citizenship and Sustainability in the Age of Globalization*, Oxford: Oxford University Press.

Crocker, D. and Linden, T. (eds) (1998) *Ethics of Consumption. The Good life, Justice, and Global Stewardship*, New York: Rowman and Littlefield Publishers.

Dewey, J. (1916/2007) *Democracy and Education*, Middlesex: The Echo Library.

Eade, D. and Sayer, J. (2006) *Development and the Private Sector: Consuming Interest*, Bloomfield, CT: Kumarian Press.

European Commission (2001) 'Promoting a European framework for corporate social responsibility', Green Paper. Available at http://eur-lex.europa.eu/LexUriServ/site/en/com/2001/com2001_0366en01.pdf [accessed 28 February 2012].

—— (2011) 'A renewed EU strategy 2011–2014 for corporate social responsibility'. Communication from the Commission to the European Parliament, the Council, the European Economic and Social Committee and the Committee of the Regions. Available at http://ec.europa.eu/enterprise/newsroom/cf/_getdocument.cfm?doc_id=7010 [accessed 28 February 2012].

Ghosal, S. (2005), 'Bad managers' theories are destroying good management practices', *Academy of Management Learning and Education*, 4(1): 75–91.

Habermas, J. (1962) *Strukturwandel der Offentlichkeit Untersuchungen zu einer Kategorie der bürerlichen Gessellschaft*, Frankfurt am Main: Shurkamp.

Hopkins, M. (2007) *Corporate Social Responsibility and International Development: Is Business the Solution?*, London: Earthscan.

Lozano, J.F., Boni, A. and Calabuig, C. (2006), 'Addressing the institutional ethos: the process of developing the ethical code for the faculty of industrial engineering at the Universidad Politécnica de Valencia', paper presented at General Conference of Institutional Management in Higher Education: Values and Ethics: Managing Challenges and Realities in Higher Education, Paris, 11–13 September 2006.

Newman, F., Couturier, L. and Scurry, J.(2004) *The Future of Higher Education: Rhetoric, Reality, and the Risk of the Market*, San Francisco: Jossey-Bass.

Nussbaum, M. (1997) *Cultivating Humanity. A Classical Defense of Reform in Liberal Education*, Cambridge, MA: Harvard University Press.

—— (2010) *Not for Profit*, Princeton: Princeton University Press.

Reed, D. (2004) 'Universities and the promotion of corporate responsibility: reinterpreting the liberal arts tradition', *Journal of Academic Ethics*, 2(1): 3–41.

Sen, A. (2010) *The Idea of Justice*, London: Allen Lane/Penguin Books.

Slaughter, S. and Leslie, L.L. (1997) *Academic Capitalism: Politics, Policies, and the Entrepreneurial University*, Baltimore: The Johns Hopkins University Press.

Ulrich, P. (1997) *Integrative Wirtschaftsethik: Grundlagen einer lebensdienlichen Ökonomie*, Bern: Haput Verlag.

Universidad Construye País (2006) 'Responsabilidad social universitaria. Una manera de ser universidad. Teoría y práctica de la experiencia Chilena'. Available at http://www.participa.cl/wp-content/uploads/2007/10/5-libro-completo-version-final.pdf [accessed 26 February 2012].

University of Barcelona (2010) 'Report on social responsibility for the academic year 2008–2009'. Available at http://www.ub.edu/responsabilitatsocial/en/memoria.html [accessed 15 February 2012].

University of Lüneburg (2010) 'Nachhaltigkeitsberich 2009. Schritte in die Zukunft'. Available at http://www.leuphana.de/fileadmin/user_upload/uniprojekte/Nachhaltigkeitsportal/Nachhaltigkeitsbericht/files/Nachhaltigkeitsbericht_2009.pdf [accessed 15 February 2012].

Utting, P. and Marques, J.C. (eds) (2010) *Corporate Social Responsibility and Regulatory Governance: Towards Inclusive Development?*, New York: Palgrave-Macmillan.

Vallaeys, F., de la Cruz, C. and Sasia, P.M. (2009) *Responsabilidad Social Universitaria: Manual de Primeros Pasos*, México D.F.: McGraw-Hill, BID.

Walker, M. (2006) *Higher Education Pedagogies*, Berkshire: The Society for Research into Higher Education and Open University Press.

Werther, W. Jr. and Chandler, D. (2006) *Strategic Corporate Social Responsibility*, London: Sage.

Yaziji, M. and Doh, J. (2009) *NGOs and Corporations: Conflict and Collaboration*, Cambridge: Cambridge University Press.

Part III

Operationalizing
a new imaginary

Chapter 10

Liberal arts education and the formation of valuable capabilities

Alberta Maria Carlotta Spreafico

A sustainable imaginary for the twenty-first century calls for rethinking the kind of education needed to enable young people to prosper individually and be capable of positively influencing social development. The European Union and the USA, among others, are faced with a worrying scenario, worsened by the economic crisis of 2008: unequal access to education, high dropout rates, widespread youth unemployment, rising cases of 'over-education', constant need for innovation and graduates' inability to relate with and shape increasingly complex and dynamic social situations and work environments. We are also coming to terms with a globalized world that rests on inequitable social, financial and environmental systems. Young people have complicated challenges ahead of them and evermore require multifaceted competences. Higher education institutions have both the potential and the responsibility to play a key role.

Neoliberal human capital theory, pioneered in the 1970s by Becker and Schultz, has greatly influenced current notion, policies, curriculum, pedagogies and quality indicators of higher education. However, while the significance of the instrumental economic role of education is undeniable, there are sound arguments for it not being the only reason for which education is important. The human development capability approach (CA) presents a broader notion of well-being and development to that of human capital theory and the associated neoliberal income-oriented approach. As proposed by Sen (1999) we should evaluate well-being in terms of functionings and capabilities. The importance of income is not disregarded, but it is redefined as a means – among others – and not as an end of human well-being. Sen (1997) affirms that we must go beyond the notion of human capital, after acknowledging its relevance and reach. The broadening that is needed, he argues, is additional and cumulative, rather than an alternative to the human capital approach. Fundamentally, education policies and institutions should help to remove obstacles from the lives of young adults in order to enable them to have the freedom to live the lives they have reason to value. This comprehensive and transversal focus requires (and allows) education to take into full consideration people in all their multidimensional elements and their relation with the social and global context. The purpose of education, pedagogy and commonly used quality indicators would be innovatively redefined by this different notion of development and well-being.

However, Sen's formulation of the CA does not suggest a fit-for-all method of operationalization or a list of capabilities that an education system or institution should foster. Although other scholars, most notably Nussbaum, have argued for the endorsement of a definite list of capabilities, according to Sen the process of selecting capabilities and subsequent quality assessments involve value judgments that cannot be isolated from the stakeholders who will experience the education.

In this chapter I follow Sen's procedural claim and attempt to address the concrete possibility of operationalizing the CA. The aim of the chapter is twofold. The first is to suggest a methodology for deriving a list of capabilities that is: (1) coherent with the human development framework; (2) tailored to an area of study that is of interest; and (3) situated in a specific chosen context. The second is to illustrate the application of the methodology. In this case, I focus specifically on higher education and on the particular case study of Barnard College – a women's liberal arts college in New York, affiliated to Columbia University. I derive a list of nine education capabilities that Barnard College intends to foster; I then also try to test the quality of the selected capabilities and of the college education from a human development perspective.[1] Although I shall apply the methodology to education, and higher education in particular, I would like to suggest that it is applicable across subjects.

Methodology

The method presented in this chapter is arranged in two parts, each comprised of three steps: the first part results in a list of derived situated capabilities and the second concentrates on testing them in relation to stakeholders' value judgments and assessments.

I follow Robeyns' (2003) five criteria for drawing up a list of capabilities: (1) explicit formulation; (2) methodological justification; (3) sensitivity to context; (4) different levels of generality; and (5) exhaustion and non-reducibility.[2] I also build upon and partly modify Walker's (2006) five-steps methodology, which she used to derive a list of education capabilities focused on contemporary South African schools and gender equity: she (1) considered the CA and the specificity of education; (2) analysed core aspects from South African education policies; (3) interviewed 40 girls from local schools; (4) then engaged with other existing lists of capabilities that were not specifically tailored to the topic in order to identify any that could apply to the field of education and ultimately derived her list; (5) she submitted her list to open debate.

Hence, my suggested methodology begins with an analysis of the CA as a general framework in order to infer the inherent fundamental concepts. Second, concentration is placed on a specific subject area of interest: in this case, education and higher education in particular. The related literature is analysed and previously derived education capabilities are acknowledged. These first two steps serve the purpose of giving academic legitimacy to the list. Also, the key concepts outlined at this stage will shape the standpoint for implementing the third step, which involves zooming into a specific context; here I take the case study of Barnard College. Building upon the first two steps, I examine Barnard's education policies from a CA perspective and derive a list of nine situated education capabilities.

The second part of the methodology turns to address the key stakeholders – in this case, the students. First, I verify whether they in fact value the capabilities – an important condition defended by the CA. Second, they are asked to assess whether the capabilities have been strengthened by their college education. I discuss these two steps together by revealing the results of a senior student survey answered by a sample of 349 students who were graduating in 2008. Finally, I investigate what a college education inclusive of these comprehensive capabilities actually enabled graduates to be and do. This last step is accomplished by addressing the alumnae through a survey completed by a sample of 668 alumnae who graduated between 2004 and 2007.

Part 1. Extrapolating education capabilities

Step 1. The capability approach: identifying the fundamentals

The key elements of the general human development framework that are particularly relevant for developing a broad analysis of higher education in modern societies are: substantive freedom to be and do (capabilities); achieved beings and doing we have reason to value (functionings); agency – including participation, empowerment, voice and autonomy; reasoning – encompassing critical thinking and open reasoning for oneself and in respect of others; sustainability; endowments; conversion factors and equity. They should be kept in mind throughout the analysis and captured by my list of capabilities.

Step 2. The subject area: acknowledging the literature and previously derived capabilities

In analysing the literature and in particular the works of Walker (2006, 2010), Nussbaum (2010), Unterhalter (2009) and Boni and Gasper (2012), I derive as core education capabilities those of: autonomy; knowledge; paid work; voice; aspiration; social relations; respect and recognition; empathy; bodily integrity and bodily health; emotional integrity and emotions; critical and analytical thinking; and use and appreciation of the creative arts. Educating institutions should also promote social goods through enhancing: personal development; contributions to society; fair participation in the economy; well-being; participation and empowerment; equity and diversity; sustainability; world citizenship; imaginative understanding and freedom.

Step 3. The specific context: extrapolating situated capabilities

By focusing on a case study I build upon the previous analysis and complete the process by deriving a context-sensitive list of education capabilities. A list of nine situated education capabilities that Barnard College sets out to foster in line with the CA will be derived.

A brief explanation of why Barnard College was chosen is necessary. Barnard is a liberal arts college in the USA: this form of education is, at least theoretically, very much in accordance with the CA. Nussbaum (2010) argues in favour of liberal arts education from a human development perspective, underlining the importance of an 'education for freedom' and the development of imaginative understanding, critical thinking and active participation through the humanities and creative arts. Moreover, Barnard is a women's college and the CA puts emphasis on empowering women. It is also an academic institution of excellence partnered with the renowned Columbia University. It is in the position to educate young women who have a higher probability to become what Walker (2010) refers to as 'influential elites': holders of positions that have a greater political weight in society. Consequently, it is ever more important for them to be educated in institutions that enhance their ability to contribute to social development. Finally, Barnard College is situated in New York, USA: using this case study can contribute to the literature that applies the CA to education in the so-called developed world. I proceed to extrapolate education capabilities that the college should foster in compliance with its own mission statements and a human development framework.

The mission statement[3] of Barnard College immediately resonates with the CA, although without directly referencing it and without necessarily defining capabilities in terms of freedoms: 'Barnard enables [students] to discover their own capabilities'. The content and the language used throughout its policies suggest an empowering kind of education that focuses on the needs, strengths, interests and choices of individual students. Barnard allows for substantial personal choice over specific subjects within and beyond an interdisciplinary and flexible set of requirements, the 'Nine Ways of Knowing', that range across the sciences, arts and humanities. Interdisciplinary knowledge and experiences can also enable students to make more genuine, critically thought, experience-based choices. Further statements suggest that the college also pays attention to equity and to what may be read as conversion factors, which impact and may limit students' ability to convert resources into concrete opportunities and achievements:

> [A]s a college for women, Barnard embraces its responsibility to address issues of gender in all of their complexity and urgency, and to help students achieve the personal strength that will enable them to meet the challenges they will encounter throughout their lives.
>
> (Barnard College Mission Statement)

And further:

> [I]n seeking to provide support for all of our students, we are especially mindful of those who come from groups that have not, in the past, been strongly

represented at highly selective colleges. A commitment to equity and justice dictates such concern.

(Barnard College Diversity Statement[4])

The pedagogy is also described as being participatory and 'problem-posing', with particular focus being placed on developing the ability to think critically and analytically, as well as to act effectively and have freedom of voice to speak out for oneself. On this basis, and reaffirming the concepts derived from my first and second steps, I extrapolate the first broad education capability dimension: *being able to be empowered and to be an active agent.*[5]

Barnard College also intends to be instrumental to graduates' professional lives. The career development office '[supports] women in cultivating a career of their own that connects the liberal arts education, leadership and work-life planning'.[6] I extrapolate the second capability: *being able to lead a professionally satisfying life.*

However, coherent with the CA (while going beyond the human capital theory) Barnard College also upholds the intrinsic (and not exclusively instrumental) value of education. Explicit worth is assigned to being enriched by, 'the love of learning' (Barnard College Mission Statement) and the president of the college underlined, in a speech in 2010, the 'sheer joy that comes from undertaking [education]'. Additionally, in line with the liberal arts tradition, Barnard assigns fundamental importance to fostering students' creativity and ability to appreciate and learn through the creative arts. We derive the third inclusive capability dimension: *being able to learn for the pleasure of learning and be creative.* I separate the capability to acquire knowledge that is instrumental for one's professional life from the capability to choose intrinsically valued subjects – being able to use and appreciate the creative arts and become a creative agent. In this manner, identifiable importance and space is given to both, emphasizing the claims of the CA, of the related literature and of Nussbaum's works in particular, and of this specific liberal arts college.

Barnard underlines its commitment towards students' capability to develop meaningful social relations. It is also important to note that being able to relate, collaborate and develop relationships, build teams and work effectively in groups are fundamental skills increasingly required in most jobs (Schleicher 2009), and that the capability of social relations is a constant across capability lists found in the literature. I derive the next inclusive capability dimension: *being able to develop meaningful social relations.*

Furthermore, Barnard refers to diversity as being one of its constitutive elements. The college's dedicated diversity statement recalls concepts and approaches associated with the CA and in particular Nussbaum's and Walker's capability for respect and recognition:

> Diversity is a key component of this institutional ethos. We learn through encountering different ideas, beliefs, and cultures, and by seeing how our own stand up to others. What we think we know is constantly expanded and

transformed by exposure to radically different ways of seeing the world. This does not mean that we should descend into mindless relativism; on the contrary, all ideas must be tested so that they can be held wisely and reflectively . . . Engaging with difference in a spirit of curiosity, integrity, and courage is about transcending one's own parochialism and narrowness. It is also basic to the academic freedom that defines the intellectual life of great academic institutions . . . At Barnard, the respect for different points of view, tempered by a commitment to common standards of inquiry and debate, is fundamental to the curriculum.

I extrapolate the fifth capability: *being able to be respected and relate in a constructive manner with diversity.*

Barnard College also undertakes the responsibility to 'promote the health of body, mind and spirit within the student community'.[7] The link between education and health is seen as being reciprocally enhancing: assuring opportunities for students to be healthy enables them to reach their full potential in college; in turn, education is intended to equip them with the basis for becoming knowledgeable users of health care throughout their life. Additionally, Barnard is committed to crime prevention and safety. On this basis, I derive the sixth comprehensive capability: *being able to be healthy in one's body, mind and spirit.*[8]

Moreover, 'the College seeks to impart every student with self-renewing intellectual resourcefulness . . . to respond both critically and creatively to a rapidly changing world',[9] as well as to become 'agile [and] resilient'. The next capability dimension that is extrapolated is: *being able to adapt and relate to different and changing situations.* Throughout the literature this capability is less commonly seen as self-standing; however, it is particularly apt in this case for three reasons: the human development framework recognizes the dynamic and inherent evolution of circumstances (Sen 1999); current social and labour market conditions are increasingly undergoing fluctuations that require young adults to readjust and reinvent themselves in order to flourish; finally, Barnard College itself singles out its importance.

Further aligned with the CA, Barnard College's policies resonate with the CA's demand for shared global responsibility, the core inclusive concept of sustainability, and with Nussbaum's derived notion of 'global citizenship'. As Debora Spar, the president of the college, affirms:[10]

[We have] an ambitious goal – to create a world renowned center dedicated to the advancement of women leaders. Not just any women leaders, but women who are visionary, bold, courageous, resilient and globally aware; women who embrace diversity and are determined to make the world a better place.

I extrapolate as the eighth capability: *being able to be a responsible global citizen.*
Last, I deduce the personally and socially valuable capability: *being able to*

appreciate and respect the natural environment. This is consistent with the broader framework (Sen 1999), Nussbaum's and other scholar's lists of capabilities and Barnard College's affirmations.

In conclusion, the fundamental concepts derived from an analysis of the CA, followed by a more subject-specific review of the literature that has applied the framework to the field of education, provides legitimacy to my third step: deriving a list of education capabilities from a context-specific analysis. Table 10.1 presents the nine comprehensive education capabilities in relation to extracts from the college's policies; it also reveals the sub-elements of each dimension. It is undeniable that the CA, compared with the mainstream human capital theory, allows for a broadening of the roles and realms reserved to tertiary education. The responsibilities of tertiary education are expanded to address, foster and respect the holistic development of well-rounded young people. Moreover, the table exemplifies that it can also prepare graduates to address important current social challenges and develop a sense of global citizenship (Table 10.1, Column 3). Finally, although the list of derived education capabilities is rooted in the specific case study of Barnard College, the methodology is indicative of an innovative and generally applicable process for deriving lists of capabilities coherently with the human development framework.

Part 2. Testing the list of situated capabilities

Through the procedural method presented in this chapter one can also assess the derived list and the corresponding quality of an institution in a manner that reflects human development. This is important, given that national and international quality rankings more or less directly act as incentives to the shaping of policies and services of institutions as the latter tend to adapt in order to rank higher. First, I want to verify whether the main stakeholders, in this case the students, in fact consider the capabilities of importance; second, I want to find out whether these capabilities have indeed been enhanced as a result of experiencing the institution; and third, whether these capabilities have been enabling throughout their lives so far and for what. I accomplish the first two steps through a senior student survey and the last with an alumnae survey.

Step 4. The stakeholders: value judgments and Step 5. The stakeholders: assessment of the degree of development[11]

To complete both steps I draw on a senior student survey that Barnard College was already using without specifically tying it back to the human development approach.[12] Although the questions were not designed for the extrapolated education capabilities, nor consciously grounded in the human development approach, only the capability to appreciate and respect the environment was not addressed and was therefore temporarily excluded from an assumed pragmatic version of my list.[13]

Table 10.1 Derived education capabilities in relation to Barnard College's policies and global challenges or needs

Barnard College's goals	Capabilities	Global needs and challenges
'Barnard enables its students to discover their own capabilities . . . [and] find new ways to think about themselves.' Barnard College promotes 'identity and leadership development'.	1. *Being able to be empowered and be an active agent* Being able to: • Function independently. • Evaluate and choose between alternative courses of action in one's life. • Have and find information on the basis of which to make choices. • Question beliefs, statements and arguments, and accept only those that survive personal and open critical scrutiny. • Think analytically and logically. • Understand oneself: abilities, interests, limitations, personality, etc. • Attain valued ends. • Plan one's life. • Plan and execute complex projects. • Speak out (have voice) and stand up for oneself. • Participate actively in one's experiences.	Political and social inclusion and participation
Students 'graduate prepared to lead lives that are professionally satisfying and successful.'	2. *Being able to lead a professionally satisfying life* Being able to: • Have effective freedom of choice over which job to engage in. • Reach leadership positions in one's professional life. • Experience jobs in different fields. • Lead a professionally satisfying life. • Earn one's living. • Acquire knowledge from school subjects that are instrumentally useful for post-school choices of study, paid work and a career (Walker 2006). • Have internships and work experiences in fields of interest.	Social inclusion

- Meet and address professionals from all fields.
- Learn and have advice on how to prepare for participating in the labour market (curriculum writing, cover letter, networking, letter writing, interview preparations, etc.).

Innovation

3. Being able to learn for the pleasure of learning and be creative
Being able to:
- Take school subjects that are of intrinsic interest and acquire intrinsically valued knowledge.
- Appreciate learning.
- Engage in fulfilling activities, hobbies and interests.
- Gain in-depth knowledge of a field.
- Acquire broad knowledge in the arts and sciences.
- Engage in any of the following: arts, music and theatre.
- Appreciate art, literature, music and theatre.

4. Being able to develop meaningful social relations
Being able to:
- Develop meaningful social relations.
- Be a friend.
- Participate in a group for friendship and for learning.
- Be guided and be a guide to others.
- Work with others to form effective or good groups for learning and organizing life (at school).
- Develop emotions and imagination for understanding and empathy.

Human coexistence, social inclusion and personal well-being

5. Being able to be respected and relate in a constructive manner with diversity
Being able to:
- Carry out autonomous critical thinking and combine it with the ability to engage in inquiry and open debates; listen to and consider other people's points of view in dialogue and

Human coexistence

Students 'graduate prepared to lead lives that are ... personally fulfilling, and enriched by love of learning.'

'Each student studies, from analytical, quantitative, and artistic perspectives, the major means by which human knowledge has been constructed.'

'Students soon discover that their classmates are among the principal resources of their undergraduate years.'

'Committed to diversity in its student body, faculty and staff, Barnard prepares its graduates to flourish in different cultural surroundings in an increasingly inter-connected world.'

Table 10.1 Continued

Barnard College's goals	Capabilities	Global needs and challenges
'At Barnard, the respect for different points of view, tempered by a commitment to common standards of inquiry and debate, is fundamental to the curriculum.'	• Question one's thoughts accordingly. • Appreciate and relate well with human diversity (intended broadly: culture, nationality, language, religion, race, social class, sexual orientation, disabilities, etc.). • Respect others. • Demand respect from others • Be responsible for one's reasoning. • Be self-confident and have self-esteem. • Act inclusively. • Identify, understand and appreciate moral and ethical issues.	
'The safety and well being of students, faculty, staff, and guests have always been of paramount importance at Barnard.' 'To promote the health of body, mind and spirit within the student community.' 'To educate students to become knowledgeable and effective users of health care.'	6. *Being able to be healthy in one's body, mind and spirit* Being able to: • Be healthy in one's body, mind and spirit. • Use health care. • Balance work and recreational time. • Feel safe and be effectively safe from any kind of crime or assault.	Healthy living and safety
'Barnard prepares its graduates to flourish in different cultural surroundings.' 'Barnard students become agile [and] resilient.'	7. *Being able to adapt and relate to different and changing situations* Being able to: • Relate and adapt to different situations. • Feel comfortable in new and different situations. • Transfer, relate and apply one's knowledge to a multiplicity of contexts and realities. • Acquire new knowledge quickly.	Complex and dynamic social and labour contexts

Global civic responsibility

8. *Being able to be a responsible global citizen*
Being able to:
- Go out there to make the world a better place.
- Be aware of social and global challenges.
- Understand the causes and effects of deprivations, inequalities and discrimination practices.
- Engage in civic and global development projects.
- Feel obligations to others/contribute to justice in society.
- Be responsible
- Be compassionate, decent and tolerant towards others.
- Be informed about international news and politics.
- Feel part of a global society and be a global citizen.

'We promote active and involved citizenship through inter-cultural education and identity and leadership development.'

Barnard students become 'responsible, and creative, prepared to lead and serve their society.'

Barnard's graduates are 'women possessed of … a cosmopolitan perspective, and moral courage; women who will go out into the world and make it a better place.'

Environmental sustainability

9. *Being able to appreciate and respect the natural environment*
Being able to:
- Enjoy the natural environment as a space for recreation.
- Appreciate and respect the natural environment and be aware of and contribute to environmental sustainability.

'Barnard College is fully committed to environmental sustainability and to doing all we can to conserve energy, decrease consumption, and reduce our carbon footprint.'

In relation to the first derived capability dimension – *being able to be an empowered and active agent* – I found that 70 per cent of the students thought that the ability to think analytically and logically was essential, while no one considered it as unimportant. The majority also declared that it has been strengthened throughout their college education. Similar results were found for the ability to evaluate and choose between alternative courses of action, to understand oneself, to lead and supervise tasks and to function independently.

With reference to both the intrinsic and instrumental value of interdisciplinary liberal arts education, approximately equal proportions of students assigned value to acquiring a broad knowledge in the arts and sciences; to appreciating art, literature, music and drama; as well as to developing in-depth knowledge of a field. According to the vast majority of students, college education succeeded in strengthening them all. Also notable is that none of the students were completely undecided on what would be their principal activity after graduation. Forty-five per cent of the students aimed at being employed full time and 12 per cent to continue their education full time. Moreover, 40 per cent of those who aspired to work as their primary activity had already found a position before graduating. The job sectors mostly chosen were: medicine, finance, education and the non-profit sector. In addition to the confirmed intrinsic value of education and the appreciation and use of the arts, the success in enabling an effective transition from school to work and the variety of areas of focus – some highly renowned as profit making and others as socially enhancing – are positive results.

The majority of students also declared that during college they had critically questioned[14] their beliefs regarding: their own political, ethical and moral values, the nature of humans or society, a race or ethnic group other than their own, a religion other than their own and people with sexual orientations other than their own. The vast majority of students also had some or substantial interaction with people from outside the USA, of a different religion and with a different economic background. Eighty-four per cent also considered somewhat important, very important or essential the ability to resolve interpersonal conflicts positively and declared that it had been strengthened by their college education. All these results strongly indicate coherence with the CA – in particular with the claim for appreciation of diversity – and a successful, broad, responsive and enabling education on behalf of Barnard College.

Positive value judgments and effective enhancement are also expressed in relation to the capacity to: function effectively as a member of a team; acquire new skills alone; find innovative and creative solutions; place current problems into historical, cultural and philosophical perspective; and develop awareness of social problems. The majority of students were also very satisfied with the student health service.

Step 6. An ex-post evaluation: which capabilities have been enabling and for what?

Finally, it is significant to investigate whether the enhancement of the selected capabilities has in fact been enabling for people's lives and in terms of which functionings. This is particularly important when arguing in favour of new practices rooted in the CA for a university of the twenty-first century. I thus examined a survey completed by 668 alumnae of Barnard College who graduated between 2004 and 2007 and present some of the key insights from the results.[15]

The vast majority of alumnae were very satisfied (58 per cent) or generally satisfied (35 per cent) with their Barnard education. Most striking are the results summarized in Figure 10.1. When asked to: 'rank the skills or experiences in college that were most important in preparing you for your post-graduate activities', 87 per cent of the alumnae ranked the ability to think analytically and critically first. Following, in descending order were: practising writing skills, ability to communicate well orally, completing a thesis or capstone project, completing an internship, experience in leading organizations, participating in study abroad, collaborating with faculty research, participating in community/civic engagement, doing required readings, attending or participating in an artistic performance, developing ability in quantitative reasoning and last, engaging in entrepreneurship opportunities. It is interesting that the latter two would tend to be the only ones defended by an education rooted in the human capital theory and by much of the ongoing public policy debates.

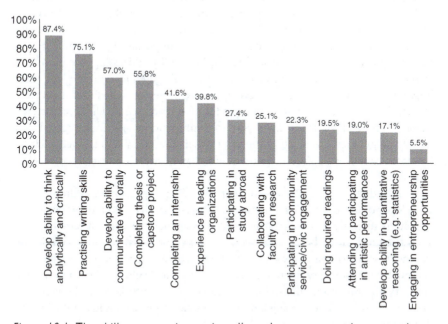

Figure 10.1 The skills or experiences in college that were most important in preparing alumnae for their postgraduate activities.

Moreover, the vast majority of Barnard graduates are engaged in full-time paid employment, or enrolled in full-time graduate or professional school. Approximately equal proportions of employed alumnae are active in for-profit (28 per cent) and not-for-profit organizations (27 per cent). Further data show that Barnard graduates decided to engage in supporting civic development when it was not part of their actual job: only 2 per cent of Barnard alumnae did not participate in non-profit or other charitable organizations. These results show that Barnard's graduates are capable of and actually choose to fulfil both socially and economically enriching lives.

Conclusion

This chapter had a twofold aim: first, to suggest a procedural methodology for the operationalization of the CA that allows for deriving and partly assessing a list of situated capabilities and second, to apply the method to the specific subject area of education, in particular higher education, taking the case study of an American liberal arts women's college.

I have therefore demonstrated how I derived a list of nine education capabilities that Barnard College aims to foster and that are coherent with the human development framework. The list indicates multidimensional goals, which include and go extensively beyond the economic instrumental role of education envisioned by the human capital theory. Elements aimed at enabling holistic flourishing of each student, as well as enhancing their responsibility as global citizens, became requisites. Through a senior student survey I then ascertained that the abilities related to each capability were indeed considered important by the students and that the college generally enhanced them. Finally, by addressing the alumnae I learned that they were still satisfied with their college education. Yet, the most important skills and experiences developed in college for their future lives were aspects that would be excluded from an education strictly rooted in human capital theory – first and foremost, the ability to think critically and analytically. I also found that graduates were either continuing their education or employed in either for-profit and non-for-profit sectors, and that nearly all participated in civic activities.

I conclude that the CA is a particularly suitable perspective for addressing the complexity of social scenarios. It is especially appropriate as a grounding framework in matters of education policies and quality assessments because it requires (and allows) education to be an effectively empowering social resource. While the general structure of this framework is its strength in terms of inclusiveness, plurality and multidimensionality, there is a need to operationalize it in relation to specific contexts; the suggested methodology is intended to contribute to the literature in order to enable an increasing amount of applied work grounded in the human development perspective.

Notes

1 In this chapter, in particular when dealing with the case study of Barnard College, I will largely draw on an unpublished master's thesis (Spreafico 2010).

2 Robeyns' (2003) five criteria are more fully defined as: (1) explicit formulation: the list should be explicit, discussed and defended; (2) methodological justification: the method that has generated the list should be clarified, scrutinized and its appropriateness for the issue at hand justified; (3) sensitivity to context: the level of abstraction and language undertaken should be coherent with the specific context; (4) different levels of generality: an ideal list unconstrained by limitations of data availability should be produced, followed by a more pragmatic one in the case of measurement limitations; and (5) exhaustion and non-reducibility: all important elements should be included without one being reducible to the other, although there may be unsubstantial overlap.

3 Barnard College mission statement. Available at http://www.barnard.edu/about/mission.html [accessed 10 June 2010].

4 Barnard College diversity statement. Available at http://barnard.edu/about/womens-college/diversity/statement [accessed 10 June 2010].

5 This category includes Walker's (2006) capabilities of autonomy, of voice and to aspire, given the known interrelation between them also observed in Barnard College's mission statements.

6 Barnard College Career Development Office mission statement. Available at http://barnard.edu/cd [accessed 18 June 2010].

7 Barnard College Student Health Service. Available at http://barnard.edu/primarycare/about [accessed 29 June 2010].

8 The education capability dimension of *being able to be healthy in one's body, mind and spirit* unites those of bodily and emotional health and bodily and emotional integrity, which are often presented as separate capabilities in the CA literature.

9 Barnard College. 'The curriculum: requirements for the liberal arts degree'. Available at http://barnard.edu/admissions/education/the-curriculum [accessed 18 June 2010].

10 Barnard College. 'Athena Center for Leadership Studies'. Available at http://athenacenter.barnard.edu/about [accessed 16 January 2011].

11 Steps 4 and 5 are discussed together to avoid repetition.

12 The survey is not crafted by Barnard but by the Consortium on Financing Higher Education (COFHE). COFHE is 'an unincorporated, voluntary, institutionally supported organization of thirty-one highly selective, private liberal arts colleges and universities' (Dillon 2010 in Spreafico 2010). It is not a financing institution but a research organization that 'focuses on matters pertaining to access, affordability, accountability, and assessment, particularly as they relate to undergraduate education, admissions, financial aid, and the financing of higher education'. Barnard has chosen to be part of COFHE and to yearly submit COFHE's Senior Survey.

13 This refers to Robeyns' (2003) fourth criterion for selecting capabilities – 'different levels of generality' (see note 2).

14 In the survey, critical questioning was explicitly defined as: 'seriously question or rethink your beliefs . . . you need not have changed your beliefs or values in order to answer "yes" to having questioned them in a fundamental way'.

15 A complete analysis of the results is carried out in an unpublished master's thesis (Spreafico 2010).

Acknowledgments

I am honoured to acknowledge Professor Amartya Sen for his initial advice on the research. I thank Professor Melanie Walker and Professor Alejandra Boni for the opportunity to contribute to this book and for their support; Professor Enrica Chiappero-Martinetti and Professor Joseph Paul Martin for their guidance; and Barnard College's faculty and students for their collaboration.

References

Boni, A. and Gasper, D. (2012) 'Rethinking the quality of universities: how can human development thinking contribute?', *Journal of Human Development and Capabilities*, 13(3): 451–70.

Nussbaum, M.C. (2010) *Not for Profit: Why Democracy Needs the Humanities*, New Jersey: Princeton University Press.

Robeyns, I. (2003) 'Sen's capability approach and gender inequality: selecting relevant capabilities', *Feminist Economics* 9(2–3): 61–92.

Schleicher, A. and Stewart V. (2009) 'International benchmarking', Asia Society. Available at http://asiasociety.org/education-learning/learning-world/international-benchmarking [accessed 12 May 2010].

Sen, A. (1997) 'Editorial: human capital and human capability', *World Development*, 25(12): 1959–61.

—— (1999) *Development as Freedom*, New York: Anchor.

Spreafico, A. (2010) 'Applying the capability approach to higher education policy and quality assessment: the case study of Barnard College', unpublished master's thesis, University of Pavia, Italy.

Unterhalter, E. (2009) 'Education', in *An Introduction to the Human Development and Capability Approach*. The International Development Research Centre. Available at http://web.idrc.ca/en/ev-146724-201-1-DO_TOPIC.html [accessed 8 March 2012].

Walker, M. (2006) 'Towards a capability-based theory of social justice for education policy-making', *Journal of Education Policy*, 21(2): 163–85.

—— (2010) 'A human development and capabilities 'prospective analysis' of global higher education policy', *Journal of Education Policy*, 25(4): 485–501.

Chapter 11

Teaching for well-being

Pedagogical strategies for meaning, value, relevance and justice

Luisa S. Deprez and Diane R. Wood

In the USA, higher education – and public higher education in particular – is perilously close to forsaking long-standing educational aims such as personal and moral development, democratic citizenship, and the pursuit of a life with value. In their stead, marketplace priorities threaten to eclipse traditional and humanistic aims – long-standing bedrocks for justifying public higher education. Critics increasingly limit their appraisal of college and universities' quality to provisos centred on national global competitiveness and individual employability. Marketable knowledge and skills are of primary concern. In fact, the pressure to steer higher education to adopt marketplace, corporate interests has distressed many in the academic disciplines. Previously the cornerstones of higher education, liberal arts disciplines increasingly grapple with how to secure their status in an academy being reconceived as job preparation. Academic fields, especially in the humanities, social sciences, and the arts, are under considerable pressure to demonstrate relevance defined almost exclusively in terms of post-college job acquisition. However, while economic responsibility and stability are important, they should not be education's *raison d'être*, particularly at the cost of discarding aims directed toward human well-being.

Market pressures have negatively affected efforts at curriculum reform in many institutions. Admittedly, seemingly impenetrable discipline boundaries have served as impediments to reform efforts in the past, but over the past 20 years notable progress has been made (see Association of American Colleges and Universities reports, for instance). Current pressures to ensure employability and increase graduates' incomes, however, have resulted in many academic units 'circling the wagons' to reaffirm their place in the academy, to protect academic freedom, and to compete for resources. Consequently, in some institutions, far less inter-disciplinary and exploratory learning has occurred, which in turn undermines the university's potential to address complex human problems – problems that almost always require interdisciplinary solutions. Diminished funding contributes to the difficulty as traditional academic fields have been hit the hardest. Universities now run the risk of attempting to produce graduates who know how to 'do' what the workplace needs but who do not know how to 'think' in order to live a meaningful life. Inevitably, constricting education to one life goal – employment – severely limits ways in which students make connections between college learning and contemporary social and personal problems.

Reducing higher education to preparation for employment runs two other serious risks. The first has to do with the notion of 'adaptive preferences' (Deneulin and Shahani 2009); that is, learning to desire what one is being socially constructed to want, rather than what one has reason to value. Without a strong commitment to the liberal arts, universities and colleges cannot help students discover genuine relevance; that is, the ability to think critically while exploring a wide horizon of perspectives, experiences, interpretations, and theories. Students need the opportunity to discover connections between theories and lives, ideas and actions, values and learning – all indicators of genuine relevance that help students envision and develop options for who they want to be and what they want to do.

The last thing students (already saturated with marketplace values due to the pervasiveness of global capitalism) need is a higher education system which has relinquished its responsibility to teach critical and independent thinking. Hence a second, and perhaps to some, more pragmatic problem arises from what many social and economic theorists explain will be people's job descriptions in the future – enough flexibility to change jobs multiple times, little loyalty from employers, rapid change and continuous learning on the job, collaborative working environments, and so forth. Preparing students for jobs as they now exist ensures an obsolete set of knowledge and skills. Moreover, such an approach fails to instil in students the lifelong curiosity and continuous learning capacity that future work lives will ultimately demand.

Despite this bleak picture we gather strength from the capability approach (CA) to education because it affirms student and social well-being as education's central concern. Social settings, the CA professes, must be assessed on an ongoing basis through a process which must consider each individual's real opportunities, as determined by both agency and freedom as well as by each individual's capacities to live lives they value. At its most fundamental level, the CA is a comparative and practical approach for negotiating just social institutions, including education, through an emphasis on human capabilities and freedom. Thus, the CA, as Sen (1999a, 2009) and Nussbaum (2000, 2011) have developed it, serves as a powerful counterweight to the dehumanizing trends we outline above because it emphasizes holistic notions of well-being against monodimensional ones. Higher education cannot afford to construct students only as workers and not as multidimensional human beings. If public colleges and universities are going to be more than vocational training centres, faculty must insist on students developing a wide-ranging knowledge base, one necessary for enhancing capacity and freedom so people can choose agentive and valued lives, critiquing social conditions, and extending human capacities and freedom to the lives of others. As the CA reminds us, economic well-being is only one facet of human flourishing.

The CA invites both teachers and students to become publicly engaged 'intellectuals' concerned with contributing to the creation of a just society. For us, two central questions prevail: (1) how might teaching and learning take shape in institutions that define education as a foundational capability essential for each individual to live the life s/he values? and (2) what would education look like if the individual well-being of every student was the key aim? In this chapter, using a heuristic we developed to guide our thinking, course development, and assessment practices, we reflect on what we have tried and learned in our efforts to incorporate the CA into our own classrooms.

Educational aims in the classroom and the capability approach

In other works (Wood and Deprez 2012, 2013 forthcoming), we have argued that curriculum ought to be responsive and flexible and connect to students' concerns, desires, interests, and aspirations. We harkened to three core professional commitments from liberatory educational movements which had guided our approaches to teaching. The first, democratic education, immerses students in the democratic ideals and practices necessary for participatory, committed citizenship (e.g. Dewey 1916; Greene 1988; Gutmann and Thompson 2004). The second, critical pedagogy, encourages exploration of, and critical reflection upon, historical and contemporary human experiences, including material contexts and economic power relations (e.g. Shor 1992; Freire 2000, 2005). The third, feminist pedagogy, foregrounds the often sublimated relational, emotional, and intuitive dimensions of teaching and learning and discloses how socially constructed categories, like gender, race, location, and class, can constrain identity and life possibilities (Miller 1977/1987; hooks 1981; Belenky *et al.* 1986/1997; Harding 1991; Minnich 1991/2004; Addelson 1992; Grosz 1992). These three commitments, which have deep resonance with the CA, particularly in terms of the mutual commitment to well-being and justice, remind us continuously that what students learn ought to *matter* to them.

Like David Crocker (2006), we believe that Sen and Nussbaum's vision of ongoing comparative analysis through public justification necessarily requires deliberative democratic practices. Whether through the lens of Sen's theory of justice or Nussbaum's principle of central capabilities, both viewpoints rely on 'small d' democratic practices (Crocker 2006) as people come together to weigh and make decisions. Essential to this process is public reasoning and justification conducted in good faith. As Nussbaum (2010: 7) describes, such democratic practices are necessary for 'the creation of a decent world culture capable of constructively addressing the world's most pressing problems'. It is precisely these capacities that education ought to practise and promote.

Thus, a CA to education focuses on democratic practices leading to greater social justice. Educators can draw inspiration from the inclusive vision of the CA, with its attendant concern for the flourishing of every individual: Sen's (1999b: 10) deep attention to 'the kind of lives that people can actually lead'. A CA approach to education also aligns with many feminists (Harding 1991; Addelson 1992; Butler 2005), who argue for a theory of justice which is oriented towards and continually assessed and tested by lived experiences. Emphasizing social *practices*, the CA gestures towards curricular and pedagogical processes that are not only dialogic and relevant, but also normative. Education, then, ought to build students' capacities for critical reasoning and reflection and help them rationally justify their opinions so their participation in a democracy is powerful and effective.

Sen (2009) quite precisely identifies education as a fundamental or basic capability that one must have to be able to be or to do . . . to live a life of value. Education, he asserts, contributes not only to the quality of one's life but also contributes to and allows for the formation and expansion of all other capabilities. Human beings who have the opportunity for an education are more likely to free themselves from unreflective adherence to tradition so they can develop the capability 'to be and to do what [they] value' (Walker 2008: 116). Education prepares persons for thoughtful, responsible, participatory citizenship while opening up spaces for them to experience and model such citizenship (Wood and Deprez 2012). It is these aims and values that we must ensure remain primary in public higher education and ones to which we, as educators, must remain diligently committed.

Obligated by our power

The moral vision of the CA has classroom implications that are both challenging and revitalizing. It reminds us of our responsibility, as educators committed to deliberative democratic aims, to do everything we can to invite students to participate while carefully considering the disparate range of capacities they bring with them to the classroom. It emphasizes to us the importance of setting high expectations for students while also setting high expectations for ourselves in terms of scaffolding learning for all students, particularly those who need extra help in order to participate. It reminds us of how crucial it is to engage students in building civil classroom communities characterized by inclusive participation, careful listening, and public rationality. Finally, it reminds us that the success of a deliberative classroom depends on the well-being, freedom, and agency of every individual (Wood and Deprez 2012: 26).

But Sen (2009) pushes us beyond this responsibility, arguing that if we have the power to make change that will reduce injustices in the world we must do just that. In other words, there is obligation that goes with one's ability and power; an obligation to 'right' the injustices being done to others. As educators, we are invested with power and authority. Power, we remind ourselves, is justified if used justly. But how, we wonder, do we 'exercise' this obligation in a way that both promotes learning and honours student well-being within the confines of the CA? How do we establish a balance between directing student learning and validating student knowledge with 'professing' our experience and our 'seasoned-ness' as educators and experts in our field?

We know how important it is to help students develop skills that enable them to engage in intellectual development and inquiry, helping them to distinguish simplistic notions of right or wrong and black or white from multiple and complex perspectives on important issues. Building knowledge, developing critical thinking and problem-solving skills, embracing an attitude of openness to the unknowns, reading with understanding both of content and context, and a healthy scepticism and willingness to question are among the attributes of an educated person. And while these skills will develop over time, encouraging students' contributions – knowledge, skills, attitudes, daily concerns, values, and motivation – to this learning process is central to their success.

So, we began in earnest a conversation about how to fulfil our obligation to share our experience and expertise without robbing students of theirs. It is, we assert, a juggling act, but one in which we must engage. Using the CA's central tenet that each individual ought to have the freedom and agency to be and to do what they value, educators have a responsibility and an obligation to create classrooms where students can debate, deliberate, and justify various positions on social issues, as well as reflect on, develop, and express values. Consequently, we must create opportunities for students to consider who speaks and who listens, who takes centre stage and who lives on the periphery, who makes decisions and who lives with them, who sets terms and who follows them. Students also need opportunities to express opinions and to justify them. As Gutmann and Thompson (2004: 24) explain: 'A fundamental aim of deliberative democracy is to offer reasons that can be accepted by free and equal persons seeking fair terms of cooperation.' Such an approach demands that there is mutual respect within public forums so that all participants listen in good faith to others while also considering the common weal. In this process, students learn that human perspectives are necessarily contingent and partial and to work dialogically toward deeper insights and ever-evolving forms of knowledge.

Because education is a foundational capacity on which other capacities depend (Nussbaum 1997, 2000; Sen 1999a, 2009), professors have a responsibility to enable students to be educated. This often requires efforts to ensure students feel sufficiently safe to take intellectual risks so that what they can and cannot do becomes audible and visible and so that extra support can be provided for those who lack background knowledge and skills (or encouragement provided for students to be proactive in seeking that support). Professors can encourage students to move beyond reductionist modes of thinking and memorization, embrace interdisciplinarity, and apply what they learn to complex issues.

Looking deeper: curricular and classroom implications of the capabilities approach

As we attempted to translate principles of the CA into practice, we heeded Nussbaum's (1997: 293) words that education must enable students to become intellectually 'free . . . [to] call their minds their own . . . [and] have looked into themselves and developed the ability to separate mere habit and convention from what they can defend by argument'. To make our dialogic inquiry more systematic we created a heuristic (see Table 11.1) based foundationally on our commitment to democratic education, critical theory, and feminist theory. These commitments are represented as columns. Elements of the CA – education for human well-being, for developing reasoned values, for relevance to actual lives being lived, and as a foundational basis for agency and freedom – which would challenge and extend our commitments – became the rows of the grid.

As we held the principles of the CA in dialogue with each of our long-held commitments, questions emerged. Consequently, the heuristic disciplined and focused our conversations, enabling and encouraging us to interrogate our present practice as we sought ways to improve it in the future. The heuristic suggests a systematic way of thinking through curricular decisions and assessing curricular materials. Our approach can be called both an archaeology of past practices and a form of action research on present practices.

We initially designed two questionnaires premised on questions that appear on the heuristic. The first questionnaire, distributed early in the semester, asked students about their experiences in earlier college classes taught by other professors; the second we reworded to refer to our own courses and handed out at the end of the semester. In two rounds of administering these questionnaires (over two semesters and assuring students' anonymity) students indicated that they experienced a greater sense of well-being, more connection to their own values and lives, more opportunities for public critical reasoning, and a greater sense of agency in our classes than in others. While this comparison is far from conclusive, creating the questionnaire and learning of students' responses focused both our conversations and our pedagogical efforts, and helped us consider what we have yet to accomplish. We outline in the next section what we have tried, referencing fundamental ideas captured in our heuristic and describing our experiences in translating CA principles into practice.

Elements of the heuristic

How do we educate for human well-being?

Human well-being is the core principle of the CA and, according to Sen (1999a, 2009) and Nussbaum (2000, 2010), is inextricably bound to social justice. A just society aimed at well-being grants the substantive freedoms necessary for capabilities development. We have come to adopt human well-being, and the capabilities development on which well-being depends, as core educational aims.

In our classes, students are engaged in questions like: What constitutes human well-being? How does education contribute to it? What kinds of teaching practices and learning experiences might promote human well-being? With CA principles in mind, we operationalized well-being as being able to hold on to one's identity and values as one learns, to feel safe as one learns, and to be a part of an authentically engaged learning community. For example, in Wood's class, students were

Table 11.1 A heuristic for translating capability approach principles into practice

Elements of capability approach	Commitments			
	Democracy: choice, deliberation, and inclusion	Critical theory/pedagogy: material life, praxis, social justice	Feminist theory/pedagogy: identity, relationship, epistemology	
	What opportunities do students have to:			
Education for human well-being	1. explore relationships between democracy and human well-being?	1. unearth and interrogate assumptions about human well-being?	1. examine their own and others' adaptive preferences in light of alternatives?	
	2. experience just and inclusive democratic practices in the classroom?	2. engage in critical reflection and dialogue on competing notions of human well-being?	2. interrogate identity constructions and individual agency freedom?	
	3. express and justify their conception of human well-being and to deliberate effectively about competing notions of human well-being?	3. explore power relations and their impact on human well-being?	3. analyse and assess human well-being across populations?	
	4. collaborate with professors and other students to create a classroom centred on student well-being?	4. explore the relationship of economic and material resources to human well-being?	4. explore links between curriculum and social practices that support human flourishing?	
Education for reasoned values	1. express and reflect upon their own values in light of the curriculum and others' values?	1. interrogate embedded values in the curriculum?	1. express emerging ideas about who they want to be and what they want to do within the classroom and without?	

Table 11.1 Continued

Elements of capability approach	Commitments		
	2. entertain, deliberate and negotiate contrary and competing values in a social context? 3. consider and deliberate the relationship between individual values and democratic contexts?	2. critically reflect on the relationship between learning, values and life choices? 3. assess contrary and competing values and publicly justify their values? 4. consider one's values over and against material life?	2. incorporate emotion, intuition and imagination in thinking about values? 3. explore values crucial for human affiliation?
Education for lives people actually can and do live	1. express and deliberate a reasoned stance on course themes and topics and apply them to lived realities? 2. deliberate curricular themes/topics in light of multiple perspectives and current social conditions/problems? 3. choose concepts and skills relevant to their own lives and apply them?	1. critically reflect on course learning in light of lived experiences and political/economic power relations? 2. interrogate the curriculum in light of larger economic and political interests? 3. explore connections between curricular topics/themes and contemporary inequities involving power, privilege and material resources?	1. imagine new possibilities for their own life and identity as a result of course learning? 2. empathically entertain others' lived experiences and express unfolding insights? 3. explore current cultural constraints on human freedom/well-being?

Education as foundational capacity for agency, and freedom

1. make choices as to what they learn and how they demonstrate what they learn?

2. participate effectively and productively in a deliberative and democratic classroom?

3. experience and extend inclusivity in the learning environment?

1. develop critically reflective and dialogic habits of mind?

2. discern and articulate economic and material constraints to freedom and agency?

3. ask whose interests are served by curricular concepts and skills and social institutions, including schools and universities?

4. explore relationships between theories and realities?

1. fully participate in the classroom?

2. recognize constraints on people's sense of the possible and develop a widening spectrum of alternatives for choosing who they want to be and what they want to do?

3. ask whose perspectives are embedded in codified forms of knowledge?

4. recognize cultural constraints on agency and freedom and take action toward a more just future?

asked to report honestly and anonymously whether their learning needs and interests were being met. Student feedback informed plans for the next class.

One of us (Wood) works with experienced teachers who are returning to college to earn a graduate degree in educational leadership. At the beginning of a course entitled 'Seminar in Supervision', students wrestled with the idea that well-being ought to be the pre-eminent goal for the schools where they worked and for the university in which they studied. During the second class, students wrote two autobiographical stories, one in which they captured a specific incident when their own well-being or their students' well-being was ill served and another when it was well served. Sharing these stories in small groups, they analysed them for what they had to say about schools as sites for human well-being. The following are selected student reactions from that process:

> This class is helping me to see how we've gotten off track with what we're doing. We claim raising test scores will help kids have great futures and happy lives, but we're making a lot of them hate learning and school in the process.

> Morale is low in my [school] building, kids don't like school, and everybody seems to be blaming everybody else that they're miserable. Now that I'm thinking kids' well-being ought to be the purpose of all this, I have to ask: what are we doing?

> This class made me feel like I could say what was really on my mind even if other people in the room didn't agree. I also learned that the professor and my classmates cared about what I thought and wanted me to do well.

Throughout the course, students were encouraged to reflect on their own well-being. Two students complained about the writing load and the number of revisions required to 'get it right', which signalled the need for professor–student conferencing and back-up help from the writing centre. Another student complained about the class being 'too liberal because teachers and professors tend to be that way'. This student sparked conversations about politics and schools and politics and learning. Raising the point emphasized for the whole class the need for civil democratic dialogue and the danger of a single viewpoint. All but one student in each of the classes claimed that their learning experiences contributed to their own sense of well-being and helped them to think about *their* students' well-being. Nevertheless, from a CA perspective, these two students loom large. We cannot simply dismiss or ignore students who cannot or will not participate fully or who do not feel they belong. They are the very students who offer us opportunities to learn and grow professionally. Thus, the CA's uncompromisingly inclusive perspective – every individual matters – continues to fuel our reflections and efforts.

How do we educate for reasoned values?

Because the CA demands a focus on each student becoming increasingly able to be and to do what they have reason to value, we asked ourselves how we might ensure opportunities for students to explore and examine a range of values. We examined the pre-digested, embedded values underlying our pedagogical and curricular approaches and asked ourselves how to make them more explicit and open for critique.

We asked students to express and justify their own values regarding human well-being, to listen to ideas from others, to consider and deliberate about competing values, and to explore the effect of power relations (in and out of the classroom) on human well-being. We encouraged candid conversations during which students could safely speak while also hearing from others. One of us (Wood), in a course on curriculum, repeatedly raised the question of values: what values underlie educational practices and structures? What values matter to you as an educator? In answering this question, students expanded their notions of curriculum to include all that *their* students learn from attending P–12 schools,[1] including what they learn from rules, policies, and norms. Students brought in school codes of conduct and classroom rules and then analysed them through the lens of human values. They listened to *their* students' talk in the halls and interviewed some about school culture. At the end of the course, students wrote:

> At first, I thought all the talk about values was dangerous. I mean who is a teacher to teach values? But now I 'get it'. You're just saying to get kids to think about values. This class has helped me see that, whether you think you're teaching values or not, you are.

> Throughout the semester, I've felt like my inside and my outside matched. I mean I didn't feel fake; I could talk about what's bothering me and people listened. Sometimes people would say they didn't agree but I always felt like they understood me better because they knew what I cared about.

> I've learned learners can't learn if you disrespect their values.

> Some stuff I thought I valued I now think I don't. People in this class have changed my mind.

Meaningful, sustained learning cannot occur when students don't value it, and values cannot mature and develop without learning in a context of multiple perspectives. Making classrooms hospitable for the expression and examination of values is essential for capabilities development; it is essential for moral development; and it encourages civility amidst diversity.

How do we educate for lives people actually can and do live?

Sen (2009: 10) bases his conception of justice on deep attention to 'the kind of lives that people can actually lead'. His vision for justice embraces democratic ideals and requires deliberative practices. Education, he claims, contributes not only to the quality of one's life but also to an individual's relative capacity to participate in democratic life and construct a life that he or she deems worth living; importantly, he places a clear emphasis on social practices – on living and acting justly in a real world. So in the classroom, how does one position students to think more carefully and deliberately about their own lives so they can be more purposeful in considering and understanding the lives of others? How does one help them secure 'agency' as they navigate and understand their lives? How might a classroom experience be designed that brings students a heightened realization of their own lives, enabling them to give deep attention to the lives of others?

In an undergraduate sociology course (Deprez teaches) named 'Critical Thinking' students are challenged to understand, analyse, and evaluate ways in which notions and definitions of social class shape both social relationships and individual lives, influence national and state social policies, and affect our well-being as a society. The class begins with students in a circle, both to promote conversation and deep listening among all class participants and to practise interdisciplinary pedagogy – reflective consideration of not only the content of education but also of the process as it occurs between student and teacher, and among students themselves. In the first session, students are asked why they are taking the course. This is an important first step as they articulate their expectations – of themselves and of the instructor: it also clarifies challenges that may arise. The expectation is that this opening sets the stage for an open, safe and supportive learning environment – especially important for the often difficult discussions of social class.

The first assignment, completed prior to any in-class discussions about or readings on social class, is an essay in which students locate themselves in a social class (Lower, Upper-Lower, Middle, Upper-Middle, Lower-Upper, Upper or Working if it feels more familiar). They are asked to define social class in their own words and to consider what it means to be a member of that class, to discuss transitions among classes they may have experienced or want/expect to experience, and to consider their family's class. In addition, they complete an exercise on the *New York Times* 'Class' website[2] which ranks them comparatively in the areas of occupation, education, income, and wealth. They then discuss these findings and comment on whether or not they were expected. At the semester's end, having completed 14 weeks of reading about, analysing, and discussing social class, they are asked to revisit this initial essay to review, assess, analyse, and evaluate their initial conceptions of social class and their membership in it. The final assignment concludes with a discussion of what they have learned about themselves and about social class, enhancing their opportunity to 'develop an ethical awareness of power relationships . . . and how power worked against the marginalized' (Walker 2008: 480).

A central purpose of this assignment is to give students the opportunity to look into their own lives – what is this life they actually do live? The hope is that they can consider and apply course learning to their own lived lives and invoke that learning as they imagine new life possibilities; deliberate course themes/topics in light of contemporary societal conditions while being able to listen to the lived experiences of others; explore connections between course learning and constructed cultural notions of class as they continue to explore and deepen their understanding of cultural constraints on human freedom and well-being; and more ably understand the lives of others.

When asked about their learning experience in this class, student reflections included comments such as:

> I have had opportunities to reflect on what I have learned in this course and then think about how that learning is relevant to the life I want to lead.

> This class has tweaked my curiosity because I see the potential impact on my life.

> This class has helped me see a wider range of possible paths my life might take.

> The issues under consideration in this class encouraged and motivated my engagement in the classroom.

> Learning experiences in this class have been related to my life experiences.

Paulo Freire (2000, 2005) writes persuasively about the process for empowering learners: providing an environment for them to think for themselves, bringing personal experiences to the classroom that relate to the ideas, concepts, and notions under discussion, having voice, and becoming aware, often suddenly, of ideas that they had not known of before. It is to these goals that this assignment aspires.

How do we educate for foundational capacity for agency and freedom?

Sen and Nussbaum see education as essential to be able to live a life of value. Without an opportunity for education and the wherewithal to avail themselves of that opportunity, many human beings are condemned to constrained agency and freedom. The full weight of these ideas creates an urgency for us: if student agency is paramount to students' learning as well as to their choosing lives they value, we must provide a critical, respectful, and inquiring classroom context for their agency to develop.

In an upper-level undergraduate sociology course (Deprez teaches), the intent is to ensure that students develop confidence to both deeply understand and aptly critique contemporary issues (e.g. poverty). Weekly insight papers facilitate this process. Papers include a concise summary of the key points of each foundational reading and raise three substantive questions to further class discussion. As the course progresses, they are asked to consider how, for example, each reading complements or plays off others. Thus, the papers provide students the opportunity to integrate readings with course concepts and to prepare them to be active class participants, able and confident to enrich and 'push' the dialogue.

Another assignment requires students to take on a leadership role by facilitating discussion of an assigned reading: this requires that they read closely to ensure comprehensive understanding. To begin, they first discuss key ideas of the article and comment on the logic of its presentation and conclusion. They then build on and integrate previous readings to consider implications as well as alternative interpretations beyond what the reading offers, and link the reading to issues of contemporary concern, if appropriate. The conversation with their peers opens by them introducing substantive questions to promote a deeper, more enriched exploration and deliberation.

Both exercises require students to *critically* engage with the text in order to comprehend it, question it, evaluate it, and form a deep understanding of it. Students are afforded an opportunity to develop and exercise their voices, and to develop critical capacities. The professor's commitment is to create an inspiring learning environment that confronts issues of contemporary interest from a critical, cross-disciplinary/interdisciplinary perspective by engaging students in inquiry to such an extent that they get 'hooked' on learning. As such, students are invited into an exploration of the subject matter at hand and encouraged to employ and apply concepts, ideas, and theoretical constructs to contemporary thinking and understanding.

Considering and listening to students' conceptions of themselves as learners and understanding how they conceive of themselves as thinkers, readers, and writers is key to increasing their agency. It also opens up new ways of thinking about instructional responsibilities and obligations and to developing new approaches for supporting students who maybe struggling as thinkers, readers, and writers: to create 'learning situations that respect and enhance the autonomy of the learner' (Garnett 2009: 445). It also encourages a more deliberate approach within the classroom to create a web of connections between and among disciplines and traditions of knowledge; challenges disciplinary boundaries, through an understanding of the interdependent nature of our interactions and the strong foundations we must build upon to facilitate change; and secures an awareness that there is never just one approach or resolution to an issue or problem despite rhetoric to the contrary. When asked about their learning, students wrote:

I feel as though I 'own' the knowledge I have acquired in this class.

I have had the opportunity in this class to engage in substantive thinking and consider myself an effective thinker.

I have seen myself as a good, careful reader in this class.

I have seen myself as a good writer in this class.

My professors have helped me when I lacked the background skills to be successful.

Concluding thoughts

The CA has compelled us to consider seriously every student's capacities for democratic engagement, the relative hospitality of our classrooms, the understandable resistance of some students, and the dynamics of power playing out in our classrooms. It reminds us of our responsibility and our obligation as educators to do everything we possibly can to enable students to participate. Ensuring each individual student's capacity to be successful is, as Walker (2008: 118) writes, 'a vital part of the egalitarian agenda . . . one that widens the possibilities for individuals and societies'.

The CA emphasizes the importance of setting high expectations for students while also setting high expectations for ourselves. It reminds us of how crucial it is to engage students in building civil classroom communities characterized by inclusive participation, careful listening, and public rationality; to develop pedagogies of engagement that invite students to research, serve, and learn alongside us. It reminds us that the success of a deliberative democratic classroom depends on the well-being, freedom, and agency of every individual. Walker too reminds us that:

> Higher education . . . involves a remaking of the self, a process of identity formation, as new knowledge and new understandings develop and previous knowledge of self and of the world is reframed in a process of learning. But we cannot guarantee that this reframing will occur, or insist that it occurs in the way we might wish. We can, however, provide the pedagogical conditions . . . so that educational development that supports human flourishing is enabled.
>
> (Walker 2006: 19)

Our questionnaires asking students about their college learning experiences before taking our class indicate that theory and abstraction have often trumped our students' voices and experiences. Hence, we recognize the need to provide more curricular space for deliberative conversations during which students offer public justifications for their opinions regarding controversial issues. We also need to invite students to explicitly explore values – their own and those of society. While we have a heightened sense of our responsibility to link curriculum to the lives actually being lived by our students, we also need to invite them to become more assertive in demanding of the curriculum what they need in order to live meaningful lives.

Rethinking our commitment to social justice through the lens of the CA foregrounds each individual student's capacity to be academically successful. As we continue to challenge ourselves and to document changes as we move forward with this work, we become increasingly diligent in attending to our students' capabilities development and our classrooms as just and equitable learning environments. We are inspired by the CA's potential to reclaim normative aims for public higher education and allow students 'to lead the lives they have reason to value and to enhance the real choices they have' (Sen 1999a: 293).

Notes

1   P–12 refers to the sum of primary and secondary grades in US schools; most usually pre-kindergarten through high school.
2   *New York Times* 'Class matters: How class works'. Available at http://www.nytimes. com/packages/html/national/20050515_CLASS_GRAPHIC/index_01.html [accessed 13 December 2012].

References

Addelson, K.P. (1992) 'Knowers/Doers and their moral problems', in L. Alcoff and E. Potter (eds) *Feminist Epistemologies. (Thinking Gender)*, New York: Routledge.
Belenky, M., Clinchy, B., Goldberger, N. and Tarule, J. (1986/1997) *Women's Ways of Knowing: The Development of Self, Voice, and Mind*, New York: Basic Books.
Butler, J. (2005) *Giving an Account of Oneself*, New York: Fordham University Press.
Crocker, D.A. (2006) 'Sen and deliberative democracy', in A. Kaufman (ed.) *Capabilities Equality: Basic Issues and Problems*, New York: Routledge.
Deneulin, S. and Shahani, L. (2009) *An Introduction to the Human Development and Capability Approach: Freedom and Agency*, London: Earthscan.
Dewey, J. (1916) *Democracy and Education*, Carbondale, IL: Southern Illinois University.
Freire, P. (2000) *Pedagogy of the Oppressed*, New York: Continuum International Publishing Group.
—— (2005) *Education for Critical Consciousness*, New York: Continuum International Publishing Group.
Garnett, R.F. (2009) 'Liberal learning as freedom: a capabilities approach to undergraduate education', *Studies in Philosophy of Education*, 28(5): 437–47.
Greene, M. (1988) *The Dialectic of Freedom*, New York: Teachers College Press.
Grosz, E. (1992) 'Bodies and knowledge: feminism and the crisis of reason', in L. Alcoff and L. Potter (eds) *Feminist Epistemologies*, New York: Routledge.
Gutmann, A. and Thompson, D. (2004) *Why Deliberative Democracy?*, Princeton: Princeton University Press.
Harding, S. (1991) *Whose Science? Whose Knowledge? Thinking from Women's Lives*, Ithaca, NY: Cornell University Press.
hooks, b. (1981) *Ain't I a Woman: Black Women and Feminism*, Boston: South End Press.
Miller, J.B. (1977/1987) *Toward a New Psychology of Women*, Boston: Beacon Press.
Minnich, E. (1991/2004) *Transforming Knowledge*, Philadelphia: Temple University Press.
Nussbaum, M.C. (1997) *Cultivating Humanity: A Classical Defense of Reform in Liberal Education*, Cambridge, MA: Harvard University Press.
—— (2000) *Women and Human Development: The Capabilities Approach*, Cambridge, UK: Cambridge University Press.

—— (2010) *Not for Profit: Why Democracy Needs the Humanities*, Princeton: Princeton University Press.

—— (2011) *Creating Capabilities: The Human Development Approach*, Cambridge, MA: The Belknap Press of Harvard University Press.

Sen, A. (1999a) *Development as Freedom*, New York: Anchor Books.

—— (1999b) 'Democracy as a universal value', *Journal of Democracy*, 10(3): 3–17.

—— (2009) *The Idea of Justice*, Cambridge, MA: Harvard University Press.

Shor, I. (1992) *Empowering Education: Critical Teaching for Social Change*, Chicago: University of Chicago Press.

Walker, M. (2006) *Higher Education Pedagogies*, Maidenhead, UK: Open University Press.

—— (2008) 'A capabilities framework for evaluating student learning', *Teaching in Higher Education*, 13(4): 477–87.

Wood, D. and Deprez, L.S. (2012) 'Teaching for human well-being: curricular implications for the capability approach', *Journal of Human Development and Capabilities*, 13(3): 471–93.

—— (2013 forthcoming) 'Re-imagining possibilities for democratic education: generative pedagogies in service to the capability approach', in M. Watts (ed.) *Higher Education and the Capability Approach*, Oxford: Symposium Books.

Chapter 12

Global learning for global citizenship

Hilary Landorf and Stephanie Paul Doscher

And what about the university's international mission? What does it mean? What should it mean? When we talk about the internationalization of the curriculum, what does that mean to you as a member of the faculty? Obviously it means different things to different people. My definition may not be the same as yours. But I think it is important for us to realize the opportunity that we have for developing a truly international university – a university that will use the world as its campus, a university that will be just as concerned about the problems outside our political borders as we are about those problems within.

(Charles E. Perry, Founding President,
Florida International University, Faculty Convocation, Fall 1973)

In this chapter we analyse our work as leaders of the 'Global Learning for Global Citizenship' initiative. We focus on our use of the human capability approach (CA) to help the university identify student learning needs and prepare itself to meet those needs. In the first section we examine how participatory dialogue and democratic deliberation enabled the institution to find overlapping consensus concerning three learning outcomes for global citizenship: global awareness, global perspective, and global engagement. We submit that the success of the initiative hinges on the recursive use of the dialogic process and that our learning outcomes expand upon Martha Nussbaum's capabilities for democratic citizenship – global citizenship, critical thinking, and narrative imagination – by placing additional emphasis on students' agency as global citizens. In the second section we explore how two important processes, our office's networking structure and our faculty and staff development workshops, have increased the university's collective global awareness, global perspective, and global engagement. We conclude with reflections on the cascading effects of the organization's embrace of its education capabilities and our hopes for the continued use of the human CA to maintain flexible, responsive organizational learning as we move forward.

The context

Florida International University (FIU) is a relatively 'young' North American institution that has always aspired to respond to the needs of its diverse community. When FIU opened its doors in 1972 to 5,667 students it was an institution with a non-traditional, experimental focus on teaching, service, and the promotion of greater international understanding. These founding purposes are written in the Florida statute that established the university (Florida Department of State 1976) and are visible today, engraved on a plaque prominently displayed at the entrance to Primera Casa, FIU's first building. Founding president Charles Perry articulated his understanding of the meaning of these purposes in a 1974 press release entitled 'International . . . It's our middle name':

> We realize that solutions to the problems of pollution, urbanization, and population growth which beset us can only be approached by a consciousness of their relation to the global human environment. It is this consciousness which led to the commitment of Florida International University not only to the traditions of higher education, but also to innovation in response to the changing needs of the citizens of the world.
>
> (Florida International University 1974)

Since its founding, FIU has grown considerably in size and in the scope of its activities. Located in the global city of Miami, the university now enrols nearly 48,000 undergraduate and graduate students, 84 per cent of whom are classified as minority, representing more than 125 countries. The typical FIU undergraduate is Hispanic, a first- or second-generation American citizen, and a first-generation university student living at home and juggling a full course load and a full-time job. FIU's colleges and schools offer more than 200 bachelors', masters', and doctoral programmes in fields as wide ranging as anthropology, accounting, landscape architecture, and law. In terms of engagement across borders, the faculty (academic staff) are heavily involved in collaborative research efforts outside the USA, professional schools offer degree programmes in numerous countries, and a number of centres and institutes, such as the Latin American and Caribbean Center and the Center for Administration of Justice, are renowned for their innovative work in international problem solving.

In the summer of 2008 we were asked to lead a university-wide effort to reinvigorate FIU's international curriculum. As educators and proponents of the human CA we wanted to use this approach as the underlying philosophical framework and methodology to develop the initiative. Perry's vision of FIU as an educative force for a global consciousness aligns closely with Martha Nussbaum's (2006a, 2007) call for education that develops students' capabilities for democratic citizenship in a globalized world. Nussbaum (2006a: 389) asserts that citizens of the world must 'see themselves as not simply citizens of some local region or group, but also, and above all, as human beings bound to all other human beings by ties of recognition and concern'. Indeed, an understanding of the interconnectedness of human well-being is one of three foundational habits of mind Nussbaum claims are critical to the survival of democracy, habits she maintains public universities throughout the world ought to be responsible for cultivating.

The FIU initiative was developed over three years and a plan formally launched in fall 2010 as 'Global Learning for Global Citizenship'. The components of this initiative are focused on the educative process of developing specific student learning outcomes through global learning, rather than on the number of international activities in which students and faculty are involved. FIU has defined global learning as a process composed of active, team-based exploration of real-world problems and issues. Through the process of global learning, FIU's undergraduates develop three learning outcomes:

1 *Global awareness:* knowledge of the interrelatedness of local, global, international, and intercultural issues, trends, and systems.
2 *Global perspective:* the ability to conduct a multi-perspective analysis of local, global, international, and intercultural problems.
3 *Global engagement:* a willingness to engage in local, global, international, and intercultural problem solving.

Undergraduates must take a minimum of two global learning courses and participate in global learning co-curricular activities prior to graduation.[1] Students take a global learning foundations course as part of their general education sequence and a second, discipline-specific global learning course in the context of their major programme of study. Foundations courses are thematic, problem centred, and interdisciplinary, include an integrated co-curricular learning experience, and are placed in categories throughout the general education curriculum. These courses set the stage for students to make multi-perspective connections throughout their university career. Discipline-specific global learning courses have been developed by nearly every undergraduate academic programme. These courses provide students with a global view of their discipline of study and may be taken either as required courses or as electives. All global learning courses and co-curricular activities address the student learning outcomes.

When we became involved with this initiative it was in the very early stages. Given the stated international mission of the university, many assumed that we would only need to do some 'tinkering' in order to develop and implement learning outcomes tied to our international mission. However, in adopting the human CA we discovered that our university's stakeholders wanted curriculum reform rather than reinvigoration, and instead of tinkering a paradigm shift would be required to achieve our goals.

One of our first acts was to establish a central Office of Global Learning Initiatives (OGLI). The OGLI reports directly to the chief academic officer but it does not reside within a college or school, nor is its mission solely administrative. The OGLI is responsible for coordinating all of the moving parts associated with global learning at FIU – administrative, curricular, co-curricular – everything from course development and approval to global learning programming to the coding of global learning courses on student transcripts. The office also coordinates communication among the individuals and groups that support the initiative. At the time we became involved, an interdepartmental development committee, convened by FIU's provost six months prior, was grappling with essential questions such as: What do our students need to know and be able to do in order to be successful in a globalized world? What kinds of classes and activities will prepare students for these outcomes? Do these classes and activities already exist or will we have to create new ones? These were important issues to consider at the outset, yet we saw a larger, more critical issue at hand: the committee was wrestling with these questions in isolation. Although members hailed from a broad variety of stakeholder groups, they were not representative of these groups since their opinions and recommendations had not emerged from a process involving democratic dialogue. This disconnect implied another issue: was our university prepared to educate students for the knowledge, skills, and attitudes they needed as twenty-first century citizens? We felt that the human CA could be used to great effect to not only help FIU find overlapping consensus concerning student learning, but also to help the organization develop the capabilities it needed in order to educate students for these outcomes. The CA could be used to help FIU achieve the vision of its founding president – transforming itself and the education it provided through responsiveness to the needs of its interrelated local, international, and global communities.

Dialogically developing the components of *Global Learning for Global Citizenship*

When we were appointed to lead FIU's initiative, the development committee had tentatively titled it: 'Adding an international component to the curriculum'. Several subcommittees were brainstorming and researching ways to make an FIU education more international. But missing from this process was essential input from the people affected: students, academics, administrators, staff, alumni, parents, local businesses, and community members. As proponents of the human CA, we believed that a meaningful, relevant, and contextually appropriate initiative would have to emerge from individual community members' conceptions of their valued beings and doings, grounded in Sen's (2009) 'public reasoning' as a matter of equitable and inclusive practice. For this to happen, participatory dialogue and democratic deliberation were necessary.

Dialogue is a 'process that involves reflection, respect and a joining of efforts to understand and take joint action' (United Nations Department of Economic and Social Affairs [UNDESA] 2007: 61). Participatory dialogue is an umbrella term that directs individuals to 'listen to each other, speak to each other, and in particular share the dialogue space with respect and consideration' (UNDESA 2007: 65). The purpose of deliberation is to arrive at overlapping consensus through 'talk about shared problems and disagreement over what to do about them in the presence of different perspectives' (Parker 2007: 26). Forging a decision in a group in which all members have equal rights and are respected as equals, and generating and weighing alternatives together, is the essence of democratic deliberation (Parker 2003). Participatory dialogue and democratic deliberation are central to human development, especially for Sen (2009). Sen is as concerned with the process of decision making as with the decisions themselves. According to him, decisions concerning development must always fit the needs of a particular community at a particular time and be discerned through a constant iterative dialogic process with community stakeholders. As Walker and Unterhalter (2007) put it, Sen's (2009: 12) viewpoint is that 'we make development and freedom by *doing* development and freedom'. Although Nussbaum (1997: 110) has been criticized for her list of ten central human capabilities on the grounds that any such list neglects the primacy of the participatory dialogic process, she does require that democratic deliberation is a core process in the formation of the 'world citizen' and a lynchpin in the expression of the common good.

Moving from 'international' to 'global'

We first reviewed documents produced by the development committee prior to our first meeting with them. Despite the use of the term 'international' in the title of the initiative, we noted the frequent use of 'global' in the minutes of the committee's discussions and in many of the subcommittees' working documents. We brought this to their attention and facilitated an open dialogue concerning the meanings of the two terms and their relevance to FIU. Members agreed that while international commonly refers to a relationship between nation states, global encompasses global, international, intercultural, and local interconnections. For the committee, global was a broader term and more descriptive of FIU's present character and activities.

With the committee's support, we engaged a variety of student and faculty groups in similar dialogue. The results of these focus group sessions corroborated the development committee's conclusions and provided additional insights into the meaning of global and its implications for education at FIU. Most interestingly, whereas faculty predominantly associated globally oriented education with mastery of content and analytical skills ('globalization', 'language', 'geography', 'taking a macro view', 'interdisciplinarity', 'critique of power relationships'), students referred to it as a state of being and doing in the world. Students expressed a desire for education that enabled them to navigate and shape changing, unfamiliar situations. They wanted classroom experiences that encouraged them to work with and understand people from diverse backgrounds. Students wanted their education to transform their responses to and attitudes toward the world. In the words of one student:

> International seems to always make people think about culture. Like, 'I'm an international student'. And no one's like, 'Oh I'm a globally conscious

student'. It's not the same. Global and international make people think something different.

Over and over, students described this difference as a state of mind that accepted the interconnectedness of human well-being. Another student put it like this:

We're taking a global perspective here. That means that everybody will have to be concerned with everyone else's welfare as far as the environment is concern[ed], not necessarily the US having their own environmental issues and say Africa having their own environmental issues and Asia having their own environmental issues, but instead saying that if South America is having a problem, everybody is having a problem. And so that's where the global aspect comes in.

Finding consensus on 'global citizenship'

Students were expressing a desire to become global citizens; global citizenship is a distinctly different notion than that of national citizenship. Whereas national citizenship is defined as a set of rights and responsibilities granted by the nation state, global citizenship is a disposition that guides individuals to take on responsibilities within interconnected local, global, intercultural, and international contexts (Steenburgen 1994). National citizenship is granted by virtue of birth, heritage, or naturalization, but according to Nussbaum, global citizenship is an outlook developed through education:

Cultivating our humanity in a complex interlocking world involves understanding the ways in which common needs and aims are differently realized in different circumstances. This requires a great deal of knowledge that American college students rarely got in previous eras . . . We must become more curious and more humble about our role in the world, and we will do this only if undergraduate education is reformed in this direction.

(Nussbaum 2004: 45)

The committee supported continuing and enlarging the university's dialogue to ascertain the will to educate for global citizenship and to determine what valued learning outcomes might be. We conducted focus groups, open forum discussions, open-ended interviews, meetings, and surveys. As can be seen in Figure 12.1, stakeholders from every corner of the university community were involved in our collective conversation.

To facilitate dialogue, at each discussion session we outlined the current stage of the initiative's development and posed several open-ended questions. These included:

- What comes to mind when you hear the term global citizen?
- What do global citizens need to know and be able to do?
- How do people learn to be global citizens?

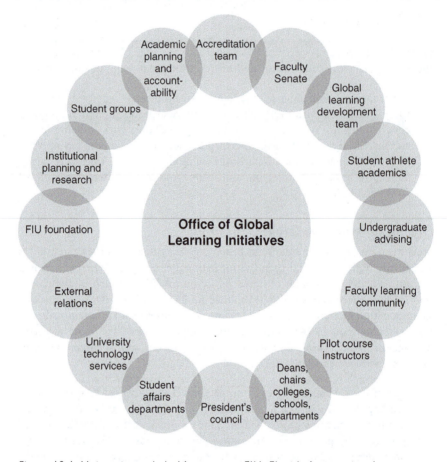

Figure 12.1 University stakeholder groups. FIU, Florida International University.

At each meeting, after an initial brainstorming period, we shared responses from other groups in order to facilitate conversation across groups. In this way we were able to identify growing consensus around several themes. Diverse stakeholders voiced the need for twenty-first century citizens to be aware of prevailing world conditions but echoed Nussbaum's (2004) contention that global citizens cannot function on the basis of factual knowledge alone. Global citizens must also possess an understanding of the interrelatedness of issues, trends, and systems. Additionally, our stakeholders consistently expressed the need for global citizens to possess a cognitive agility that allows them to view issues through multiple social, political, cultural, and disciplinary lenses. Beyond this, participants wanted FIU to graduate students who would be or become active rather than passive global citizens. While clearly stipulating that the university should not dictate what students should think or how they should behave, participants drew a sharp distinction between understanding how the world works and the inclination to do something about it. The FIU community was expressing a commitment to educate students for agency, consistent with Sen's (1999: 19) description of an agent as 'someone who acts and brings about change, and whose achievements can be judged in terms of her own values and objectives'. Agency became a focus also of our continuing deliberations as we sought to determine a coherent approach to education for global citizenship.

Framing 'global learning'

At the same time that stakeholders were coming to collective agreement concerning a commitment to action as part of global citizenship, a faculty learning community was exploring theoretical frameworks for education for global citizenship, increasingly referred to as 'global learning'. Although the American Association of Colleges and Universities describes global learning as the process by which students are prepared to fulfil their civic responsibilities in a diverse and interconnected world (Hovland 2006), there is little, if any, agreement in the higher education community concerning what constitutes the process of global learning. After a thorough literature review, an interdisciplinary group of 12 faculty members found two frameworks to be informative for our initiative. They cited Robert Hanvey's (1982) model as the best way to synthesize the discrete elements of global citizenship emerging in the university-wide conversations. Hanvey (1982: 162) contends that citizens can and must attain a 'global perspective' in order to 'deal more competently with the challenges of interdependence in their daily lives'. Unlike many other global education frameworks, Hanvey's model is developmental and composed of five interrelated dimensions: perspective consciousness; state-of-the-planet awareness; cross-cultural awareness; knowledge of global dynamics; and awareness of human choices. The faculty also looked to Gibson *et al.*'s (2008) model to provide a set of learning conditions and pedagogical strategies that would result in the development of global learning outcomes. Many of these approaches – teamwork, cultural contrast, substantive and authentic goals, reflection, and critical thinking – were drawn upon to develop faculty and staff global learning workshops and a rubric for Faculty Senate approval of global learning courses.

'Willingness'

The development committee was enthusiastic about the Hanvey (1982) and Gibson *et al.* (2008) models, agreeing with Hanvey's strong focus on preparing students for life in a diverse and interconnected world and with the mutually reinforcing nature of his learning outcomes. They also agreed that a traditional approach to teaching (i.e. primarily lecture-based and focused on content coverage) would not provide the kinds of educational experiences that students asserted would lead to a global consciousness. Comfortable with the growing consensus among university groups for learning outcomes associated with inter-relatedness and multi-perspective problem solving, the committee also began grappling with an attitudinal learning outcome for global citizenship. In their estimation, attitude was the ingredient that would transform global citizenship from being a concept into a way of being and doing in the world.

Attitudes are composed of three components: (1) affect ('I like/I don't like'); (2) behaviour ('I will/I won't'); and (3) cognition ('It is good/it is bad') (Newman 1971). Attitudes assist us in making meaning of our experiences and help us organize and structure our responses to the world. Although not equivalent to action, taken together the components of attitudes can be good predictors of action. For example, an individual's feelings about voting ('I like to vote') and evaluation of voting ('I think voting is important') are less predictive of future behaviour than adding their behavioural inclination concerning voting ('I will vote'). The development committee supported having a global learning outcome that described a predisposition towards problem solving across borders. They struggled to find an adjective that encompassed the affective, cognitive, and behavioural aspects of an attitude towards addressing local, global, international, and intercultural issues. In the end, they decided to use the term 'willingness'. This word incorporated the three components of attitude and expressed a commitment to bridging the gap between mastery of the knowledge and skills of global citizenship and exercise of global citizenship.

Deriving student learning outcomes

At the end of a full year of dialogue, democratic deliberation, and over 75 iterations of the outcomes, the university moulded three developmentally cohesive, interdependent student learning outcomes that embody students as agents of global citizenship: global awareness, global perspective, and global engagement. We contend that FIU's three global learning outcomes are constitutive of Nussbaum's (2006a) core education capabilities – critical thinking, global citizenship, and imaginative understanding – and that they expand upon them by specifying the attitude that promotes students putting their knowledge and skills to use to address issues. Nussbaum's (2006a: 388) first capability is critical think-ing: 'the capacity for critical examination of oneself and one's traditions, for living what, following Socrates, we may call "the examined life"'. She argues that critical thinking is foundational to productive coexistence and dialogue in a world of diversity. Nussbaum's second capability is that of global citizenship, or a con-ception of oneself as a functional member of interconnected communities, at once a citizen of local and national entities and responsibly bound to all earthly beings, human and non-human. Third, Nussbaum (2006a: 391) proposes that universities cultivate students' narrative imagination, a creative acuity that allows one to inhabit others' points of view in order to facilitate among individuals and groups the kind of 'responsiveness and interactivity that a good democracy will also foster in its political processes'.

FIU's global awareness outcome overlaps with Nussbaum's (1997) capability of global citizenship; global citizens must understand contemporary interconnected local and global dynamics and the connections between/among them. Nussbaum (1997: 10) argues that global citizens must not only possess an understanding of global interdependence, but also have 'the ability to see themselves . . . as human beings bound to all other human beings by ties of recognition and concern'.

FIU's global perspective outcome encompasses both Nussbaum's (1997) capabilities of critical thinking and narrative imagination. Our definition is based on Hanvey's (1982) dimension of 'perspective consciousness'; one's perspective consists of ordinarily unexamined assumptions, evaluations, explanations, and conceptions of time, space, and causality. Perspective consciousness involves two challenging facets of cognition. The first is Nussbaum's critical thinking capability. The second consists of understanding that others have different perspectives and that people use multiple methods to create meaning from experience (Tomlinson 1999). It is only by discerning the distinctive and common qualities between one's own perspective on the world and the perspectives of others that one attains insight into the experiences of others or, as Nussbaum (1997: 390) puts it:

> an ability to think what it might be like to be in the shoes of a person different from one, to be an intelligent reader of that person's story, and to understand the emotions and wishes that someone so placed might have.

To Nussbaum's three education capabilities, FIU adds another component – that of agency, expressed as the willingness to engage in problem solving. The ultimate aim of the 'Global Learning for Global Citizenship' initiative is for students to develop the capacity to accept shared responsibility for problem solving to take action to solve local, international, and global problems in the context of their own lives. We have defined global citizenship as: 'The willingness of individuals to apply their knowledge of interrelated issues, trends, and systems and multi-perspective analytical skills to local, global, international, and intercultural problem solving.'

Developing the university's potential for change

Having utilized the CA to develop the components of *Global Learning for Global Citizenship*, we were faced with the challenge of helping our university ready itself to implement the initiative. A staggering number of administrative details needed to be worked out, with new processes and structures developed to facilitate the most ambitious curriculum reform effort ever attempted by FIU. By 'readiness' we mean more than administrative capacity to offer a sufficient number of courses and activities to enable students to meet FIU's global learning graduation requirement. We contend that, in order for organizational change to take hold and flourish, not only must faculty and staff possess the educational capabilities they wish to engender in students, but the institution itself must embrace these capabilities. In leading the implementation of the global learning initiative, we saw ourselves as responsible for establishing systems that facilitate multiple opportunities in the curriculum and co-curriculum for not only students but also faculty, staff, and the institution as a whole to develop and exert global citizenship capabilities – global awareness, global perspective, and global engagement.

Sen (1999) and Nussbaum (2006b) acknowledge the importance of institutions in the development of well-being through the nourishment of capabilities and provision and protection of instrumental freedoms. Nussbaum (2006b: 308) adds that institutions possess certain 'cognitive and causal powers that individuals do not have' and she assigns responsibility to institutions to promote individuals' capabilities. We take this to mean that, although an institution may not possess capabilities per se, we can speak of institutions' derivative possession of capabilities. To that end, the CA can enable organizational learning, the process by which 'a group acquires the know-how associated with its ability to carry out its collective activities' (Cook and Yanow 1993: 378). We have used the CA to help FIU take on a 'learning orientation', achieved when everyone in the system is involved in 'expressing their aspirations, building their awareness, and developing their capabilities together' to achieve a mutual purpose (Senge *et al.* 2000). Two key elements – the OGLI's network relationship to the university's overall organizational structure and our faculty and staff development workshops – have been most successful in facilitating organizational learning and improving our ability to educate for global citizenship.

Network organizational structure

Because the OGLI must work with departments across the university, continually crossing traditional reporting lines, it is set outside of the university's formalized hierarchical structure. This enables the office to function more effectively as a central hub in an increasingly complex network of individuals and departments, both within and outside of the institution. The OGLI's network-oriented placement and function encourages and supports all three of FIU's student learning outcomes among stakeholders simultaneously. We fully agree with Nussbaum (2000: 294) that 'the capabilities are an interlocking set; they support one another, and an impediment to one impedes others'. The distributive nature of our networked leadership structure encourages information sharing and empowered decision making. We have found that many faculty and staff are willing to break through traditional academic and administrative silos when they are able to see the interrelatedness of their actions and are given the opportunity to analyse actions from multiple perspectives. However, many disciplinary departments are the site of a continuing struggle between two competing forces. One force involves university and state structures that do not recognize the vital importance of interdisciplinary teaching and learning. The other force is composed of increasing numbers of faculty, staff, and students whose experiences reveal that the silo mentality greatly hinders global learning.

This struggle has been especially evident in our efforts to implement inter-disciplinary, interdepartmental team teaching at FIU. In focus groups held during the development of the global learning initiative, students voiced a strong desire for more thematic, issues-oriented courses that capitalized on the diverse cultures, backgrounds, and perspectives of our faculty and student body. FIU's provost also supported increased collaboration among faculty for research and teaching. Fifty-two faculty members representing all of FIU's 12 colleges and schools responded to our initial request for proposals for the development of new interdisciplinary, team-taught global learning foundations courses in the general education curriculum. Yet, when we began working with department leadership to create a process to implement the courses, we were obstructed from moving forward.

In deconstructing these challenges to team teaching we found ourselves facing attitudes we initially interpreted as narrow disciplinary or authoritarian territorial-ism, only to encounter policies emanating from both the university and the state bureaucracy which precipitated such defensiveness. For example, course credit is typically only assigned to one faculty member per course section. Deeper still, we found reward structures that reinforced many of these policies, reflecting institutional values that ran counter to the valued beings and doings of students and faculty. Institutionally, faculty salary is based on a calculation comprising the percentage of time spent teaching, doing research, and managing grants. Furthermore, annual faculty evaluations and bonuses are partly based on student evaluations of teaching – evaluations that can only be keyed to the course's single professor of record. Eighteen months into the implementation of the *Global Learning for Global Citizenship* initiative, only five of the ten interdisciplinary, team-taught global learning foundations courses developed in response to our first request for proposals have survived in their original configuration, while the other five have morphed into team-developed interdisciplinary courses taught by a single faculty member.

Nevertheless, every time we come together to tackle difficult issues that negatively influence the initiative, such as the silo mentality, it increases our understanding of the complex nature of institutional barriers and our willingness to engage with others in order to overcome them. This is particularly true when people come to see that their actions will in turn better enable the same knowledge, skill, and attitude development in FIU's undergraduates.

Global learning faculty and staff development workshops

In educating students for global citizenship we understand the necessity to lead our students towards experiences of cognitive dissonance, providing multiple opportunities for them to reflect upon and resolve these dissonances. Nussbaum (2007: 39) has written that the process of becoming global citizens 'demands that students step away from the comfort of assured truths, from the nestling feeling of being surrounded by people who share one's convictions and passions'. Here we understand the term 'step away' as a reference to students' agency. Reasoned resolution of conflicting ideas can result in changes in behaviour or cognition or the adoption of new cognition (Festinger 1957). At FIU we intend resolution to take the form of increased global awareness, global perspective, and an attitude of global engagement. But at a certain point – and this point is different for each individual – students must begin to actively seek dissonant experiences on their own, for a global citizen thrives in a world of differing ideas and perspectives.

Our interdisciplinary, interdepartmental workshops are designed to nurture a global learning culture for students by facilitating cognitively dissonant experiences for faculty and staff. The strategies we use are intended to sensitize participants to the development of their own global awareness, perspective, and engagement in order to move them towards new ways of thinking about and implementing courses and activities. To do this, we have participants engage in active, problem-based learning strategies that they can later use with their own students. Participants become aware of global learning's significance for the collective and come to value the influence of collaboration on content and pedagogy. In the words of one faculty member:

> Although I was familiar with the international impact of my specialty, I was surprised to observe how many other subjects also have international (global) consequences . . . Curriculum design used to be a solitary task for me, the interactions and exchanges that occurred during this training have been invaluable to sharpen my ideas and add a broad variety of inputs to enrich the process.

We begin all workshops with a reiteration of the dialogic process in which the university engaged to determine FIU's definition of global citizenship and the global learning outcomes, and the open-ended questions, 'What is global citizenship? What must global citizens know, feel, and be able to do?' Participants take some time to consider the answer to this question on their own, gather in small groups to discuss their thoughts, and then discuss findings with the group at large. Discussions are animated and sometimes controversial and contentious. The facilitator records all responses on a large poster and together the group identifies common, overlapping themes. Knowledge themes addressing complexity, interconnectedness, and diversity emerge, as well as skills such as critical thinking and problem solving, and attitudes associated with mutual responsibility and commitment. Since the groups are interdisciplinary, different terms are used to describe these ideas, but invariably, when facilitators code for themes with the group, they are able to demonstrate how they cluster around FIU's three learning outcomes for global citizenship. The process supports the freedom of individuals to simultaneously articulate their visions and aspirations for global citizenship, while at the same time identifying overlapping consensus that lies beneath differences in language, discipline, and outlook. For some, this begins a paradigm shift in their conception of teaching; a typical observation is that this discussion leads to 'thinking about putting more emphasis on cooperation between multiple perspectives as opposed to spending all the time educating American students about how others may think'. These discussions build interconnectedness by clarifying our common project, educating students for the achievement of the global citizenship outcomes.

Faculty also see that assessment and teaching strategies are as influential as content:

> I think global perspective and learning is far more comprehensive and also somehow simpler than I originally conceived . . . I think global learning means more than simply internationalizing curriculum (in my case, assigning international readings). It also means identifying with and understanding the circumstances that create knowledge.

Indeed, the medium is critically important to the global learning and global citizenship 'message'.

During the workshops, participants draft learning outcomes for their course or activity that are aligned with FIU's global learning outcomes, including inter-connectedness, multi-perspective analysis, and real-world problem solving and the knowledge, skills, and attitudes pertaining to their own discipline. The group analyses each other's outcomes, evaluating language for clarity, internal con-sistency, and coherence. Discussion of the outcomes always involves consideration of the assessment and learning experiences in which students will engage, for well-written outcomes are both thought provoking and aspirational in their depiction of student achievement. During this iterative process, participants gain a broad view of the global learning occurring across the university and a critical under-standing of the necessary congruity between the global citizenship outcomes and the global learning process.

Conclusion

The most revealing evidence of the effects of applying the CA to our leadership efforts is the global learning initiatives that have been developed across the university *without* our leadership. In our Division of Student Affairs, every department annually chooses one of the global learning outcomes to address for its administrative goal setting and review process. FIU's Center for Leadership and Service is collaborating with Housing and Residential Life to launch a Global Leadership Living/Learning Community for the 2012–2013 academic year. Both our Chaplin School of Hospitality and Tourism Management and our College of Business Administration, two of the highest ranked programmes in the USA, are currently revising all of their courses to address the global learning outcomes. Every week we hear of new activities initiated by areas of their own accord.

As we continue to use the essential processes of the human CA to take the pulse of all members of the FIU community, and more areas of the university embrace global learning, our hope is that FIU continues to take on the learning orientation so vitally needed to enable students to connect to their local and global communities, step away from their own perspective, and make a world that supports quality of life for all.

Note

1 Co-curricular activities are out-of-class activities, often supervised and/or financed by the university, which provide curriculum-related learning experiences. Global learning co-curricular activities are designed to enrich global learning courses and, in turn, global learning courses prepare students to participate in and gain more benefits from their co-curricular experiences. Global learning co-curricular activities range from films to lectures, concerts and art exhibitions.

References

Cook, S.D.N. and Yanow, D. (1993) 'Culture and organizational learning', *Journal of Management Inquiry*, 2(4): 373–90.

Festinger, L. (1957) *A Theory of Cognitive Dissonance*, Stanford, CA: Stanford University Press.

Florida Department of State (1976) *6C8-1.001 Purpose*. Tallahassee, FL.

Florida International University (1974) 'International . . . It's our middle name', press release, Miami, FL: Florida International University.

Gibson, K.L., Rimmington, G.M. and Landwehr-Brown, M. (2008) 'Developing global awareness and responsible world citizenship with global learning', *Roeper Review*, 30(1): 11–23.

Hanvey, R.G. (1982) 'An attainable global perspective', *Theory Into Practice*, 21(3): 162–67.

Hovland, K. (2006) *Shared Futures: Global Learning and Liberal Education*, Washington, DC: Association of American Colleges and Universities.

Newman, I. (1971) 'A multivariate approach to the construction of an attitude battery', unpublished thesis, Southern Illinois University at Carbondale.

Nussbaum, M. (1997) *Cultivating Humanity: A Classical Defense of Reform in Liberal Education*, Cambridge, MA: Harvard University Press.

—— (2000) *Women and Human Development: The Capabilities Approach*, Cambridge, UK: Cambridge University Press.

—— (2004) 'Liberal education and global community', *Liberal Education*, 90(1): 42–8.

—— (2006a) 'Education and democratic citizenship: capabilities and quality education', *Journal of Human Development and Capabilities*, 7(3): 385–95.

—— (2006b) *Frontiers of Justice: Disability, Nationality, Species Membership*, Cambridge, MA: The Belknap Press of Harvard University Press.

—— (2007) 'Cultivating humanity and world citizenship', Cambridge, MA: Forum for the Future of Higher Education. Available at net.educause.edu/ir/library/pdf/ff0709s.pdf [accessed 16 November 2011].

Parker, W.C. (2003) *Teaching Democracy: Unity and Diversity in Public Life*, New York: Teachers College Press.

—— (2007) *Imagining a Cosmopolitan Curriculum*, working paper developed for the Washington State Council for the Social Studies. Available at http://education.washington.edu/areas/ci/profiles/documents/CosmoCurriculum.pdf.

Perry, C. (1973) 'We have only begun', faculty convocation speech, Florida International University.

Sen, A. (1999) *Development as Freedom*, New York: Oxford University Press.
—— (2009) *The Idea of Justice*, Boston: The Belknap Press of Harvard University Press.
Senge, P., Cambron-McCabe, N., Lucas, T., Smith, B., Dutton, J. and Kleiner, A. (2000) *Schools That Learn: A Fifth Discipline Fieldbook for Educators, Parents, and Everyone Who Cares about Education*, New York: Doubleday.
Steenburgen, B.V. (1994) *The Condition of Citizenship*, London: Sage.
Tomlinson, J. (1999) *Globalization and Culture*, Chicago: University of Chicago Press.
United Nations Department of Economic and Social Affairs [UNDESA] (2007) *Participatory Dialogue: Towards a Safe, Stable, Just Society for All*, New York: United Nations.
Walker, M. and Unterhalter, E. (2007) 'The capability approach: its potential for work in education', in M. Walker and E. Unterhalter (eds) *Amartya Sen's Capability Approach and Social Justice in Education*, New York: Palgrave Macmillan.

Chapter 13

Capabilities and a pedagogy for global identities

Veronica Crosbie

Pedagogical practice that evokes a sense of self and other and of identity development and agency in global contexts is the focus of this chapter. Using a case study methodology, I investigate a higher education language classroom to see to what extent it can be viewed as a site that lends itself to capability enhancement. I tell a story of an engagement between teacher and students about matters concerning social justice, community and diversity in the context of an English to speakers of other languages (ESOL) module centred on the theme of globalization. One of the aims of the pedagogical practice in this case is to educate the students to 'read' the world in more complex ways (Freire 1970/1996), to be able to view the negative as well as positive aspects of globalization and to engage with diversity at the level of theory as well as practice in the classroom setting. The capabilities approach (CA) is used in this study as an analytical lens in two spheres: (1) the micro level of the classroom as a space for learning; and (2) the macro level of society, dealing with freedom and justice in global contexts. Emergent pedagogical themes, such as power (Walker 2006; Leach and Moon 2008) and participation in communities of practice (Wenger 1998) that foster capabilities of voice, critical thinking and intercultural being, among others, are discussed. The CA has not been used in the context of higher education language classrooms heretofore; this study thus adds a new framework to the critical business of teaching and learning foreign languages in this domain.

I begin with a discussion of three constructs that inform the work: power, pedagogy and participation, defining and contextualizing each in turn and analysing them from a CA perspective. I then report on a case study concerning the development of global identities of international undergraduates studying English, where the three constructs are operationalized and analysed within a capabilities framework. A set of 12 capabilities that emerges from the data is presented, followed by a profile of three capabilities that indicate nascent global identity development.

The three 'Ps': power, pedagogy and participation

Power

The term 'power' is a derivative of the Latin *potere*, 'to be able to' (Collins 1994), and its link with the term 'capability' can be seen in that the latter concerns having the freedom and ability to engage in valuable beings and doings if the right structures and supports are in place (Sen 1999). Power can be perceived as being value neutral but how it is conducted, appropriated and dispersed is the critical issue. According to Foucault (1994: 120), power 'needs to be considered as a productive network that runs through the whole social body, much more than as a negative instance whose function is repression'. It is perceived thus as a current that flows rather than as a static, negative block to be countenanced. If we view the classroom as a microcosm of society, where identities, cultures and inter-personal communication co-mingle, we must be mindful of the fact that in this micro-structural domain, power is always present. As the classroom is a relatively autonomous space, teachers and students can enjoy a degree of agency to question, negotiate and resist power, thus developing countercultural discourses and pathways. This approach can lead to disorder. However, creative disorder can be viewed as a fundamental condition for 'languaging' according to Phipps and Gonzalez (2004: 78).

The issue of power is central to the CA. Notions of freedom and agency, as developed by Sen (1999), are bound up with the concept, especially with regard to having opportunities for valuable beings and doings, which are considered to be indicators of well-being. The related concept of empowerment, as articulated by Lozano *et al.* (2012: 3) in a discussion of agency in higher education, is also pertinent. The authors understand it to mean educating students to be the authors of their own lives, which they see unfolding in a threefold manner comprising personal decision making and selection of preferences; reflecting critically on global issues; and empowering them to take steps to effect desired change.

Unterhalter and Walker (2007: 246), while they acknowledge the centrality of power in the CA, urge capability scholars in education to develop the concept in more concrete ways as they say it has been under-researched to date. They advocate the incorporation of other theories to support this research as the CA is deliberately developed as a framework rather than a specific theory and, as such, is open to further elaboration. They suggest that theories that conceptualize power and participation, critical learner identity formation, critical thinking and criticality will assist research scholars understand the struggles associated with the development of learners' identities as they encounter historical and contextual constraints in the process of learning. Some studies focus on inequalities concerning class, race, gender and disability issues (e.g. Unterhalter 2003; Burkhardt 2004; Walker 2007); however, there is a need for more research of this nature, both at the 'positional' as well as at the 'intrinsic value' level concerning agency and well-being achievement (Unterhalter and Brighouse 2007: 80). The presence or absence of student voice is a case in point, as discussed by Walker (2006) in the context of higher education pedagogies, illustrating, through case studies, students' articulation of capabilities they have reason to value. I return to this issue of voice in relation to my own case study, discussed in the section entitled 'The case study'.

Pedagogy

According to Bruner (1999: 17), '[P]edagogy is never innocent. It is a medium that carries its own message.' In other words, pedagogical choices inevitably convey a conception of the learning process, the teacher and the learner. For example, the 'guide on the side' model views the teacher as facilitator rather than authoritarian figure. This compares with a critical pedagogical approach that views classrooms and pedagogical practices as highly contested political spaces (Kincheloe 2008: 2). Based on Freire's notions of 'radical love' and of the 'teachable heart' (Kincheloe 2008: 3), such pedagogy seeks to refashion knowledge in a critical way, to 'connect with the corporeal and the emotional in a way that understands at multiple levels and seeks to assuage human suffering' (Kincheloe 2008: 3). Critical pedagogy awakens and develops a critical democratic consciousness, which Freire terms *conscienticização* (Freire 1970/1996: 17) with a view to critiquing dominant cultural power structures and taking action against them.

A definition of pedagogy that also resonates is one put forward by Leach and Moon (2008: 8) who write that *authentic* pedagogy is explicit about 'visions, values and educational purposes and addresses big ideas'. They highlight the importance of establishing common goals that both teachers and learners respect and agree to.

These views of pedagogy are holistic in nature, drawing on the context, the culture and the attributes of the learner as they describe and circumscribe visions of teaching and learning that seek to challenge and transform individuals and society through moral interaction.

Nussbaum (1997, 2002, 2006, 2010) has written widely about the CA in conjunction with democratic citizenship in education, and in this context she advocates three main capabilities that inform human development. The first is the capacity for *critical examination* in the spirit of Socrates' notion of the examined life. This concept is present in pedagogical approaches that engage with critical theory (e.g. Barnett 1997; Freire 1997/2005; Pennycook 2001), where educators are called on to move beyond recognition to action. The second capability for democratic or world citizenship is that of *affiliation*, which Nussbaum (2006: 389) describes as 'human beings bound to all other human beings by ties of recognition and concern'. The third capacity is *the narrative imagination*. It refers to the capacity to walk in other people's shoes, imagining how they live, and is ideally cultivated through literature and the arts. Nussbaum (2006: 392) says that freedom is at the heart of these three 'Tagorian capacities'.

In another account, Walker (2006: 128) drafts an 'ideal-theoretical' list for capability distribution and evaluation, offering it as a starting point for educators to think and make choices around capabilities in higher education. The list, which was generated through data in which students voiced values and aspirations, comprises eight capabilities that can be seen as opportunities as well as skills and capacities for development in higher education (Walker 2006:128).[1] Walker highlights the dearth of research on the evaluative dimension of capability development in education.[2] She says that in addition to statistical indicators such as class size, degree results, etc., evaluation ought to be based on the narrative voices of learners, teachers and others involved in educational contexts. My case study, presented here, is an attempt to add to the small but growing body of empirical research on this evaluative dimension.

These accounts of research-led pedagogical practice bear the hallmarks of a pedagogical practice that is critical, agentic and community based, both in the narrower sense of the classroom as well as the social environment beyond its walls. They set the scene for the case study.

Participation

Educators today consider participation to be central to learning rather than learning being viewed as an individual pursuit (Lave and Wenger 1991; Leach and Moon 2008; Wenger 1998). Wenger (1998) highlights this in his four premises that underpin a social theory of learning. He outlines the salience of our social selves and that knowledge is construed as a set of competences based on valued activities; that knowing involves an active engagement in the world; and that this engagement should be meaningful to us to qualify as learning. In this context, the value of communities is underlined and how learners move from a peripheral to a more central position as they gain knowledge and competence. This 'learning as becoming' affects our identities: the combination of knowledge, competence and active participation changes who we are and how we are perceived to be and 'creates personal histories of becoming in the context of our communities' (Wenger 1998: 5).

From a capabilities perspective, participation is considered to be central to the well-being of individuals. Nussbaum (2006), as mentioned above, lists affiliation as one of three architectonic capabilities in education. Sen (1999) also views participation as central to well-being in that capabilities should be arrived at through a democratic process of deliberation, with all stakeholders participating in discussions about valuable beings and doings. Walker (2006: 106) cautions that the capability of affiliation is rather underspecified, however, in that it 'leaves open how relations of power might work to silence some voices in a dialogic forum'. She thus draws on the social theory of deliberative democracy as a complementary 'add in' to the approach. Deneulin and McGregor (2010) explore this notion of democratic deliberation further by highlighting the complexity inherent in the social construction of meaning. In so doing, they argue for a reinterpretation of the concept of well-being, indicating that it connotes 'living well together' (Deneulin and McGregor 2010: 503) rather than simply 'living well', as interpreted by Sen. The authors point out that our identities are co-constructed in social and cultural situations and that conflict and power lie potentially at the heart of the process of meaning making if participants do not share similar cultural or social value systems. If we look at international classroom contexts, where students of different nationalities and backgrounds are encouraged to work together and deliberative democracy is encouraged, issues of power and inequality can and do emerge. In this context, Walker's (2006: 106) 'pedagogy of recognition', which she also refers to as 'an equality pedagogy', complements participatory approaches dealing with diversity, in which knowledge formation and identity development are considered to be twin pedagogical goals.

From the perspective of the discipline of foreign language education (FLE), where my case study is located, the interrelationship between power, participation and pedagogy, while relatively absent from the literature heretofore (Pennycook 2001; Block 2007), has begun recently to be discussed by researchers as part of a new wave of critical applied linguistics (Cummins 1996, 2000; Canagarajah 2004; Norton and Toohey 2004; Phipps and Gonzalez 2004). Each has looked at different aspects of FLE to raise awareness and make a call for action to redress social injustices. Their work, in addition to Freire's and that of other pedagogical theorists already mentioned, has been influential on my praxis.

The case study

The case study that informs this inquiry was conducted in the academic year 2005–2006 in a university in Ireland, where I work as a full-time lecturer. The module which was chosen for the study is designed for international students learning English at upper-intermediate level. Using a critical pedagogical approach, it aims to develop a deeper understanding of processes and issues concerning globalization; increase fluency and accuracy in English; foster group work; and assist learner autonomy by conducting self-assessment and goal-setting exercises. Content and language integrated learning (CLIL) is one of the teaching methods adopted to realize these aims.

The mode of assessment of the module is continuous in nature rather than by formal written examination. In the year the case study data were collected, the assessment was divided into three components: (1) interactive peer-teaching sessions; (2) written reflective reports; and (3) group oral reflective discussion on the learning process and outcomes.

The enrolment for the module consisted of 29 international students. The cohort comprised a gender ratio of 21 females to 8 males, with an age range of 19 to 25. A subset of 11 students volunteered to participate in focus group interviews for the study, with the remainder of the class agreeing to allow their artefacts and transcripts of oral examinations be used as part of the data set.

Methodology

The case study is based on a qualitative insider/practitioner research approach in which data were gathered via a set of four methods throughout the semester: focus group interviews, survey questionnaires, participant observation and document analysis.[3] Mindful of bias that could influence the research outcomes, I looked for evidence of claims made by the students and me through triangulation of the data. My key research question was: 'In what ways can the language classroom be seen to contribute to the formation of learners' cosmopolitan and learning identities, which affect their capability to live and act in the world?'

In seeking to answer this question I asked a subset of questions, including whether there was evidence that valued capabilities were being developed as a result of pedagogical initiatives, whether agency and autonomy could be observed and, if so, to what extent these attributes affected students' perceptions of themselves and their place in the world, and finally, what might a curriculum of capabilities look like for an undergraduate programme of language and intercultural studies.

Roles of teacher and learner

During the course of the module the roles of teacher and learner changed substantially. I commenced practice in the traditional mode of instigator and, to some extent, controller of course content, classroom dynamics and learning. When it was the students' turn to take over for the presentations and peer-teaching sessions, our positions reversed in that I sat at the back or to the side of the class and participated in learning events of their making. Thus, the balance of power shifted back and forth, both between tutor and students and at peer level. I noted how adept the students were with the technology and how creative they were in presenting material. Much of their work was visually rather than word driven, which was quite refreshing and made me reflect on my own efforts to present material.

Classroom activities

The topics and activities that the students and I chose to work with were ones we hoped would have an immediate and visceral impact on each other, drawing where possible on our lives and immediate environment, evoking senses and emotions as well as intellect (see Freire's teachings on radical love and *conscienticização*, mentioned in the 'Pedagogy' section of this chapter). This was greatly assisted by the fact that the students were themselves in a heightened zone of global cultural awareness as they were dwelling temporarily in another culture, speaking a different language and meeting people from different walks of life, as illustrated by comments made by the students in focus group interviews.

I began teaching the course from the students' perspective, encouraging them to observe how globalization was affecting them on a personal level in terms of their quality of life, what they had in common as well as how they differed from each other, and how their lives compared with other economic, social, political and cultural groups across the world. This engagement with self and other was linked to studies and activities connected with ethnicity and identity and branched further into intercultural studies, with a focus on in-group/out-group theory. On the socio-economic front, we studied 'free' versus 'fair' trade and Developing World poverty, drawing on readings, videos and classroom debates to raise critical consciousness. I also gave a lecture on key aspects of globalization, including economic, social, political and technological dimensions. Students were then given a list of global bodies to choose from and in groups prepare short presentations for the class. They examined the history, structure and function of organizations such as the World Bank, the Organization for Economic Cooperation and Development, and the United Nations and were encouraged to develop critical lateral thinking by highlighting positive, negative and interesting points related to their chosen topic. This was a preparation for the more complex peer-teaching session due to take place towards the latter half of the semester.

For the peer-teaching sessions, eight groups were created from the class list and they self-selected the following themes: child labour, drugs, ethnicity, fair trade, McDonaldization, sport, and world music. It was interesting to note the level of creativity and dedication that many of them brought to the planning and execution of these themes. Those with technical abilities created their own videos with soundtracks and credits, others recorded interviews which they played in class, and most of them designed quizzes and other tasks to check comprehension, knowledge retention and vocabulary acquisition. They engaged well, for the most part, within a critical pedagogical framework, seeking to present different perspectives on topical issues in a bid to uncover and make sense of inequalities in the context of globalization.

Evidence of capabilities

The corpus of research material that emerged from the beings and doings of the module included many examples of students voicing values and changing beliefs. They indicate a nascent understanding of freedom and choices that they are able to make, both for their own personal benefit and as part of an expanding global identities set that encompasses intercultural learning and cosmopolitan citizenship.

The capabilities that I uncovered from the data, 12 in total, are based on functionings in evidence that were initially grouped according to themes, such as intercultural group work; metacognitive skills (e.g. understanding of the module aims); awareness of self and others; desire to create an emotional impact in peer-teaching sessions; sensory stimulus (e.g. how video materials opened their eyes); and so forth. I have grouped the capabilities as shown in Figure 13.1; however, they could arguably be grouped in different ways. Lists, as discussed further on, tend to be hierarchical in nature with the more important closer to the top. In this iteration, the ranking is based on the focus of this study on global identities. I would also like to acknowledge the influence of scholars who have drawn up lists of capabilities for normative evaluation in a variety of contexts (e.g. Nussbaum 2000, 2003; Crafter *et al.* 2006; Walker 2006, 2007).

Capabilities in the case study

The selection of capabilities generated from the case study data is shown in Figure 13.1.

In the next section, I select three of these capabilities for a more detailed analysis; linking them back to the three 'Ps' discussed earlier. They are: cosmopolitan citizenship; voice and agency; and identity and ontological being.

Cosmopolitan citizenship

If analysed from a cosmopolitan perspective, it can be said that the aim of the module to develop a deeper understanding of globalization framed by social justice was achieved to a large extent. Many students attested to the fact that they had developed greater awareness and understanding of global issues, at the same time learning more about themselves, their ethnicity and their social roles in society.

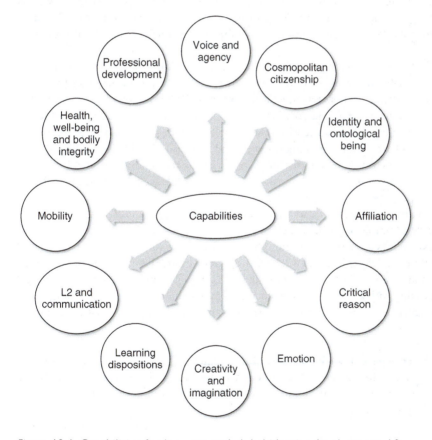

Figure 13.1 Capabilities for language and global identity development. L2, second or foreign language.

Below is an example of the comments representing these nascent cosmopolitan dispositions:

> I found out that there are really problems, huge issues in the world, and I thought that I should do something that I can do. But there are really so many problems so I am confused where to start, but at least I shouldn't pretend that I can't see. It's not like it's not my concern and I shall always care about those kind of social problems even if it's not related to my country.
>
> (Mayuko; Focus Group 2b: 7–8)

Voice and agency

Voice and agency are central features of cosmopolitan citizenship and, as discussed above, are associated with the constructs of power and empowerment, as well as with participation. An example of voice work follows, in which one of the Japanese students, Makiko, uses it in the sense of taking the initiative and speaking out:

> When we were in Japan or other classes I really don't take the initiative because maybe the other person[s] do it instead of me, the guy or the other European students . . . it's very difficult to take initiative in the world or your own life because we didn't know what the other people are thinking about. But I learnt a lot to communicate with other people. To take initiative is really important and expressing our opinion as well, and that kind of ability we can use in other classes as well [as] in our life. I think that's a really good attitude.
>
> (Makiko; Focus Group 2a: 9–10)

Turning to the corollary of voice, that of agency, the data reflect a growing understanding of global issues and the kinds of action that the students might take. Whereas at first they thought that they were too insignificant to make a difference: 'My role in the world? Oh my God! I think I am so small in the world. I don't know' (Lola, Focus Group 1C: 12); by the end of semester they were speaking with a degree of confidence about their ability to take some action, albeit in small ways, as evidenced in the following extract from a final focus group interview:

> They gave us a paper and we, I don't know, it was like, if we draw a picture about the human rights and child's education rights or something, then it will help[5] . . . Yeah. I could know that even I can do something for that big global issue.
>
> (Moe; Focus Group 2a: 11)

Identity and ontological being

Because a key aim of the study was to track developments in students' cosmopolitan and learning identities, I looked for evidence of transformation in the data. I also wanted to see if students had expressed their learning in terms of intellectual knowledge only or whether they also acknowledged ontological changes. Leach and Moon's (2008) inventory of learning identities, which, as well as voice, also includes relationships, community, language and imagination as necessary prerequisites for the development of learner self-esteem, was a useful framing device to study this capability. In the next extract I focus on relationships, as it relates to the construct of participation, discussed previously. There are many citations in the data of the value of relationships in the classroom context, both between the students themselves and the students and me, their teacher. While there are a couple of comments regarding difficulties in working as a group, by and large these were not a major issue; rather, the students often spoke of the value of working closely within their multicultural groups and, in so doing, reflecting on themselves and their own identities, as expressed in the following exchange between two French students:

> *Sandra:* Yes . . . I'm not exactly the same now. I think this course . . . taught me more tolerance and humility. You know, I found out new cultures – like Japanese culture. When I worked with Makiko, this girl from my group, it was really interesting because we shared a lot of things about food habits because we did McDonald presentation on food habit and common habits. I shared a lot of things with her.
>
> *Charlene:* Yeah. I think I also became aware of cultural differences and it makes me understand better . . . I like this . . . international environment, because I was working with a Spanish girl and two Japanese girls . . . So yes. I'm happy with that too, to be a bit more tolerant and this time better, I think.
>
> (Oral B: 3)

In the following extract Sebastian, from Germany, describes the experience of linking the course content to the experience of classroom participation:

> Because I think . . . the world is becoming kind of smaller and there is so much interaction between different nationalities and so on and so I think it's very important that people become aware of other nationalities and other customs, other behaviours and understand why people act in a certain way. Yeah, I think it is also very interesting because we are here in Ireland, a foreign country for us. You meet different cultures and different behaviour and so there is a comparison between the globalisation and what we did in the module as well as the experience and practice. It's very interesting I think.
>
> (Oral C: 3)

Freire's emphasis on dialogue as a key aspect of critical pedagogy is mirrored in the data, through the value that students themselves place on the opportunities given to engage in pedagogical work that involved a lot of explication, discussion and negotiation of meaning.

To a large extent, the relationships expressed in the above also encompass the sense of community that Leach and Moon (2008) refer to, based on Wenger's (1998) theory of community of practice. What was interesting for me to note, as the semester progressed, was how the power dynamics shifted as students, particularly many of the Japanese cohort, adapted to new forms of pedagogical practice, such as interactive group work, active participation, and speaking up and out; in so doing, moving from the periphery to more central positions as they gained confidence and pushed themselves to participate more actively – another demonstration of agency in the classroom.

Devising a list

When I began to analyse the data in my case study, as I grouped them according to themes, I realized a key finding was emerging: that the beings and doings of the module could be identified as capabilities, and thus a list of sorts began, which I later began to sort and categorize in different ways. The creation of a list of capabilities is not uncontroversial. Sen and Nussbaum have different views regarding how the CA might be defined, with Sen choosing a set of five instrumental freedoms that need to exist as preconditions for capability expansion and Nussbaum (2011: 70) advocating a list of central capabilities as 'a basis for the idea of fundamental political entitlements and constitutional law' (see also Nussbaum 2000, 2003).[6] According to Sen (1999), agreement of what constitutes these freedoms is to be arrived at through a process of democratic deliberation. His reluctance to frame capabilities in the form of a list is because he fears: (1) it will become a fixed canon; (2) it will be drawn up on the basis of theory without appropriate public consultation; and (3) the numerical ordering of a list brings the relevant value of each capability to the fore in a competitive manner (Sen 2003). Nussbaum, on the other hand, defends the use of a list as a means for agreement of minimal levels of social justice that a given society can aspire to. For her, specifying content is important in order to prioritize one set of freedoms over another; however, she clearly sees a list as a means of 'persuasion' rather than an issue of 'implementation' (Nussbaum 2011: 71). Nussbaum's methodology has been adopted by a number of scholars (Robeyns 2003; Crafter et al. 2006; Walker 2006, 2007; Terzi 2007; Vaughan 2007) and I have also chosen to describe capability expansion in the language classroom in this manner because I find that naming and listing capabilities can make freedoms and opportunities appear more tangible. Also, in the case of the list I present, the capabilities and functionings are arrived at through praxis and the active engagement of the students in consultative deliberation. It is, however, important to highlight that any list is provisional and, to an extent, context dependent.

I had not set out to design the module in the case study with a capabilities framework in mind; therefore, it was interesting to see that a range of capabilities was in evidence, including ones I had not been fully aware of when teaching the module or had not realized that the students had valued. In her overview of capabilities in education, Unterhalter (2009: 217) points out that one way educators can work with the approach is by adopting the language of capabilities to 'shed new light on old discussions regarding the value of education and the processes for evaluating it'. In my analysis of the case study, by evaluating the data through a capability lens, I found that it has allowed me to observe what is happening in FLE in new ways; thus opening up perspectives on the freedom, opportunities and aspirations that students have as they engage with the process of language and intercultural learning. Elsewhere (Crosbie 2011), I have demonstrated how the list can be adapted to take a wider set of curriculum objectives into account.

Conclusion

The results of this study highlight three key findings that are presented as a contribution to the scholarship of FLE in higher education. First, 12 capabilities were generated from the data that represent the richness and complexity of a university language classroom, belying the notion that FLE is essentially about linguistics and communicative acts, or can be captured adequately via standard measurable module learning outcomes. Second, listening to student voices and using their values to generate theory brings a vital element to the research. Finally, the rich workings of a critical pedagogy classroom, as viewed through a capabilities lens, details a nascent awareness of changing global identities as students engage with ideas and issues of a global scale that, at the same time, can be seen to relate directly to them, if they choose to see them thus. As evidenced here, many have chosen, tentatively, to value this way of engaging with the world.

Acknowledgements

This research is based on a doctoral thesis. My thanks to Professor Melanie Walker for her invaluable guidance and support; also to the students at the heart of this study. Thanks also to Professor Alejandra Boni, co-editor of this volume.

Notes

1   They are listed as: (1) practical reason; (2) educational resilience; (3) knowledge and imagination; (4) learning disposition; (5) social relations and social networks; (6) respect, dignity and recognition; (7) emotional integrity and emotions; and (8) bodily integrity.
2   More recently, Vaughan (2007) has written about the measurement of capabilities in the context of girls' schooling.

3 Seventeen sets of data were collected: five sets of student oral evidence; eight sets of student textual evidence; one set of practitioner–researcher oral evidence; and two sets of practitioner–researcher textual evidence.
4 L2 refers to second or foreign language and can be used in the singular or plural.
5 The students were encouraged to fill out dream cards for children in Nicaragua, which were designed by an NGO.
6 Nussbaum's list of central capabilities: (1) life; (2) bodily health; (3) bodily integrity; (4) senses, imagination and thought; (5) emotions; (6) practical reason; (7) affiliation; (8) other species; (9) play; (10) control over one's environment. Two capabilities are presented as overarching, setting individuals apart from animals, thus marking them as truly human. These are: practical reason and affiliation (Nussbaum 2000: 72).

References

Barnett, R. (1997) *Higher Education: A Critical Business*, Buckingham: SRHE/Open University Press.
Block, D. (2007) *Second Language Identities*, London: Continuum.
Bruner, J. (1999) 'Folk pedagogies', in J. Leach and B. Moon (eds) *Learners and Pedagogy*, London: Chapman.
Burkhardt, T. (2004) 'Capabilities and disability: the capabilities framework and the social model of disability', *Disability and Society*, 19(7): 735–51.
Canagarajah, S. (2004) 'Subversive identities, pedagogical safe houses, and critical learning', in B. Norton and K. Toohey (eds) *Critical Pedagogies and Language Learning*, Cambridge: Cambridge University Press.
Collins (1994) *Collins English Dictionary*, 3rd edn, Glasgow: Harper Collins.
Crafter, G., Crook, P. and Reid, A. (2006) *Success for All: Ministerial Review of Senior Secondary Education in South Australia*, SACE Review: Final report, Government of South Australia. Available at http://www.saasso.asn.au/wp-content/uploads/2012/10/SACE_Review_full.pdf [accessed 13 April 2007].
Crosbie, V. (2011) 'A curriculum of capabilities for language and intercultural studies in higher education', paper presented at the Human Development and Capability Association Annual Conference on Innovation, Development and Human Capabilities, Den Haag, September 2011.
Cummins, J. (1996) *Negotiating Identities: Education for Empowerment in a Diverse Society*, Ontario, CA: California Association for Bilingual Education.
—— (2000) *Language, Power and Pedagogy*, Clevedon, UK: Multilingual Matters.
Deneulin, S. and McGregor, J.A. (2010) 'The capability approach and the politics of a social conception of wellbeing', *European Journal of Social Theory*, 13(4): 501–19.
Foucault, M. (1994) *Power: Essential Works of Foucault 1954–1958*, in J. Faubion (ed.) London: Penguin.
Freire, P. (1970/1996) *Pedagogy of the Oppressed*, revised edn, London: Penguin.
—— (1997/2005) *Teachers as Cultural Workers*, expanded edn, Boulder, CO: Westview Press.
Kincheloe, J. (2008) *Critical Pedagogy*, 2nd edn, New York: Peter Lang.
Lave, J. and Wenger, E. (1991) *Situated Learning: Legitimate Peripheral Participation*, Cambridge: Cambridge University Press.
Leach, J. and Moon, B. (2008) *The Power of Pedagogy*, London: Sage.
Lozano, J.F., Boni, A., Peris, J. and Hueso, A. (2012) 'Competencies in higher education: a critical analysis from the capabilities approach', *Journal of Philosophy of Education*, 46(1): 132–47.
Norton, B. and Toohey, K. (eds) (2004) *Critical Pedagogies and Language Learning*, Cambridge: Cambridge University Press.

Nussbaum, M. (1997) *Cultivating Humanity*, Cambridge, MA: Harvard University Press.
—— (2000) *Women and Human Development*, Cambridge, MA: Harvard University Press.
—— (2002) 'Education for citizenship in an era of global connection', *Studies in Philosophy and Education*, 21: 289–303.
—— (2003) 'Capabilities as fundamental entitlements: Sen and social justice', *Feminist Economics*, 9(2–3): 33–59.
—— (2006) 'Education and democratic citizenship: capabilities and quality education', *Journal of Human Development*, 7(3): 385–95.
—— (2010) *Not For Profit: Why Democracy Needs the Humanities*, Princeton: Princeton University Press.
—— (2011) *Creating Capabilities*, Cambridge, MA: The Belknap Press of Harvard University Press.
Pennycook, A. (2001) *Critical Applied Linguistics*, London: Lawrence Erlbaum Associates.
Phipps, A. and Gonzalez, M. (2004) *Modern Languages*, London: Sage.
Robeyns, I. (2003) 'Sen's capability approach and gender inequality: selecting relevant capabilities', *Feminist Economics*, 9(2–3): 61–91.
Sen, A. (1999) *Development as Freedom*, Oxford: Oxford University Press.
—— (2003) 'Capabilities, lists and public reason: continuing the conversation', *Feminist Economics*, 10(3): 77–80.
Terzi, L. (2007) 'The capability to be educated', in M. Walker and E. Unterhalter (eds) *Amartya Sen's Capability Approach and Social Justice in Education*, New York: Palgrave Macmillan.
Unterhalter, E. (2003) 'The capabilities approach and gendered education: an examination of South African complexities', *Theory and Research in Education*, 1(1): 7–22.
—— (2009) 'Education', in S. Deneulin and L. Shahani (eds) *An Introduction to the Human Development and Capability Approach: Freedom and Agency*, London: Earthscan.
Unterhalter, E. and Brighouse, H. (2007) 'Distribution of what for social justice in education? The case of education for all by 2015', in M. Walker and E. Unterhalter (eds) *Amartya Sen's Capability Approach and Social Justice in Education*, New York: Palgrave Macmillan.
Unterhalter, E. and Walker, M. (2007) 'Conclusion: capabilities, social justice, and education', in M. Walker and E. Unterhalter (eds) *Amartya Sen's Capability Approach and Social Justice in Education*, New York: Palgrave Macmillan.
Vaughan, R. (2007) 'Measuring capabilities: an example from girls' schooling', in M. Walker and E. Unterhalter (eds) *Amartya Sen's Capability Approach and Social Justice in Education*, New York: Palgrave Macmillan.
Walker, M. (2006) *Higher Education Pedagogies*, Maidenhead: McGraw-Hill, SRHE & Open University Press.
—— (2007) 'Selecting capabilities for gender equality in education', in M. Walker and E. Unterhalter (eds) *Amartya Sen's Capability Approach and Social Justice in Education*, New York: Palgrave Macmillan.
Wenger, E. (1998) *Communities of Practice*, Cambridge: Cambridge University Press.

Chapter 14

Educating development professionals for reflective and transformative agency

Insights from a master's degree

Jordi Peris, Sergio Belda and Iván Cuesta

Within the field of development management, there is a growing concern about the role of the university in the education of development professionals, which is deeply related to the underlying concept of what a development professional is expected to be and what are the essential capacities to develop during their education. For example, McFarlane (2006) notes that development management is dominated by a rationalist teaching and learning perspective which understands knowledge as objective, universal and instrumental. In contrast, he raises a claim in favour of exploring a critical–communicative perspective based on action and practice as spaces where different types of knowledge are articulated. Similarly, Johnson and Thomas (2007) explain that learning and teaching in the field of development policy and management are currently being confronted by two different perspectives. On the one hand, learning is understood as a linear process of acquisition and subsequent application of knowledge, and on the other as 'an interactive and complex process involving several kinds of opportunity for practice and reinforcement, including a positive organizational environment' (Johnson and Thomas 2007: 40), which contributes not only to developing knowledge and skills but also values, attitudes, sense-making and responsibility. These discussions seem to be essential when it comes to considering development education programmes from a critical perspective. As Clarke and Oswald (2010) put forward in their proposal, capacity development of professionals has to be oriented toward emancipatory social change. In the same way, Walker *et al.* (2009), in their discussion on how a university can contribute to reduction of poverty through professional educational programmes, suggest the need of a 'praxis pedagogy which is transformative, critical and attentive both to knowledge and to responsible action in society' (Walker *et al.* 2009: 568).

It is precisely in the framework of these critical trends that we aim to discuss how postgraduate programmes in the field of development management can contribute to what can be called a 'critical development practice' (Clarke and Oswald 2010). For this aim, our discussion will focus on a notion which is crucial to the capability approach (CA), namely, the notion of agency. The tags 'reflexive' and 'transformative' are introduced to underline two essential features of agency as formulated in the CA, which clearly resonate with what in the field of development management studies is known as 'critical development practice'. In tune with that, participation and critical thinking make up the conceptual axis around which our educational proposal revolves. Therefore, the specific goal of the chapter is to explore the way a master's degree in development management puts into practice a critical education for reflective and transformative agency of development practitioners. Particularly, it focuses in the institutional and organizational context constraining and enabling the overall educational process and shaping the spaces where graduates perform their activities as development professionals.

We base our analysis on the study of the Máster en Políticas y Procesos de Desarrollo[1] (MPPD) of the Universidad Politécnica de Valencia (UPV) in Spain, an experience framed by the specific dynamics of the Spanish university and international aid system. The study of the experience, of which the authors are part, is based on direct observation as well as on the outputs of both internal and external evaluations throughout the four years the MPPD has been held, between 2007 and 2011. To this end, semi-structured interviews were carried out with students, lecturers, master's managers and people from the organizations where the students' internships are conducted. In addition, a wide range of participatory workshops were held to enable a dialogue and discussion among the different actors involved in the MPPD on the questions under discussion.

In the second section of this chapter we present the MPPD in order to provide the reader with some basic information. We then frame the notion of agency and link it to the notions of critical thinking and participation, whose implementation in the MPPD is explained. In the following sections we discuss the relevance of the university and aid sector contexts in enabling and restricting the possibilities of the educative project. We discuss the educative results from the point of view of the students and, finally, we draw some conclusions.

The Master's Degree in Development Policy and Processes

The MPPD is a 66 European Credit Transfer System (ECTS)[2] degree including a specialization in Development Processes and Project Management. It has been promoted by the Department of Engineering Projects of the UPV, a technical university imbued with a rational and instrumental vision of the capacities that university students should acquire for their 'employability'. The first student intake for the MPPD took place in 2007, and the course has been taught for four academic years. Teaching staff with a background in the field of project management are complemented by staff with a social science perspective to development and international aid interventions. From the beginning, continuous feedback has been received from different evaluation spaces, where academic staff, students, non-governmental organizations (NGOs) and other organizations have taken part. These insights have slightly reoriented the MPPD's curriculum and methods throughout the years.

The structure of the programme aims to facilitate the participation of active professionals, combining distance learning and autonomous work periods of two-and-a-half weeks with intensive classroom sessions and workshops at the UPV during two-and-a-half days. The course starts with an initial training period of 15 ECTS, in which the economic, social and political forces shaping development processes are studied and the international aid system is presented. Afterwards, a specialization training period of 30 ECTS focuses on development planning and organizations, research techniques and aid project management. To complete the programme, an internship is carried out in a development institution (16 ECTS), which is the basis for a research study synthesized in the form of the master's final dissertation (five ECTS). The student profile is quite diverse; 28 per cent have a background in engineering, 27 per cent in social sciences, 16 per cent in economics, 9 per cent in architecture and the rest in other degrees. Career opportunities for graduates include government agencies, NGOs, international organizations, private consultancy or academia.

Framing agency, critical thinking and participation

The concern of providing students with the appropriate knowledge, skills and competence for performing what Clarke and Oswald (2010) call a 'critical development practice' has been present in the MPPD from its very beginning. This type of practice assumes the complex and political nature of development processes and locates the principle of social justice at the core of values and practices of development professionals (Clarke and Oswald 2010). Specifically, it entails understanding development as a process for 'emancipatory social change' (Clarke and Oswald 2010). This clearly resonates with the idea of professional capabilities for poverty reduction professionals developed by Walker *et al.* (2009). From this perspective, university commitment to human development entails enabling students to 'practise as professionals working for social transformation' (Walker *et al.* 2009: 565). Their approach is based on Sen's understanding of capabilities as a kind of power which involves a responsibility 'to bring about the changes that would enhance human development in the world' (Sen 2008 quoted in Walker *et al.* 2009: 567).

Consequently, the discussion leads us to the idea of agency as a core notion of the CA (Deneulin and Shahani 2009), which underpins Sen's idea of freedom as not only the primary end but also the principal means of development (Sen 1999). Sen understands agency as 'what a person is free to do and achieve in pursuit of whatever goals or values he or she regards as important' (Sen 1985: 206), so that 'people who enjoy high levels of agency are engaged in actions that are congruent with their values' (Alkire 2007: 3). In that sense, agency freedom goes beyond well-being freedom as it does not have to be necessarily related to the agent's own well-being but responds to 'what a person does or can do to realize any of her goals and not only the ones that advance or protect her well-being' (Crocker 2008: 3). Consequently, agency has to be studied within the social context in which it is exercised as it is conceptually linked to the notion of social change and trans-formation processes which go beyond the well-being of the individual exercising agency. Sen specifically states that 'I am using the term of agent as someone who acts and brings about change' (Sen 1999: 19), and emphasizes that agency 'may incorporate commitments to other individuals or to causes' (Burchardt 2009: 6).

Although Sen explicitly recognizes that 'the freedom of agency that we individually have is inescapably qualified and constrained by the social, political and economic opportunities available to us' (Sen 1999: xi–xii), incorporating a sociological perspective enriches the discussion by considering the complex relations among agency and social structures. In that sense, the agency of social actors would be enabled but also restricted by structures, which take on the form of distributive patterns, roles, organizations, institutions, cultural norms, theories and doctrines (Archer 2003; Mdee 2008). Consequently, social structures not only constrain the opportunities that people have to exercise agency but also play a crucial role in framing the goals and values they regard as important. In this line, Ibrahim (2006: 403) emphasizes the intrinsic importance of social structures and their two-way relation with individual agency by reaffirming the 'social embedded-ness of individuals' and denounces as a serious mistake the attempt to interpret individual agency regardless of social relations. In addition, Cleaver (2007: 225) claims the necessity to place 'understanding of agency in wider contexts and frameworks, and think beyond the assumption of agency as purposive action' by taking into consideration its complex relations with social structures, institutions and organizations that create patterns which, in turn, are modulated by the agency of social actors. This opens the possibility for social change because 'creative agents are sometimes able to overcome constraints and generate transformational change' (Cleaver 2007: 227).

Provided that structural power is partly anchored in our imaginaries, beliefs and assumptions, critical reflexivity and Freire's (2002) conscious awareness of being an agent become crucial in developing transformative agency of development professionals. According to Chambers and Pettit (2004), to consciously reflect on our assumptions and modes of thinking carries with it transformative power, particularly if it helps to look at power relations as a key element that constrains or enables transformative action. In Drèze and Sen's (2002 cited in Crocker 2008: 11) words 'what is needed is not merely freedom and power to act, but also freedom and power to question and reassess the prevailing norms and values'.

In addition to critical thinking, we consider participation skills as essential for developing professional agency in the field of development processes. In that sense, we understand participation as not only the ability to effectively participate and exercise agency in the public space (Deneulin 2009), but also as the aptitude to enable the participation of others to influence the processes that have an effect on their own lives (Leal and Opp 1998). We assume that this participation takes place in a pre-established institutional framework that constrains and limits the forms of action (Houtzager et al. 2003). Hence, opposite to instrumental conceptions, we look at participation as a process of empowerment, aimed at deepening the democratic nature of institutional governance systems (Gaventa 2006), by emphasizing issues related to accountability, power relations and rights (McGee 2010).

Critical thinking and participation in the MPPD

In accordance with this, the MPPD aims to develop skills, knowledge and attitudes for critical thinking oriented to transformative action. Following Brookfield (2005), critical thinking is incorporated in the master's degree through three different strategies. Firstly, we conceive learning from a constructivist perspective in which knowledge is collectively produced in an interactive and intersubjective process in the classroom through dialogue and debate. Therefore, pedagogical methods have emphasized participation and creative reflecting on previous experience through, for instance, role playing or drama in the classroom. Secondly, we present the students with a range of theoretical frameworks and conceptual approaches which are intended to underpin and build up reasoning and analysis skills for the shaping of their own rigorous judgments. As a consequence, a serious concern for confronting and challenging the prevailing values, ideas and practices in the field of development and international aid has been developed. Rather than working from a unique perspective on development, the students are confronted during the whole MPPD process with different approaches in order to enrich their vision on the complexity of development issues. Thirdly, we emphasize self-reflection as a way of linking theory and practice, which allows us to reflect on the way individuals learn to construct and deconstruct their experiences and meanings. In a specific way, an interpretative approach to knowledge creation enables us to introduce the idea and practice of deconstructing and denaturalizing 'reality' in order to become aware of our own prejudices.

Turning to the issue of participation, the MPPD has developed its own participatory approach through four different strategies. Firstly, participation played a key role in the design of the master's degree. Through different workshops, development practitioners from different backgrounds were asked for the knowledge, skills and values that they would expect from a master's graduate. The results were translated into a draft educational programme, which was submitted to peer review evaluation by university professors, lecturers and researchers in Europe and Latin America. This provided us with valuable feedback to define a syllabus which was responsive to the requirements of both professionals and academics. Secondly, participation is an essential and defining feature of the pedagogical approach and teaching methodology, which takes advantage of all kind of participatory techniques to build collective discussions and deliberations in the classroom. Thirdly, participation has a preeminent space in the master's degree contents by incorporating a critical analysis on participatory development issues. Finally, participation plays a crucial role in the continuous evaluation of the master's degree: (1) students openly assess each subject in a small evaluation workshop; (2) a steering committee made up of lecturers and students quarterly assess each module for cohesion and coherence; and (3) an advisory board composed of development organizations meets once a year to discuss evaluations and recommend strategic actions.

The relevance of the context: barriers and enablers

As shown in this section, the university context has been essential in determining the way in which the MPPD has developed an educational process based on participation and critical thinking for transformative and reflective agency of development professionals.

Regarding the introduction of critical contents, the location of the MPPD in the Engineering Projects Department has to be taken into account. Within the development studies context, a focus on 'the project' as the key strategy of aid intervention may be assumed to be detrimental to a deeper analysis of the way development processes take place. In that sense, disciplines such as sociology or political science seem to be closer to this approach than project management, the major discipline of the lecturers in this department. This fact is compensated for by the presence within the department of the Development, Cooperation and Ethics Study Group,[3] which is of a more interdisciplinary nature and was in charge of the MPPD implementation with a significant degree of autonomy. Coexistence of disciplines is reflected in certain tensions between the different understandings of participation as developed in the teaching curriculum. Specifically, the notion of participation from a project management perspective has been complemented with a broader vision focused on governance, rights and accountability as processes of empowerment and democratic deepening.

Finally, it is worthwhile mentioning that the prevailing educative culture in Spain underpins an initial passive attitude towards learning by the students entering the MPPD. This means that participatory and critical methodologies have to gain legitimacy during the courses in a progressive manner. However, students with experience in NGOs tend to show the opposite attitude, so their contribution to active dynamics in the classroom has become truly positive.

Enablers and constrainers that constrain and enable the implementation of the acquired capacities for a reflective and transformative agency can be observed also in the aid sector. Although each particular student's experience within a particular organization has been of a different nature, there are some shared aspects that could be considered as structural features of the development aid system in the Valencia region.

Generally speaking, the participative orientation provided within the MPPD's training process appears as a counterpoint to the dynamics of a bureaucratized sector mainly focused on the financial and technical management of their interventions. The day-to-day work of these organizations is strongly conditioned by the requirements of formulation, management and monitoring of projects, which are based upon results-oriented models and financed on the basis of public calls in accordance with the structure of the Logical Framework Approach. In addition, the development NGO sector in Valencia, as in most Spanish regions, is characterized by weak organizational structures with an overload on administrative and bureaucratically oriented work. Although we find some notable exceptions, the political dimension of organizations tends to be eclipsed, they benefit from little social support, do not incorporate a strategic conception of learning and self-reflection and are detached from academia (Unceta 2004). Moreover, organizations usually lack coordination and have to compete for the scarce public funds on which they depend. Nevertheless, according to our assessments NGOs positively judge graduates' knowledge, skills and positions regarding participation. For example, SETEM, a development NGO devoted to fair trade, believes that 'the working methods of people trained in the masters are more participative, open and democratic' (SETEM practitioner). This seems to be recognized as a positive contribution by some NGOs that understand participation as a mechanism to bring their practices closer to a critical conception of development.

In other cases, graduates' participative orientation is seen as distant from what, in reality, 'is done in this sector' (lecturer and expert on project management). They consider that such a political vision on development clashes with a more practical and realistic vision of what the education of a development practitioner should be. In this regard, some organizations do not seem to approve the MPPD emphasis on participation and self-reflectivity because it hinders other technical competences for 'proper' project management. This seems to be representative of an institutional context in which public funding of NGOs, as well as project management based in logical models, seems to play a crucial role in framing the strategies and day-to-day practices of organizations. This way, some actors consider that the main contribution of the MPPD to the Valencia aid sector should be providing professionals with the ability 'to elaborate logical frameworks with divine perfection' (private consultant). Even when talking about participation skills, interviewees from organizations refer more to the learning of participative techniques for project management than to an understanding of participation as a process of empowerment within institutional governance systems.

Paradoxically, this point of view is partly shared by development NGOs of a more political and activist nature. This is the case of Engineering Without Borders – Valencia, an organization working in food sovereignty and engaged in local and global processes of social mobilization. It assumes that the participative and political component of development is already present in the organization, so its interest in the MPPD is mainly related to the capacities of the organization to access public aid funding. Again, public financial support is what determines the demands of a postgraduate programme in development management such as the one offered by the UPV.

In contrast, new frameworks for critical development practice are not acknowledged by organizations as 'benefits' that the MPPD can provide their members with. Therefore, a clear divergence appears regarding the expectations of organizations and the intentions of the MPPD promoters, even if they seem to share similar perceptions on development essentials. This could be due to two reasons. On one hand, the underlying notion of what a university can offer to organizations (and specially a technical university) seems to be related to technical training rather than critical reflection on development issues. On the other, this divergence reveals an institutional gap between the MPPD and the organizations that has restricted dialogue and mutual learning.

As a consequence of all the above, the MPPD's content and teaching approach reflect the conflicting demands and intent of both academic staff and aid sector professionals. Therefore, a balance between two different perspectives has been present. On the one hand, and due to the nature of the course contents, a focus was placed on technical–instrumental training in 'useful' tools and methodologies for effective and efficient project management, in line with the requirement of donor institutions and professional NGOs. At the same time, a concern about social and power relations inequalities has been developed in the form of alternative and critical approaches to development processes and the role of development interventions. Consequently, the MPPD tried to be sensitive to the tension among mainstream development management approaches and practical tools (such as logical models) and other perspectives of a more progressive slant (participatory, rights and power-based approaches).

Educational results and processes: the students' view

As shown in the different interviews and participatory evaluation workshops, the dominating perception among students reveals that technical and strictly managerial capacities are given little value or even ignored when valuing the key learning developed through the MPPD. In contrast, the most valued skills are related to shifts in values and their perceived position as professionals; the capacity for reasoning, analysing and discussing development ideas and social change; and the capacity to understand and handle dynamics of power (Frediani and Terol 2011). As outlined before, this is congruent with the perception the organizations have of the students they have been working with. Among the results of the learning processes the ideas of participation and critical thinking occupy a central position. It is worth noting that virtually all the individual interviews and collective workshops establish a connection between these concepts and the idea of power.

In that sense, power seems to be considered as essential in two ways. First, it allows understanding and engaging participation processes by unmasking interests, hidden agendas and cooptation processes (Frediani and Terol 2011); second, it underpins reflexivity and critical thinking in the sense of 'deconstructing' and 'denaturalizing' reality. The master's is said to contribute to the acquisition of new 'lenses' through which reality seems to be looked at in a different way by 'broadening and widening the view of particular situations and problems' that reveals implicit meanings and hegemonic views and, thus, enables proper reaction. Specifically, 'gender lenses' are the most prominently mentioned by students (Cascant 2010).

A large number of the students seem to believe in the importance of participation as a process of empowerment and that they have the tools to encourage a more transformative participation within their spaces of action. By contrast, the idea of capacity to encourage critical thinking within collective spaces, such as organizations, is rarely mentioned. In that sense, although they have developed a very critical view of the aid system, a feeling of disappointment and frustration exists due to their own 'paralysis' when it comes to promoting change within the organizations in which they are committed. This is partly attributed to the lack of frame by the MPPD of a precise outline on how an alternative idea of development practice could be reached.

According to our inquiry, participation and critical thinking have been emphasized as not only educational results but also as crucial methods and drivers for enabling active learning processes (Belda *et al.* 2012). Nevertheless, students also mention issues that have limited the scope and depth of these processes. Regarding methods and learning processes, participatory methodologies are considered to be crucial for the internalization of core concepts and to enable self-reflective and critical thinking, particularly when they include an open reflection on how power dynamics operates in the classroom itself. In that sense, it has allowed students to become aware of their own positions in a specific participatory experience. That way, participatory methodologies have become central not only to 'learn' how to participate but also to facilitate others' participation. Alongside this, critical and reflexive guidance have become a core element as well. According to students it has taken the form of educative methods, attitudes encouraged by lecturers, axis for autonomous work, and theoretical approaches to specific notions and concepts.

In relation to this, there are two specific issues that have played an important role. On the one hand, the diversity of students' profiles is acknowledged to have encouraged a more productive and critical learning. However, according to some of the interviewees, gaps in 'previous student knowledge' seemed to generate particular power dynamics undermining learning processes as reflected in inhibitions in classroom debates. On the other hand, the structure of the master's degree enabled different spaces for critical participation and reflexivity which were of an informal nature but of major importance, such as spontaneous debates outside the classroom in different spaces (breaks, hangouts, etc.). These informal spaces clearly contributed to improve the quality of in-class participation and collective reflection by building ties of confidence among students.

In another respect, students who throughout the MPPD educational process were involved in development organizations did not feel that these experiences 'outside' the course were capitalized 'inside' the course through encouraging a reflection on the relations of their own experiences with the master's curriculum. Although experiences provided by lecturers were valued as positive, students did not think that the newly acquired knowledge was built upon their previous experiences as development practitioners. A general claim was that the MPPD does not link knowledge to 'local reality' and the diversity of local processes promoted by grass-roots organizations in Valencia. This was particularly striking at a time when social mobilization in Spain was increasingly visible.[4] In general, students do not seem to have the impression that the educational process is based on a 'learning by doing' philosophy as learning seems not to be connected with action (Frediani and Terol 2011). This perception changes during the internship period, where they acknowledge a valuable experiential learning in contact with the 'ground'.

Conclusions

This chapter builds on the premise that the role of the university in educating critical development practitioners has to be linked to the idea of emancipatory social change. In that sense, the notion of reflexive and transformative agency has allowed us to create a framework for approaching the critical educational proposal that also underpins the MPPD. This proposal locates the principle of social justice in the heart of values and practices and takes into consideration the complex and political nature of development processes. Additionally, the focus on agency has led us to broaden our perspectives and explore the way in which the institutional and organizational context defines the room for manoeuvre for both the educational process and the practice within the organizations. In that sense, it is of the utmost importance to reflect critically on the structural factors conditioning the articulation and implementation of a critically oriented educational process.

Hence, the fact that the MPPD is located in a specific institutional and organizational context has enabled and, at the same time, constrained the advance of critical and transformative agency through participation and critical learning. The integration into a technical university and into a project management department, the process of convergence in the European Higher Education Area, the demands of the aid sector and the values and attitudes of both students and teachers towards learning have clearly modulated the process. It is mainly perceived that the acquired capacities are strongly related to changes in attitudes and values; reasoning and analysing development and social change; and understanding and handling dynamics of power. Therefore, participation and critical thinking seem to have been two key issues in both the learning processes and results.

Nevertheless, except for the final internship stage, a deficiency in terms of 'learning by doing' has been pointed out throughout the teaching period. That is, synergies between personal experiences of participation and critical reflexivity outside the MPPD and the educational process itself do not seem to have been properly established. Hence, an important challenge emerges to deeply align educational strategies to the type of learning the MPPD wishes to encourage.

From the perspective of the organizations, the critical approach imbued by the education process of the MPPD contrasts with the dynamic of a sector which is highly focused on the technical management of interventions. Hence, two opposing assessments emerge: on the one hand, organizations acknowledge graduates' knowledge, skills and dispositions towards participation, but, on the other hand, they believe that this knowledge has been detrimental to the development of more sound technical skills in project management. The structure and approach of the aid system regarding projects' public funding seems to account for this attitude, as it clearly sets the agenda and concerns within the organizations.

Therefore, the current context of rapid changes and uncertainties, resulting from the economic crisis and drastic cuts in development public funding, calls for the necessity to rethink the roles of both development organizations and universities as development actors and to jointly define the challenges of the education of development practitioners. Throughout this chapter we have intended to show how moving a capacity building to a capability development perspective in terms of reflexive and transformative agency requires a deep acknowledgment of institutional and organizational elements, which constrain and enable the forms of action that university postgraduate programmes can perform in their contribution to a critical development practice.

Notes

1 Master's Degree in Development Policies and Processes.
2 European Credit Transfer System (ECTS) is the standard unit for comparing the study attainment of students of higher education across the European Union and other collaborating European countries. One ECTS is equivalent to 25–30 hours of learning (autonomous work, classroom attendance, etc.).
3 The Development, Cooperation and Ethics Study Group is a research group belonging to the Engineering Projects Department.
4 Several interviews and participatory workshops that have formed the basis for this research were carried out over the weeks in which the Spanish 'indignants movement' (15 M movement) was having greater public visibility.

References

Alkire, S. (2007) *Concepts and Measures of Agency*, OPHI Working Papers Series 7. Oxford: Oxford Poverty and Human Development Initiative.

Archer, M. (2003) *Structure, Agency and the Internal Conversation*, Cambridge: Cambridge University Press.

Belda, S., Boni, A., Peris, J. and Terol, L. (2012) 'Rethinking capacity development for critical development practice: inquiry into a postgraduate programme', *Journal of International Development*, 24(5): 571–84.

Brookfield, S.D. (2005) *The Power of the Critical Theory for Adult Learning and Teaching*, Maidenhead: Open University Press.

Burchardt, T. (2009) 'Agency goals, adaptation and capability sets', *Journal of Human Development and Capabilities*, 10(1): 3–19.

Cascant, M.J. (2010) *Evaluación de los 3 primeros años del Máster en Políticas y Procesos de Desarrollo*, internal report to Universitat Politècnica de València.

Chambers, R. and Pettit, J. (2004) 'Shifting power to make a difference', in L. Groves and R. Hinton (eds) *Inclusive Aid: Changing Power and Relationships in International Development*, London: Earthscan.

Clarke, P. and Oswald, K. (2010) 'Why reflect collectively on capacities for change?', *IDS Bulletin*, 41(3): 1–12.

Cleaver, C. (2007) 'Understanding agency in collective action', *Journal of Human Development and Capabilities*, 8(2): 223–4.

Crocker, D. (2008) *Ethics of Global Development: Agency, Capability, and Deliberative Democracy*, Cambridge: Cambridge University Press.

Deneulin, S. (2009) 'Democracy and political participation', in S. Deneulin and L. Shahani (eds) *An Introduction to the Human Development and Capability Approach*, London: Earthscan.

Deneulin, S. and Shahani, L. (eds) (2009) *An Introduction to the Human Development and Capability Approach*. London: Earthscan.

Frediani, A. and Terol, L. (2011) *Informe de evaluación de la 4ª edición del Máster en Políticas y Procesos de Desarrollo*, internal report to Universitat Politècnica de València.

Freire, P. (2002) *La Pedagogía del Oprimido*, Buenos Aires: Siglo XXI Editores.

Gaventa, J. (2006) *Triumph, Deficit or Contestation: Deepening the "Deepening Democracy" Debate*, IDS Working Paper 264. Brighton, UK: Institute of Development Studies.

Houtzager, P.P., Lavalle, A.G. and Acharya A. (2003) *Who Participates? Civil Society and the New Democratic Politics in São Paulo, Brazil*, IDS Working Paper 210. Brighton, UK: Institute of Development Studies.

Ibrahim, S. (2006) 'From individual to collective capabilities: the capability approach as a conceptual framework for self-help', *Journal of Human Development and Capabilities*, 7(3): 397–416.

Johnson, H. and Thomas, A. (2007) 'Individual learning and building organizational capacity for development', *Public Administration and Development*, 27(1): 39–48.

Leal, P. and Opp, R. (1998) *Participation and Development in the Age of Globalization*, Ottawa: Canadian International Development Agency.

McFarlane, C. (2006) 'Crossing borders: development, learning, and the North-South divide', *Third World Quarterly*, 27(8): 1413–37.

McGee, R. (2010) 'Procesos de desarrollo, participación, gobernanza, derechos y poder', *Cuadernos de Investigación en Procesos de Desarrollo*, 1. València, Spain: Universitat Politècnica de València.

Mdee, A. (2008) 'Towards a dynamic structure-agency framework: understanding patterns of participation in community-driven development in Uchira, Tanzania', *International Development Planning Review*, 30(4): 399–420.

Sen, A. (1985) *Commodities and Capabilities*, Amsterdam: North Holland.

—— (1999) *Development as Freedom*, Oxford: Oxford University Press.

Unceta, K. (2004) 'La Universidad y la cooperación al desarrollo: hacia un marco de colaboración con las ONGD', in Plataforma 2015 y Más (coord.) *La Palabra Empeñada: Los Objetivos 2015 y la Lucha contra la Pobreza. Segundo Informe Anual de la Plataforma 2015 y Más*. Madrid: Los Libros de la Catarata.

Walker, M., McLean, M., Dison, A. and Peppin-Vaughan, R. (2009) 'South African universities and human development: towards a theorization and operationalisation of professional capabilities for poverty reduction', *International Journal of Educational Development*, 29(6): 565–72.

Chapter 15

Re-imagining universities
International education, cosmopolitan pedagogies and global friendships

Shanti George

How can university education contribute to urgently needed societal and global change towards an equitable and compassionate world? Part of the answer lies in building shared visions of global challenges and shared identities of global citizenship, as argued by the present book and the chapters that constitute it. A nuanced position concurs neither with the view that education can be expected to right all society's wrongs nor with the other extreme position that education serves only to reinforce existing societal and inter-societal inequalities. University education can contribute to rethinking in society and of society, including even global society, especially if, as argued by Nussbaum (1997), it promotes qualities connected to citizenship, notably sensitivity and compassion within global perspectives. The regrettable truth, however, is that university education today increasingly fails to promote what Nussbaum argues for.

The prevailing demand is for a type of higher education that is driven mainly by a combination of individual aspirations and corporate needs in changed international contexts (Nayyar 2008). Higher education tends to serve only small affluent segments of the population rather than orient itself towards collective well-being and equality (Vessuri 2008). International higher education is oriented towards attracting foreign students who pay high fees, in order to bolster finances available to universities in rich countries, instead of responding to moral responsibilities and civic engagement within the global environment (Stuart 2008: 80).

Nonetheless, this chapter argues that 'other universities are possible', following de Sousa Santos' (2008) assertion that 'another knowledge is possible' and Susan George's (2004) affirmation that 'another world is possible' – maintaining the logical link that the emergence of a better and more just world is dependent on the availability of transformative and emancipatory knowledge that, in turn, can be generated through the strengthening of capability approaches (CAs) and orientations towards human development within universities across the world.

The present chapter offers a glimpse of what is possible for universities by drawing on a case study from the margins of current university education, highlighting the relatively atypical nature of international development studies as taught and learnt at schools or centres of development studies, usually located on or near university campuses. Courses in international development are increasingly offered at the graduate level (and even to undergraduates). This chapter, however, uses a case study from one of the older schools of development studies in Europe, founded in 1952 as part of the death throes of the Dutch colonial empire. I argue that although much 'international development studies' in this early form – and also in more contemporary forms – can be described as 'colonialization by other means', the subject of classroom discussions as encapsulated by various development debates and the preponderance of experienced and articulate people from Africa, Asia and Latin America among the 'students' allows the contestation of dominant knowledge and the emergence of transformative friendships, both of which are significantly different from the pedagogies and friendships that typify conventional university campuses.

The case study

The focus of this study is on 'international education' at a graduate school of international development studies in Europe, as previously noted. The study draws on detailed interviews with 124 men and women from 27 countries in Africa, Asia, the Americas and Europe, who passed through this school in the course of the second half of the twentieth century.

Schools or centres of international development studies are typically situated within universities, or are affiliated to them, but offer education with a somewhat different orientation. For example, the International Institute of Social Studies, located in The Hague, the Netherlands (the school under discussion here), describes itself as providing interdisciplinary problem-oriented and policy-focused studies at the graduate level, through master's and diploma programmes as well as doctoral work. Those who attend its programmes are often professionals in mid-career and largely come from Asia, Africa, Latin America and Eastern Europe, usually supported by fellowships from various sources (including nowadays one-third with Dutch government fellowships). Small numbers from Western Europe and North America also attend programmes at the institute.

The institute emerged in 1952 through collaboration between the Netherlands government and Dutch academe, in response to the restructuring of global relationships within a postcolonial world. It is now a graduate school within Erasmus University Rotterdam. English was adopted from the beginning as the working language, not Dutch, since the institute has always recruited over-whelmingly and widely from developing countries. The master's programme nowadays lasts 16 months, so that each annual intake (close to 200 students) also interacts with the earlier and the later intake – for the first few months with the outgoing group of students and for the final months with the new intake – and thereby trebles its potential exposure. The specializations have mutated over a half-century, but with persistent tracks in economics, public policy and management, urban and regional development, rural development, and later in gender studies and 'alternative development'. More recent tracks include international political economy, governance, human rights, conflict studies, environment, children and youth, and other current subjects of debate. Activists and employees of civil society organizations have long been prominent in the student body, along with large numbers of civil servants, university teachers and researchers.

This type of international education has been explored in a set of publications in which the theme of 'global conversations' emerged as central in students' personal narratives (George 1997). Individual experiences and perceptions from countries around the world were woven together during the intense informal exchange that can typify international education, along the lines of what has been called a conversation of cultures in international society (Blaney and Inayatullah 1994), a polylogue (Kavolis 1991) and a 'community of conversation' within a 'global dialogical community' (Benhabib 1995: 247). At a school of development studies in a small Western European country that draws its students mainly from developing countries, a global microcosm emerged that was in some important ways free from the structural and psychological barriers that hinder open exchange – or 'conversation' – in global society, as will be discussed later in this chapter.

The protagonists

The research used in-depth interviews with a wide selection of graduates of the institute, from all continents except Australia, who had studied at the institute at various times between 1952 and 1999 (George 1997, 2000, 2001, 2002).

Narratives of professional development and personal change were extremely varied for these 'children of the twentieth century' whose dates of birth varied from 1928 to 1970, but with striking commonalities across the regional differences. Life journeys were described that commenced in diverse homes and continued through state or private schools, until the experience of university dramatically expanded horizons; choices were then made between disciplines of study, and career decisions were taken and often later reconsidered.

Many of the students' direct life environments included numerous fellow humans living in dire poverty. Exposure to these realities was often inevitable despite the efforts of relatively fortunate families to cocoon their children. 'If you live in Colombia and have any social sensitivity, you can't ignore the disparities around you' (George 1997: 92; all quotations in this section are from former students of the institute):

> During one school vacation, when I was ten years old, I accompanied my elder brother on a business trip to the provincial town. On my way home, we were accosted by some beggars. I asked my brother, and later my father, why some people were poor and others rich. They couldn't give me an answer. I kept thinking about this, and later decided that I should do something about it.
>
> (George 1997: 92)

The Thai man who narrated this later rose to a senior position within the country's administration. Such positions often gave individuals a wider view of injustice. In the words of two other people interviewed:

After I joined the Indian Administrative Service, one of my early postings was in an area characterised by much agricultural development but also by much social disparity. Occasionally I lost control of myself when I saw the injustices the rural rich perpetuated on poor, powerless people.

(George 1997: 92)

My first job was with the unit of the Ghana Public Service Commission that handled complaints from dismissed personnel. One day a man turned up to complain about being dismissed from a development corporation. He was illiterate, dirty and had only one eye. I telephoned his boss, who explained in a polished voice that this was a chronic case of absenteeism. I dismissed the complaint. The man then untied the knot of his bundle and produced documents from the hospital for every day that he had been absent from work, and explained that he had lost his eye because of stone chips at the workplace. I became emotionally involved and fought and won his case. Since then I have never belittled such people.

(George 1997: 92)

Human solidarity and sensitivity could thus emerge against the odds, although the odds continued to hold strong against efforts to strengthen social justice. Contrasts between metropolis, province and periphery within a country, or between urban and rural situations, further sharpened a burgeoning sense of an unfair world. Some of the personal narratives conveyed a feeling of relative deprivation that might well be combined with an awareness of relative privilege in other respects. Experiences of inequalities and contradictions in terms of power, class, gender, race, culture and religion – within the family as well as the world outside – were often recounted. The Europeans and North Americans who were interviewed for this study described the additional leap of consciousness required to grasp the structural inequality between themselves and the rest of the world. A Dutch woman reported:

I'll never forget going to listen to a Namibian freedom fighter who had been tortured to the point of mutilation. I found myself in tears, moved and grieved not only by his condition but by my own country's imperialist record.

(George 1997: 43)

Cosmopolitanism also permeated the personal narratives. Deep as each individual's roots lay in a particular locality, the broader view had been sought from early on. An African man said, 'I chose to go to high school in a district far away from my home. I wanted to see the coast and steamers, to experience life outside my home town' (George 1997: 303). Where physical relocation was not possible, the mind could still travel. Another African reminisced:

My father was active in local politics and interested in wider politics. Although he was just a farmer, he bought the *Daily Graphic* every morning and I read it after he'd finished with it. From the sixth standard onwards, I read the *Reader's Digest* regularly.

(George 1997: 306)

While a Latin American man reminisced:

I attended a private non-religious school in Mexico City. It was the product of American–Mexican co-investment. It was somewhat socially isolated, but there I gained fluency in English and learned to think freely despite growing up in a Catholic society.

(George 1997: 306–7)

Several of those interviewed echoed the following interests: 'I liked geography, history and literature. I was always curious about other places, other ways of life' (George 1997: 308).

At least in the cases of reflective individuals like these, the school of real life – especially in 'developing' countries – provided enough exposure (both positive and negative) to encourage sensitivity to the suffering of fellow human beings as well as openness to the lives and ideas of other people at varying radius of distance. A formal school of development studies then provided an environment within which these qualities and perspectives could be further stimulated. Two key aspects are highlighted in the next section.

Wider systematic analysis of poverty, marginalization and exclusion

The global curriculum of development studies presented in classrooms and seminar halls provided digests of current understandings about privation and deprivation from various disciplinary viewpoints. In a setting where the major regions of the world were directly represented by people who possessed first-hand familiarity with various local realities, the formal curriculum could be affirmed, refined, modified or challenged. 'The other day in class,' a Caribbean man reported, 'we were looking at the literature on famines. An Ethiopian classmate was able to speak from first-hand experience and could present empirical evidence that challenged the literature' (George 2001: 13). Conversely, such study could provide a prelude to actual exposure to realities on the ground for those who had grown up in Europe or North America. A young Dutch man recounted:

Nine months after I graduated from the institute, I found myself in a developing country for the first time. At first I almost laughed, at the small houses and twisting roads and the people everywhere. Then I became more affected. How could I write about major issues in another country for my research paper without ever having been there, and just from documents? And how could I have criticised a government's policy on that basis? At the same time, I felt that although I didn't come from a developing country, I had the right to study development issues.

(George 1997: 242)

Self-education constituted a major component of such trajectories of study, and faculty members proved most effective where they acted as co-learners and coaches rather than 'transmitters' of knowledge (George 2001). Development studies is a relatively young academic field that addresses parts of the world that are largely neglected by most traditional disciplines. The hierarchies that generally separate faculty from students are less entrenched in development studies, where quite often students can speak more authoritatively about a context where they have grown up than a European or North American lecturer can. The ambitious coverage of issues and areas around the world that development studies attempts is very much work in progress, and the students in this field who were interviewed described how they had to draw on the ideas and experiences of classmates from other continents as well as on contributions from faculty and the literature when trying to understand global realities.

Such an environment stripped away many of the privileges that students from North America and Europe tended to take for granted. They were not eligible for fellowships held by classmates from developing countries and were sometimes very short of money during their period of study. They were usually far less able to contribute first-hand insights and experiences of development on the ground than their peers from other continents, and were therefore often at a disadvantage in discussions. Their affiliation to countries in globally dominant positions proved something of an embarrassment in a discursive environment that laid bare the structural features of an unfair and grossly unequal world. The colour of their skins – in a minority in the institute's classrooms – might feel an uncomfortable reminder of all the foregoing points.

Cosmopolitanism at all levels from the local through the national and regional to the global

The cosmopolitan value of international education at a school of development studies could be as great for a Dutch person who comes to feel like a foreigner in his home country as for someone leaving an Asian or African or Latin American country for the first time in order to study at the institute. As graduates of the institute put it:

> During discussions . . . this year and among ourselves, we found that the most remarkable element of our experience here, outside of the lectures and academic reading, was the sharing of ideas, identities, cultures, ambitions, concerns and experiences with our fellow students. Where and when would we be in a position like this again, able to speak so fluidly, freely, candidly and without (as much) pretence with peers who represent more than 60 nations?

Where else would we have this opportunity to see our own reflections in the actions, emotions, behaviours and eyes of others with whom we may not initially have believed we shared certain characteristics? Perhaps to an even greater extent, we began to value the characteristics we do not share and learned from them as well.

(Alluri *et al.* 2006: iv)

Such interactions across a diverse and disparate global society could sometimes prove extremely stressful but also extremely rewarding (George 2000). Often such a setting provided unprecedented opportunities for those from a region to become closely acquainted with each other and to explore joyously their similarities and differences. The 'downside' of this was often a perceived regionalism that worried those who looked for similar bonding across all developing countries, or even across the globe. That appeared to be often a dream too far; but in the later months of the 16-month master's programme webs of close friendship typically did emerge that wove together individuals from different regions.

Indeed, many people interviewed for the study argued that a global site of professional learning that was located somewhat outside the dominant core of university education – as with a school of development studies positioned on the margins of the university world – *and* situated in a less hegemonic part of the Global North (i.e. within a small country in Western Europe) was more nurturant of expressive friendships between people from distant continents than were the 'world class universities' at the apex of the pecking order within global education.

My brother studied at the Massachusetts Institute of Technology, and his degree is recognised worldwide. People do rank you according to where you've studied, and such a qualification enhances your career prospects. But I don't think he found that living in the USA was a personally enriching experience. It's a competitive society, in which people are more isolated. You may meet people from other countries but you don't have the right setting for deep friendships . . . Maybe I'd have had more tools for analysis if I'd studied at Harvard, but I don't think that I would have been happy with the personal experience there. Being at the institute wasn't just about studies – it was an opportunity to discuss all kinds of things with a great variety of people.

(George 1997: 259)

A Thai woman described her acute personal experience of breakdown under the demands of international education at the institute, as well as the peer support that aided recovery:

English was such a major problem that I almost felt like giving up. It made the course very difficult, I had to struggle both with the content and with the language. Halfway through my period at the institute, I failed a test. I was so upset – it was the first time in my life that I had failed anything. My self-confidence was eroded, and I felt depressed for weeks afterwards. I found that I couldn't read, couldn't write, couldn't understand or absorb things, and couldn't communicate. I was unable to make decisions, not even about what groceries to shop for. I was completely burnt out. But people helped me – a lecturer to whom I was close, the student counsellor, my close friends . . . Funnily enough, those friends weren't Thai because I'd tried to make a wide circle of friends. They were women from the Dominican Republic, South Korea, Myanmar, Ethiopia, and especially one from Surinam who did my shopping for me. I made a long distance call to my parents who were very loving and supportive. Gradually I got better, but I learnt a lot about myself during that state of burn-out, about my real self as opposed to my self-image. I found out who I was and what I was able to do and not able to do. I also discovered sisterhood without barriers, and communication through feelings rather than words.

(George 1997: 208)

The expressive friendships that were described embodied strong international-ization (Appadurai 2001), which contrasted with the weak internationalization and instrumental friendships, typifying more competitive educational environments in universities and jockeying to maintain their positions at the narrow 'world class' apex. 'I was sent to an old elite private university and I'm very thankful today. I mixed with the children of important people and later I could use those networks to get a good job' (George 1997: 105). The shocking case of a young woman student at Harvard who was at the centre of a suicide–homicide provides a tragic illustration (see George 2000 reviewing Thernstrom 1998) of the social struggles and sufferings that students from Africa, Asia or Latin America sometimes experience within the student subcultures associated with global elite education. The distinction that Nederveen Pieterse (2006) makes between capitalist cosmopolitanism and emancipatory cosmopolitanism resonates in the difference between hegemonic global friendships that maintain the world as it is and transformative global friendships that illuminate the world as it could be – and also highlights the difference between universities as they are and as they might be (George forthcoming).

A contrasting case of 'international education'

The sensitivity and cosmopolitanism stimulated by international development studies contrasts with what Rizvi (2005) has described from another type of 'international education' that is increasingly encouraged by a globalized economy. His sample consisted of 79 young people from China and India who studied business, engineering, information technology and management at universities in Australia. One of them said: 'My parents and I have invested a large amount of money on the assumption that the returns will be considerable. They now want me to take advantage of the globalization in which they have invested' (Rizvi 2005:

6). On return to India, one of the group worked on an Indian equivalent of Pepsi and another two were successfully selling Australian pastries to affluent urban people: 'We are selling something that is global . . . to young people who are citizens of the world' (Rizvi 2005: 7). Rizvi muses:

> Note here the assumption that in India to consume Western goods is to be a 'citizen of the world' . . . The underlying logic thus speaks of a space that is . . . located within the dominant cultural logic of global capitalism that it does not question. If universities are to profit from international education in ways that are not merely commercial, then they have a major responsibility . . . If they are to be serious about preparing their students for the new world, then they need to teach them not only how to build effective professional careers within the global economy, but also how to lead productive moral lives . . . global interdependence is . . . a way of helping students to expand their moral universe in cosmopolitan terms . . . To produce morally cosmopolitan identities, universities need to provide forms of education, through which students learn about themselves in relation to others, so that mobility and cultural exchange do not contribute to the economic exploitation of others but open up genuine possibilities of cosmopolitan solidarity.
>
> (Rizvi 2005: 10)

What are some of the main differences between the two types of international education just described? The first case was about international development studies that attempt to address – within the limitations of the field – the inequalities and injustices that characterize today's world. In contrast, the case discussed by Rizvi involves fields of study (business management and engineering, for example) that generally lead to advancement in the world as it is and not the world as it might be. International development studies builds on sensitivities to the sufferings of others, and extends this through systematic and shared analysis of how suffering in various contexts might be redressed. This is not so in the fields of study described by Rizvi that are typically oriented towards individual advancement in a disparate and unfair world and require – if anything – the suppression of any awareness of negative outcomes for the many people excluded from the prosperity generated by private corporations.

The world views of those interviewed by Rizvi were permeated by competitive individualism, as epitomized by the statement: 'My parents and I have invested a large amount of money on the assumption that the returns will be considerable. They now want me to take advantage of the globalization in which they have invested.' This metaphor of investment (Norton 2000) characterizes many 'biographical solutions made by students from the Asian nations to plot personal trajectories in a global field of educational opportunities' (Doherty and Singh 2007: 125). Competitive individualism also characterized the relationships between peers in fields such as business management, despite the emphasis on teamwork and on 'client orientation'. In the case of international development studies, however, most people returned to governments or universities or civil society organizations in different countries, and there was usually no direct competition for jobs but instead keenness to share as much as possible with each other in whatever time was available during a relatively brief period of study together.

A school of development studies in a small Western European country thus encouraged a different view of the world. Travel to Australia to study was undertaken – by contrast – with reference to an international pecking order of educational institutions, wherein those located in rich Anglo-Saxon-dominated countries enjoyed special prestige and charged high fees to foreign students for the privilege of studying there. According to Eisenchlas and Trevaskes (2007: 179), 'Universities in Australia have become increasingly dependent on this population of students to supplement their income', benefitting from 'the proliferation of foreign, mainly Asian students on campus'. More generally, beyond Australia: 'International student mobility is big business. Approximately 2.8 million students study abroad, distributing an estimated $50 billion around the globe annually' (Reisberg and Altbach 2011: 12).

Towards change

The two contrasting cases suggest lessons that conventional educational institutions can learn from what are – at the moment – relatively small-scale initiatives in non-conventional education provided at schools or centres of development studies. The purview of education should broaden the perspective on the world from Europe or North America to a more global picture to which those from other parts of the world can contribute their experiences and perceptions. The pedagogical processes recommended are not those where Europeans or honorary Europeans transmit knowledge to others who are ignorant, but instead involve mutually respectful co-learning (e.g. George 2001). The relationships between peers should encourage sharing, rather than competition, in a cosmopolitan environment that values both differences and similarities. The moral orientation would then be not towards reproducing the world as it is but towards nurturing the world as it might become (George 2000, forthcoming).

International development education does not always attain these ideals, but its stated aspirations towards a changed world can generate dynamics, as described above, that pull against the status quo and against the relationships that sustain it. The present book argues that universities across the planet should reorient themselves towards human development and CAs, within a new imaginary of what higher education can contribute to the transformation of global knowledge and thus of global society, thereby increasing the pull against the status quo and the entrenched interests that maintain it.

References

Alluri, R., D'Souza, S., Nunez, C., Peterson, J., van Staveren, T. and Zepeda, C. (2006) 'Foreword: the ways of worldmaking', in *An Exercise in Worldmaking: The Institute of Social Studies Best Student Essays of 2005/06*. The Hague: Institute of Social Studies.

Appadurai, A. (ed.) (2001) *Globalization*, Durham, NC: Duke University Press.

Benhabib, S. (1995) 'Cultural complexity, moral interdependence and the global dialogical community', in M. Nussbaum and J. Glover (eds) *Women, Culture and Development: A Study of Human Capabilities*, Oxford: Clarendon Press.

Blaney, D.L. and Inayatullah, N. (1994) 'Prelude to a conversation of cultures in international society? Todorov and Nandy on the possibility of dialogue', *Alternatives*, 19(1): 23–51.

de Sousa Santos, B. (2008) 'The role of the universities in constructing an alternative globalization', in Global University Network for Innovation (ed.) *Higher Education: New Challenges and Emerging Roles for Human and Social Development*, Basingstoke and New York: Palgrave Macmillan.

Doherty, C. and Singh, P. (2007) 'Mobile students, flexible identities and liquid modernity: disrupting Western teachers' assumptions of the "Asian learner"', in D. Palfreyman and D.L. McBride (eds) *Teaching and Learning Across Cultures in Higher Education*, Basingstoke and New York: Palgrave Macmillan.

Eisenchlas, S. and Trevaskes, S. (2007) 'Intercultural competence: examples of internationalizing the curriculum through students' interactions', in D. Palfreyman and D.L. McBride (eds) *Teaching and Learning Across Cultures in Higher Education*, Basingstoke and New York: Palgrave Macmillan.

George, S. (1997) *Third World Professionals and Development Education in Europe: Personal Narratives, Global Conversations*, New Delhi, London and Thousand Oaks, CA: Sage.

—— (2000) 'International education and multiculturalisms: The Harvard foreign student killings in a comparative perspective', Working Paper No. 321, The Hague: Institute of Social Studies.

—— (2001) '"Self-educators" and "coaches" at a school of development studies: a case study of Third World professionals in Europe', Working Paper No. 345, The Hague: Institute of Social Studies.

—— (2002) 'Technocrats and humanist intellectuals in the Third World: cases from a school of development studies in Europe', Working Paper No. 364, The Hague: Institute of Social Studies.

—— (forthcoming). *Reimagined Universities for Global Citizen Professionals: International Education, Cosmopolitan Pedagogies and Global Friendships*.

George, Susan (2004) *Another World is Possible If. . .*, London and New York: Verso Books.

Kavolis, V. (1991) 'Nationalism, modernization and the polylogue of civilizations', *Comparative Civilizations Review*, 25: 124–43.

Nayyar, D. (2008) 'Globalization and markets: challenges for higher education', in Global University Network for Innovation (ed.) *Higher Education: New Challenges and Emerging Roles for Human and Social Development*, Basingstoke and New York: Palgrave Macmillan.

Nederveen Pieterse, J. (2006) 'Emancipatory cosmopolitanism: towards an agenda', *Development and Change* (Forum 2006), 37(6): 1247–58.

Norton, B. (2000) *Identity and Language Learning: Gender, Ethnicity and Educational Change*, Harlow: Pearson Education.

Nussbaum, M. (1997) *Cultivating Humanity: A Classical Defence of Reform in Liberal Education*, Cambridge, MA: Harvard University Press.

Reisberg, L. and Altbach, P.G. (2011) 'Third party recruiters: essential dilemmas', *The Hindu*, 12 February: 12.

Rizvi, F. (2005) 'International education and the production of cosmopolitan identities', in A. Arimoto, F. Huang and K. Yokoyama (eds) *Globalization and Higher Education*, Japan: Research Institute for Higher Education, Hiroshima University..

Stuart, M. (2008) 'The concept of global citizenship in higher education', in Global University Network for Innovation (ed.) *Higher Education: New Challenges and Emerging Roles for Human and Social Development*, Basingstoke and New York: Palgrave Macmillan.

Thernstrom, M. (1998) *Halfway Heaven: Diary of a Harvard Murder*, London: Virago.

Vessuri, H. (2008) 'The role of research in higher education: implications and challenges for an active contribution to human and social development', in Global University Network for Innovation (ed.) *Higher Education: New Challenges and Emerging Roles for Human and Social Development*, Basingstoke and New York: Palgrave Macmillan.

Chapter 16

Social engagement and universities

A case study from Mexico

Jadicha Sow Paino

Educational systems all over the world have always been very closely related to their historical, economic and social context. Most recently, financial investments in education policies based on the theory of human capital (Becker 1993) have predominated. These investments have been focused towards obtaining a trained population able to provide countries with one more means of production, as well as to facilitate their development. From this point of view, education becomes a tool to encourage productivity growth and economic development.

Nevertheless, within these conceptions of education, one issue has not been sufficiently taken into account – namely the relevance of educational processes as catalysts for other processes which are less instrumental, which have an effect on people's decision-making capabilities and on the conception of themselves as active and decision-making individuals within society.

The present chapter therefore intends to explore this less instrumental dimension of education and to analyse its transformative capacity. For this purpose I have chosen the theme of universities and social engagement, and, more specifically, a non-formal education system: Community Learning Centres (CLCs). The aim is to observe and interpret in which way these spaces can contribute to improving the quality of life of a group of women who are following or have completed a course at a CLC. For this aim, I have applied the capability approach (CA) (Sen 1999) as a framework for the analysis. This approach focuses on the various dimensions of the individual and allows a broader view of education benefits beyond academic and economic achievements.

The present research work has focused on the study of a group of female students from two CLCs. These spaces are designed and managed by a Mexican university institution, Instituto Tecnológico de Estudios Superiores de Monterrey (ITESM), together with other actors of the Mexican government and civil society. Throughout this chapter, voices of the interviewed students will be presented to support the exposition of their development and results of this research. Thus, I will look at the functioning and achievements of this non-formal educational system from their particular point of view.

What are Community Learning Centres?

I will begin by providing background information on the concept and context of CLCs from their early beginnings to their current situation. A CLC is defined as a 'learning centre where participants gain access to educational programmes and interact with teachers by means of computer technology . . . They have access to specialized databases which allow them to transcend borders and to integrate into the knowledge-based society' (ITESM 2010). The CLCs emerged in 2001 with the joining together of the concepts of responsibility and service. In an agreement signed between the ITESM and the Secretaría de Desarrollo Social de México (SEDESOL)[1] the basis for collaboration was established to promote comprehensive development in several Mexican municipalities by setting up various CLCs. In accordance with this agreement, ITESM provides a virtual working platform (WebTec), educational programmes available on the web portal, and ITESM students who provide online tutorials and course assistance to CLC students. SEDESOL provides the necessary tools for the implementation of conventions and agreements with state and local governments or with private companies in order to set up centres and supply computer equipment, as well as for the functioning, maintenance and management of the CLCs. In addition, SEDESOL is responsible for the promotion of the centre within a given municipality by meeting its educational needs. This initiative has encouraged particular partnerships between different actors involved in management and operational issues within the centres, namely municipal, state and federal authorities, private companies, non-governmental and civil society organizations, municipalities and community committees. Currently, there are 2,099 centres spread mainly across Mexico and the USA, and, to a lesser extent, in Guatemala, Colombia, Ecuador, Panama and the Dominican Republic.

But, which are their specific goals? To give an answer to this question I focus on the mission and principles of ITESM. First of all, ITESM takes on a social responsibility in training 'whole, ethical individuals, with a humanistic and competitive perspective; individuals, which are, at the same time, committed to the economical, political, social and cultural development of their community' (ITESM 2010). The institution aims at producing graduates with particular values, positions and skills, such as responsibility as citizens and sensitivity to social reality, or collaborative working and a spirit of service. Hence, one of the ways in which this responsibility materializes is by integrating social service[2] provided by ITESM students in several projects, in which CLCs are included. Secondly, a commitment to service is established by providing a quality education and by offering training spaces with access to information; this commitment goes beyond higher education and is addressed to society in general. For this purpose, several strategies have been implemented, such as the setting up of centres for the transfer of knowledge for sustainable social development.

Aims and methods of the CLCs

As previously stated, the ultimate goal of the training provided in the CLCs is to contribute to the comprehensive development of the different communities in Mexico. However, it is important to note that centres put this goal into practice in the form of two specific and differentiated groups of objectives. On the one hand, there are objectives aiming at specific skills oriented towards production processes, or towards access to better employment which, in turn, allows social mobility, higher living standards and social inclusion. In this sense, the availability of training and information spaces, as well as the provision of quality education, is considered crucial in order to reduce the digital divide and to generate communicative and participative skills, among others. On the other hand, we can distinguish objectives dealing with the creation of informed citizens, having at their disposal particular tools to use and transform information for their individual and collective benefit. For this purpose, centres advocate for processes that democratize information and that contribute to the requirement for accountability and transparency in order to help to prevent corruption. I consider how this duality of objectives has been achieved by exploring different cases involving working, training and personal issues within my reference group of female students.

In order to understand the educational and learning process developed at a CLC, we first need to take into account the personal motivations of students. In this respect, the educational experience begins with the students themselves and with their identifying of personal needs and aspirations: their aspiration to acquire new knowledge, training requirements, willingness to address new challenges, etc. Once students have decided to start their training, they will start this educational process with the guidance of the head of studies of the CLC. This person is in charge of identifying the needs of the students and advising them on the use of the centre's resources, available self-learning courses and guided learning.[3] The centre's opening hours are flexible in order to enable access to all people regardless their personal situation or pace of study. In addition, group work sessions monitored by the head of studies of the CLC are carried out, encouraging collective learning. This enables the students to have access to online distance learning through the virtual platform, WebTec, with the assistance of the head of studies and without time limitation. The successful completion of each course is credited by a certificate granted by the ITESM.

The profiles of students at the CLCs are very mixed, as there are no age, gender or occupational restrictions in order to enter the centre, and the available educational programmes are designed for children, adults and young people. This fact promotes the coexistence among people of different ages and conditions, which in a formal educational system would be less likely.

The capability approach as a framework for the analysis of the CLCs

The study I describe has been developed in two CLCs located in two Mexican municipalities: Monterrey, in the state of Nuevo León, and Saltillo, in the state of Coahuila. Both centres are located in important industrial enclaves in the north-east of Mexico; and the students' profiles are predominantly female (70 per cent of the students are women), ranging from 40 to 70 years old.

I have already mentioned that the defining aspect of this research is the attempt to reveal how a non-formal educational system can improve the quality of life of a group of students by understanding the training provided as a transformative experience concerning several personal dimensions (individual and collective). This is the main reason for choosing Amartya Sen's CA as the theoretical framework for this research. The CA advances the idea of understanding development (or quality of life in this case) by taking into account a wider range of information and from a broader perspective through which various dimensions of the human being are considered in order to assess well-being (Unterhalter *et al.* 2007). In addition, it attaches great importance to what individuals are capable of doing and being, namely learning different disciplines, acquiring new tools which can be put in practice within their contexts, etc.

As noted in the introduction, instrumental and economic approaches that traditionally have tried to understand and explain education as a producer of human capital hardly integrate the diverse dimensions that make up human beings and society. In contrast, the CA focuses on the ability of individuals to direct their lives towards what they really appreciate and towards the realization of desires, responding to their capacity to make choices. Hence, the actual benefits of education go beyond the human role as a production good as it has an effect on the expansion of other human capabilities or freedoms (Sen 1999). Along this line of reasoning, he states that 'the capacity of exercising freedom can be, to a considerable extent, directly subject to the education we have received and, therefore, the development of the education sector can be connected in its foundations to the capability approach'.

But which are the roles of education that can have an influence on the expansion of other capabilities? According to Drèze and Sen (2002: 38–40) and Robeyns (2005), education can play various roles. First of all, education is important in itself. Individuals can give value to knowledge just for the personal satisfaction of knowing something they are interested in. But, in addition, there are certain instrumental roles that have an effect on economic aspects and living standards of an individual's life, and on the capacity to choose among particular goods; there are also roles related to the access to information and the ways to interact and engage with others. This role is especially relevant, as it affects the way individuals conceive their life within society and it can even determine the lifestyle they wish to have. These qualifications on the roles of education are relevant in this chapter, since they build one of the basic principles for the definition of the specific capabilities which will be studied among the group of students of the CLCs.

In order to complete the delimitation of our theoretical framework, and with the aim to show similarities to the present study, I refer to Pedro Flores-Crespo's (2005) study *Educación Superior y Desarrollo Humano: El Caso de Tres Universidades Tecnológicas* [Higher Education and Human Development: The Case of Three Technological Universities]. In his research, Flores-Crespo assesses, from the perspective of the CA, whether education has expanded the freedoms of a group of graduates from three different Mexican technological universities (TUs). His work is relevant to the present study due to several reasons:

- Both our research studies have been carried out in Mexico.
- Flores-Crespo's work is of a novel nature on account of his proposal of operationalizing the CA within higher education by suggesting a specific methodology to evaluate capabilities and functionings.
- Both studies share the objectives of identifying the factors that enable trained individuals to address, with better and diverse tools, any social and economic disadvantages, and of elucidating under what circumstances education can contribute to expanding the capabilities of graduates in different fields.
- Although the educational space in Flores-Crespo's work is represented by three Mexican TUs – that is, a formal educational framework – his investigation is based on the study of the graduates' expansion of freedoms after their educational training. In addition, the technological nature of the ITESM – the scenario of the current research – has parallels with the TUs with regard to infrastructure and resources.

In his work, Flores-Crespo understands the concept of capability as a sort of freedom which enables the realization of different lifestyles. Hence, the expansion of capabilities and functionings is what enables human development. In this sense, he shapes his framework of analysis by defining six capabilities in accordance with Martha Nussbaum's (2000) list of basic capabilities. Connected to these capabilities, he lists a series of functionings that match the reality of the studied individuals. Finally, Flores-Crespo refers to instrumental freedoms related to economic means and to the social opportunities proposed by Sen, as he considers they are likely to improve people's capabilities. Thus, by using several tools (assessment of particular cases, data collection and comparative analysis) Flores-Crespo intends to evaluate functionings and instrumental freedoms with the aim of revealing to which extent the education provided by a TU is likely to expand individuals' capabilities.

Nevertheless, if we consider that capabilities represent the main information space for the evaluation of well-being (Alkire 2002), Flores-Crespo's conceptual approach is liable to attract some criticism: to base the analysis of the expansion of freedoms on functionings could not reflect the same capabilities for all the analysed cases. The focus should not only be on the individuals' achievements or lifestyles, but also on real possibilities of choice to lead one type of life or another. This criticism could reflect the multiple methodological and conceptual challenges posed by the implementation of the CA. However, as we have previously mentioned, Flores-Crespo's novel proposal provides the starting point for the methodological and, partly, conceptual setting of this research work.

Analysis of the CLCs in Monterrey and Saltillo

First of all, in order to define the methodology of my research, certain issues were raised which should help to look into the expansion of capabilities related to personal, professional and educational aspects of my group of CLC students. In addition, in order to define capabilities, I have taken into account to a large extent of the previously mentioned work carried out by Flores-Crespo. I also had the opinions of several actors of the CLC system (heads of studies, representatives of the ITESM, etc.), who confirmed the hypothesis related to the possible influence of the training provided by the CLCs on the proposed capabilities.

The first capability to be analysed posed the question whether the educational experience within the CLC is likely to expand the students' capability to gain more self-esteem and self-confidence. Taking into account the non-instrumental role of education, acquiring new theoretical and practical knowledge which the student considers valuable can have a powerful influence on the way students regard themselves and on their self-esteem. This fact becomes even more significant as we are dealing with adult women who, in most cases, started their training at a CLC after being out of the educational system for many years. The second capability to be defined referred to whether the training and experience within the CLCs contributes to develop broader educational capabilities according to the instrumental role of education. This role broadens the range of information available and enables access to further types of training and educational levels. Finally, I focused on the economic and professional role of education, which can translate into economic benefits and working improvements. For this aim, I assessed whether the training received and the experience at the CLCs is able to expand the student's capability to achieve economic and professional improvements.

With this purpose, and along the lines of Flores-Crespo's methodological proposal, I established eight functionings related to the analysed capabilities (Table 16.1). These functionings are inspired by Flores-Crespo but they are different from the ones he outlines in his work, as they need to respond to the reality of the students taking part in this study.

My main source of information was a series of semi-structured qualitative interviews held with the selected group of students. These interviews aimed at presenting evidence of the students' achieving the functionings suggested in Table 16.1. Interviews were held with ten students from two different centres (Table 16.2): eight of them from the CLC of Col. Tecnológico, and two of them from the CLC of Saltillo. All of them were attending a course on basic computer skills or had already completed it and were taking part in other courses. The participants involved in this study were adult, female students of the CLCs. Women between the ages of 40 and 70 account for 70 per cent of the students at the CLCs

Table 16.1 Functionings related to the analysed capabilities

Capabilities	Suggested functionings
Capability to feel self-esteem and self-confidence	Feeling more confident to face new challenges – improved self-esteem and self-confidence Improving and/or strengthening the capacity to interact with others
Development of broader educational capabilities	Gaining access to further training levels at the community learning centres Gaining access to further training levels in other institutions Increasing the capacity to communicate and be informed
Capability to achieve economic and professional improvements	Increasing incomes Being able to find employment Improving the quality of work

Table 16.2 Students' main characteristics

Student	Place of birth	Age (years)	Period of time at the CLC (months)	Course	Employment status
S1	Monterrey	NA		BCS, English	Catalogue-based seller/housewife
S2	Edo. México	57	12	BCS	Catalogue-based seller
S3	Monterrey	57	12	BCS	Office worker
S4	México	77	1	BCS	Retired. Social service in conferences on clinical psychology
S5	Monterrey	60	3	BCS	Retired
S6	Monterrey	63	2 weeks	BCS	Retired
S7	Monterrey	55	18	BCS	Catalogue-based seller
S8	Monterrey	68	4	BCS	Housewife
S9	Saltillo	64	3	BCS	Housewife

BCS, basic computer skills; CLC, community learning centre; NA, not available.

and represent examples of successful experiences in the completion and continuation of the courses taught at the centres.

Nevertheless, in order to complete this analysis I must consider other issues that determine the students' actual capability to make choices (Walker 2007). For this reason, I have included in this research two further dimensions crucial to the CA: the students' initial endowments and their conversion factors.[4] Due to the complexity of the analysis when introducing these new variables, and to the lack of enough information (caused by time limitation and the small size of this example), only endowments which were closely related to the suggested functionings, as well as conversion factors of a personal nature, were taken into account for the discussion of the results.

I also interviewed the heads of studies of both centres with the aim of looking at the educational and personal evolution of the students from a different point of view. The issues discussed addressed the students' further training after the completion of courses at the CLC; the conditions they considered necessary for a proper educational development; the subsequent implementation of the acquired knowledge; and the personal evolution of the students. The opinion of the heads of studies is particularly relevant since they manage various aspects of the CLCs and deal directly with the students during the entire educational process.

To gain a better understanding of the motivational, functional and operative aspects of the CLCs, I interviewed two persons in charge of the ITESM programme. In this case, the information on the possible reasons for the feminization of the CLCs was particularly interesting and determined the selection of the study sample for this research. Finally, since the role played by social service students in the monitoring of CLCs students is crucial, I split them into three discussion groups where, among other issues, they were asked about the skills CLC students had acquired throughout their educational process.

From skills to capabilities

At this point, I will present the results, which reveal in which way a non-formal educational system such as a CLC can contribute to improving the quality of life of a group of female students; excerpts from the interviews will be added to support the presented evidence. In addition, I will outline several estimations on the definition of the suggested capabilities and functionings.

The capability to increase self-esteem

Firstly, I raised the issue whether the CLCs contribute to encouraging the capability to increase self-esteem and self-confidence, which posed a methodological and interpretative challenge. From the interpretative perspective, and according to the interview results, I noted that eight out of the ten interviewees affirmed feeling more confident to address new challenges and maintained that their self-esteem and self-confidence had increased. They added that, despite the initial fears and once they had experienced the results, it was very gratifying to prove themselves capable of carrying out the training, and this fact enhanced their self-concept as individuals able to face new challenges. These are some of the statements from students:

> Sure, in order to increase self-confidence and feel more secure . . . I thought it impossible to work with the computer but I am convinced I am going to make it . . . I was thinking I must be able and learn.
>
> (Student 6)

This helps, it also helps us to feel more confident, to feel we are able to do a lot of things from home. It is a tool for empowerment.

(Student 5)

I think it helps building the self-esteem of many women who, although being professionals, have devoted their whole lives to the household; they gave up their profession, they did not practice it. Now that they are into this, I notice they feel renewed, chat, make comments, invite one another, gather in groups, go out for dinner.

(Student 4)

I already feel this is something very positive . . . because I myself don't feel the same as before. I feel more capable . . . if you had asked me five months ago I would have told you: I am willing to learn, but, how, where, what should I do? So now I do feel this is a triumph.

(Student 8)

Regarding this capability, eight women stated that once they had begun the courses at the CLC, their ability to interact with others increased or improved. However, I must note that this improvement occurs mostly within the family context. It is usually with close relatives of younger age that ties are strengthened because a new common element has emerged, namely, computer knowledge and the support students receive from family members if any questions arise. Often students mention the pride of their families for them taking part in these courses:

Now it is much easier to have a conversation with them [their children]. We are on the same wavelength! And they ask me questions, and that is beautiful.

(Student 10)

Your conversation is now more varied. Now you are able to talk to younger people, before you couldn't know what they were talking about because you didn't even know what a software was. So I think this does open new possibilities.

(Student 3)

It is also important to note that friendship relations emerge among students at the centres. In some cases, coexistence generates groups that share knowledge and leisure activities outside the centre during their free time. Many of the interviewees state that it has been very worthwhile to coexist at the CLC with male and female students of different ages and conditions, as all of them have learnt something from their peers.

From the methodological perspective, the evaluation of this capability by means of the specified functionings posed the following questions:

- The difficulty in specifying the achievements or states of being that confirm the expansion of the capability to feel self-esteem and confidence.
- The need to review the suggested functionings ('feeling more confident to face new challenges – improved self-esteem and self-confidence'; 'improving and/or strengthening the capacity to interact with others'; see Table 16.1), as I noticed that the answers obtained in the interviews were more related to capabilities than to functionings.

The development of broader educational capabilities

Secondly, I tackled the issue of the development of broader educational capabilities after the training at the CLCs. For this aim, I studied two types of achievement: those related to the access to further educational levels at the CLC or in other institutions, and those related to the capacity to communicate and be informed.

In the first case, I observed that seven of the interviewees were attending a further course at the CLC or had the intention to do it; and two of them intended to start some kind of training within formal educational systems. They assume that if they have been able to learn computer skills, which initially posed a great challenge, they will be able to study more complex things, such as languages, countries and cultures or financing:

> I wish to learn more, know what's next, find out what else am I able to do, because if I have already had this chance, I say to myself, what comes next? There are a lot of issues here, it is very open, I have seen something on business, or accounting . . . and I want to learn more, I don't want to be limited to just one thing.
>
> (Student 8)

> And I wish to study a degree and I always doubted because all tasks were to be done on the computer, and that's the reason, and keep updated and continue with the training. It is never too late.
>
> (Student 5)

Regarding the issue of being informed and being able to communicate, the experience of independent learning at the CLC has been crucial. On the one hand, being able to seek information beyond the conventional resources they had at their disposal before the starting of the course makes them believe that the limitations to access particular knowledge can only be set by themselves:

> In the evening you used to watch the soap or any other programme on TV, but now what's on TV doesn't interest you anymore. Then you turn on the computer and see what you can find. And you could really spend a lot of time searching for whatever you want.
>
> (Student 3)

On the other hand, taking into consideration Mexico's migration situation and the fact that many of the students have relatives and friends living outside the country, we note that their command of computers enables them to communicate more frequently and at lower cost.

> Communicating with the family was also very important. All the members of my family are alive, one of them lives in California, some in New Mexico, others in Arizona, and I communicate with them. And you also spare time and money with computers. Now I communicate with all my friends through the computer . . . Now I read the news. I do things that I didn't use to do before; I enter the Internet and read the news directly.
>
> (Student 1)

Therefore, they give value to the possibility to find and obtain any kind of information or knowledge on the Internet, as through other means would become more difficult. They referred to their experience with the Internet as a 'window to the world', 'panorama' or 'to open the eyes'.

The capability to achieve economic and professional improvements

Thirdly, I studied the capability to achieve economic and professional improvements after finishing the courses at the CLC. The study of this capability could have been simpler, as the specification of possible achievements allows more precision. However, due to the interviewees' socio-cultural situation, the access to employment and/or the need to provide income to the household, in most cases this was not a priority or an immediate need. Yet, some of them did contribute to the household economy to a greater or lesser extent by working in formal or non-formal contexts. In the case of women who already had a job – mainly catalogue-based selling – computer skills enabled them to improve the contact and access to their customers, which led to greater incomes. In the case of women who did not have an occupation outside the household, some of them, after having acquired computer knowledge, considered the possibility of developing some kind of online business:

> You earn more money because you are better organized? Sure! As it saves time, I have more time to do other things.
>
> (Student 1)

> I am considering the fact of setting up an online business, sell something, I don't know. I need assessment on that. Yes, it opens an important perspective. Being able to earn more money instead of doing nothing, accepting just what I receive.
>
> (Student 5)

Another important issue pointed out by some of the women who had an occupation was the significant improvement of the employment quality encouraged by their computer knowledge. The development of new and more efficient procedures and skills brought about an important and positive change at work:

> I have to use the computer at work, but I was not able to abandon my 'little system' of salaries, accounting . . . because I was stuck . . . And if I had to do any other kind of work it was very complicated. Now I am not afraid of the computer any more and I dare to work on Excel on my own, or on Word . . . so, it has been very useful for my work, to lighten the burden. To me it has been like a big door opening.
>
> (Student 3)

Although this capability could be considered secondary within the context we are dealing with, we must bear in mind that providing higher incomes to the household economy or reducing the time devoted to household activities can lead to a significant change in the quality of life of individuals and in the way they see themselves.

Endowments and personal conversion factors

As I have previously mentioned, in order to analyse capabilities, I have looked at some endowments I consider essential and at particular conversion factors of a personal nature. With regard to the endowments emerging from the interviews, I identified several material issues, such as receiving support from the ITESM, having access to a computer either at the CLC or at home, or the role of the CLC's head of studies, etc. Having enough time to attend courses and surf on the Internet, as well as the availability of transport, are also relevant endowments, as sometimes the centres are located far away from the students' homes. To be more precise, having official certification and training would be considered a required endowment in order to achieve certain functionings, such as 'being able to gain access to further educational levels'. Having an occupation or the adequate tools in order to enter the work market are specific endowments for the functionings of 'being able to find employment' or 'improve the quality of the employment they already have'.

With regard to personal conversion factors, I suggest, firstly, that the will to do better, common to all the interviewees, is necessary to start out and to take advantage of the information. Initial motivation is required, as well as curiosity and the will to overcome challenges. Secondly, I perceived that the students' lowest level of education is secondary education; this fact raises the question whether the involvement in previous educational processes is decisive as a conversion factor to the successful completion of the CLC training. In this sense, previous gratifying and successful experiences could be understood as a relevant conversion factor. Finally, family support stands out as a decisive and necessary conversion factor for success. This support is put into practice by helping the student to solve doubts related to the study subjects, by driving her to the CLC, by sharing household tasks so that she is able to devote enough time to studying, or by providing moral support which should make the student feel appreciated.

Conclusions

In this chapter, I have aimed at revealing the improvements in the quality of life of a group of women who have taken part in a joint educational process. However, we intended to go beyond the instrumental benefits provided by education. For this reason, I have used the CA as the framework for evaluation, as it permits to have and analyse more information, and to reveal the various benefits that education might provide in the various dimensions of the individual. In addition, the CA enables rethinking those benefits provided by initiatives and interventions launched by university institutions, which are key actors in contributing to create a more just and inclusive society and in the democratization of knowledge.

How about the CLCs? By assessing the operational activities of the centres and the students' achievements, I observed that training in computer skills can be a catalyst for more complex processes which affect the personal and professional levels. To be precise, I have seen how these instrumental skills have helped to enhance the students' self-concept and to establish new relationships within the family and within the CLCs' educational context. Furthermore, the acquisition of new skills and knowledge in a particular field enhances the capacity to answer to new educational challenges and reinforces the access to information involving a high degree of self-teaching. Finally, and from a more instrumental perspective, it is worth mentioning the potential or actual achievement of economic improvement in the lives of the students which stems from the acquisition of knowledge and the optimization of their usual working processes. However, my research also reveals a series of factors which could constrain the achievement of these improvements. In order to achieve educational success and to acquire the explained capacities, it is regarded as necessary that students are highly motivated and that they have a basic educational training and support from the family.

Within the framework of this educational proposal, it is also worth mentioning that centres, besides providing knowledge, often become spaces where coexistence is encouraged among individuals of different ages and social strata who, otherwise, would not find common working and meeting spaces. The personal relationships formed among students, heads of studies and social service tutors represent a small but essential part in the mechanism of social empowerment; they must be taken into account when conceiving and shaping the relationships among all the actors involved in the educational experience.

Finally, I must mention that the research has particular limitations as it was developed within a small sample of students, with a possible bias in the selection of examples, with an innovative methodology still subject to a process of continuous improvement, and in a very specific location within the Mexican context.

In this sense, for future interventions and evaluations under the scope of the CA, it would be advisable to specify the capabilities to be studied by means of participative and deliberative processes in which several actors of the CLCs would take part; this is, with the aim to reflect the various contexts and to include as many voices as possible.

Notes

1 The Mexican Department for Social Development. SEDESOL's participation in the creation of the CLCs is framed within the context of the 'Strategy for Micro Regions'. Its aim is to overcome poverty and to promote comprehensive development in the most socio-economically disadvantaged regions and municipalities of the country.
2 By university social service we understand the compulsory carrying out of temporary activities by students of technical and professional degrees, which involve the implementation of the acquired knowledge and the exercising of the professional activity for the benefit or in the interest of society.
3 The guidance of the courses is carried out by the students of the ITESM Social Service.
4 According to Robeyns (2006), there are three types of conversion factor, namely personal, social and environmental, that have an influence on how individuals achieve different states of being and the procurement of goods.

References

Alkire, S. (2002) *Valuing Freedoms: Sen's Capability Approach and Poverty Reduction*, New York: Oxford University Press.

Becker, G. (1993) *Human Capital: A Theoretical and Empirical Analysis, With Special Reference to Education*, 3rd edn, Chicago: University of Chicago Press.

Drèze, J. and Sen, A. (2002) *India: Development and Participation*. Oxford: Oxford University Press.

Flores-Crespo, P. (2005) *Educación Superior y Desarrollo Humano. El Caso de Tres Universidades Tecnológicas*, México: ANUIES.

Instituto Tecnológico y de Estudios Superiores de Monterrey [ITESM] (2010) 'Publishing on the Internet'. Available at http://www.itesm.edu/ [accessed 3 December 2011].

Nussbaum, M.C. (2000) *Women and Human Development: The Capabilities Approach*, Cambridge: Cambridge University Press.

Robeyns, I. (2005) 'The capability approach: a theoretical survey', *Journal of Human Development*, 6(1): 93–114.

—— (2006) 'Three models of education: rights, capabilities and human capital', *Theory and Research in Education*, 4(1): 69–84.

Sen, A. (1999) *Development as Freedom*, Oxford: Oxford University Press.

Unterhalter, E., Vaughan, R. and Walker, M. (2007) 'The capability approach and education', *Prospero*, 13(3): 13–21.

Walker, M. (2007) 'Pedagogías en la educación superior relacionadas con el enfoque de las capacidades humanas: hacia un criterio de justicia', *Revista de Educación Superior*, XXXVI(2)(142): 103–19.

Index